FINDING STRENGTH
in Weakness

REVISED & EXPANDED EDITION

A STUDY OF TRIBULATION AND
OUR APPROPRIATE RESPONSE

WILLIAM D. BLACK, M.D.

FINDING STRENGTH

in Weakness

REVISED & EXPANDED EDITION

A STUDY OF TRIBULATION AND
OUR APPROPRIATE RESPONSE

WILLIAM D. BLACK, M.D.

The Tennessee Publishing House

ISBN 978-1-58275-274-7

Dedication:

To my wife Barbara, who has taught me much over the years.

Book Endorsement

Finding Strength in Weakness by Dr. William D. Black will be of help to anyone who has or will experience circumstances that can be identified as "tribulation."

Dr. Black's varied personal and professional experiences, coupled with his diligent study of both Biblical and non-Biblical literature, have resulted in a book of genuine insight.

One of his strong points is the ability to analyze and classify into manageable annotated lists the information gained from his study.

His insights will be helpful not only to an individual working his way through a tribulation experience but also to a pastor or Christian counselor trying to help such an individual.

Lawrence N. Lunceford, missionary to Korea, public school educator, and pastor in the Kansas City, MO area.

Dr. Black writes from the pathos of the examination room, where physicians observe both human bodies and souls passing through the shades of misery and despair. But his message is not one of foolish optimism, always looking for the silver lining. Instead, from a lifetime of immersion in Holy Scripture, intermixed with his own multiplex of personal setbacks and devastating family illnesses, he brings us a book that the anguished and heartbroken will turn to again and again for solid help. In offering solace to the suffering, Dr. Black does not take the easier, often-used solution to the question of sin, sickness and pain offered by many a theologian, i.e. a limitation of the sovereignty of God. Rather he boldly avers that suffering is a part of God's purpose for His people and that it is through suffering that God does His greatest work. In the reading of this book the Christian will be spared the waste of his pain in self-pity or the hope of immediate relief. Rather, he will join in the noble purpose that God has for those whose calling it is to suffer.

Rev. Ronald L. Siegenthaler
Minister of Christian Education
Coral Ridge Presbyterian Church
Fort Lauderdale, FL

No one can better speak to the needs of humanity than those who have been in the crucible of suffering themselves. William Black has been there—as a participant and as an observer. Dr. Black is a combination of compassionate physician (MD), Bible teacher, and wise observer of human nature.

In his book *Finding Strength in Weakness* Dr. Black addresses one of our oldest concerns—difficulty, suffering, and what we learn traversing the dark valleys of life. I like the balance of Scripture, wisdom, and personal experience woven into the pages of this readable book and recommend it without reservation.

Harold J. Sala, Ph.D.
Bible teacher, author and President of Guidelines International

The following is a transcript of a letter from Warren Howell. He is retired after serving forty years as a Methodist minister. He has end stage renal disease and is being treated with chronic hemodialysis at LaFollette Dialysis Center.

JAN. 21, 2001

Dear Doctor Black:

Greetings in the name of our Lord Jesus Christ. I read the manuscript of your book *Finding Strength* in times of *Weakness* this last week. It is **good good good**. I read it to my wife since she is all most blind. She lost one eye through Glaucoma and the other one is almost gone from sugar. We both were blessed and I could say overjoyed from all of God's wonderful promises and His wonderful providences. Really God has done some wonderful leading in your life, so when God's word declares that all things work together for good in the end, look what God's providence has produced. – a wonderful book through His leading a good Dr. by obedience.

Dr. Black when your book has been printed, I would like to know. I would recommend it to the brethren. I believe any ministry could get a lot of good from it and God would get the Glory. Thank you again. It gave my spirit a lift when I need it the most.

I hope that your wife is still doing better. God's word declares *I am the Lord which healeth thee. Please pray for us* and we will be praying for you.

In Christian love
Warren & Peggy Howell

Aug. 21, 2001

This is a note of thanks to you for sending me a copy of *Finding Strength in Weakness*.

It is a fine book, bringing together a great deal of biblical wisdom that to my knowledge is not to be found between any other two book covers. The clinical way in which you present everything, especially the harrowing things, gives extra force to the thoughts. . . . It is a powerful piece of writing, and will surely do its readers a great deal of good.

The way you share your life-experiences is telling, too, for it is so free from egocentrism. That's grace!

You say some kind things about my own writing. Thank you. It is always ministry to the writer to be told that his book have been doing the job for which they were designed.

God bless you and yours as you walk on with him in the future.

Sincerely Yours in Christ,

J.I. Packer
Professor
Regent College
Vancouver

CONTENTS

PREFACE TO THE REVISED EDITION

It's been four years since the first edition of Finding Strength in Weakness was published. I've been amazed at what a platform the book has given me to share my faith and tell others about God's love and His principles for life. In order to keep the information fresh in my mind, I've reread the book several times. There have been a few places where I thought a minor revision in the text was appropriate, and in those revisions, I've tried to be as faithful in the wording as possible.

During these last four years, I've continued to read my Bible. In that reading, God has shown me countless passages that confirm the principles espoused in the initial publication. When I would come across such a passage, I would write down the reference in the margin of a copy of my book. As I made preparation for this revised and expanded edition of the book, I studied those passages, and inserted the extra Scripture references as it seemed appropriate. I tried not to include new passages that repeated exactly the same idea as the old, but tried to stick with those where the message seemed more compelling or perhaps offered new insight not found in the Scripture passages already quoted.

Even though a large number of Scripture passages have been added to this expanded edition, the main content of the book is essentially unchanged. Were I to try to write the book now, it would be impossible. I don't have the same mind-set as I did when I originally wrote it. Barbara died about year after its publication. Since I am no longer a spousal caregiver, I don't think the same way as I did before. My mood is different. Also, after Barbara died, I had to go back to work. While Barbara was ill, I had been working only part-time. I still don't take night call, as my impaired vision makes it dangerous for me to drive at night, but otherwise, I am working what most people would consider full-time. From what I can tell, my transition back to working full-time was smoother than what many other people have experienced on returning to work after being spousal caregivers and then losing their mates. I thank God that I am doing as well as I am. My associates in our practice were very good to me while Barbara was ill, to cover for me, and they are still good to me now. They know that I appreciate, more that I can say, what they did and are doing for me. Now that I've gone back to work, I would not have time to write a book.

I have remarried. When we started dating, Kay had been a widow for about five years. We had known each other for over twenty years, both working at St. Mary's Medical Center in Knoxville. Kay is a wonderful person, and God really blessed me when He brought us together. I now have some idea about what it is like to be in a blended family. However, compared to some of the stories I've heard about other people's experiences with second marriages and blended families, we are doing very well.

I am still learning and hope to continue to do so. I am seeking to know God better and to be one of His many lights in a dark world. I offer this material to you the reader, and pray that the information will bless your heart.

ACKNOWLEDGMENTS

The Bible tells us that out of the overflow of the heart, the mouth speaks (Matt. 12:34b). This book is an overflow from my heart. It is only by the grace of God that I am who I am, and this book is a product of my inner being as fashioned by the work of Jesus Christ.

I would like to express gratitude to the many people God has used, over the years, to shape me into the person I am. My father taught me a work ethic. He set high standards and expected me to meet them. My mother nurtured me as a child; she read me Bible stories and taught me to say my prayers. When I was a teenager, she encouraged me to read my Bible. For the last twenty-three years, since we returned home to Knoxville, she has been my friend. I would like to thank my older brother John for being the first person to tell me about the forgiveness from sins, available through faith in Jesus Christ.

I would like to express my appreciation to Mr. Beeler. While I was at Camp Ta-Pa-Win-Go he helped me understand that I could have the assurance of my salvation. The summer I was a counselor at that camp, Reverend Mike Birkner taught me a great deal about living the Christian life. When I was in college, Pastor Robert Wood of Park City Presbyterian Church in Knoxville had a great influence on me. At Bryan College, several men made special efforts to instruct and encourage me: President Theodore C. Mercer, Dr. Irving L. Jensen, Dr. John Anderson, and Dr. Fred Donehoo.

When I was in medical school, I was greatly influenced by Dr. James Gibb Johnson. During my junior year, when he was the chief medicine resident, he spent time with me teaching me things I needed to know. Later as a mentor during my internal medicine training, he helped me see that my ego support as a physician should not come from patient gratitude but from knowing within my own soul that I did what was right. He could not have given me a higher standard. My Nephrology Chief, Dr. Fred Hatch, led me by the hand in helping me learn to present medical papers and become published in the medical literature. Since I have been in practice, I have been influenced by such Christian authors as C. S. Lewis, James D. Mallory, Jr., Tim LaHaye, D. Martyn Lloyd-Jones, J. I. Packer, and Ron Dunn.

My wife Barbara has taught me much over the years. She has influenced my attitudes and actions and because of her, I have had the privilege to learn what it is like to be a spousal caregiver. During her illness these last three and a half years, we have spent much time together, and our relationship has grown closer and closer. Many other people have encouraged me and helped me in writing this book. I would like to express my appreciation to our rector, Father Henry Swann of Church of the Good Shepherd in Knoxville. He read an early copy of the manuscript and encouraged me. My brother-in-law, Dr. Ron Proctor, and I have exchanged ideas over the years. During a time when I was ready to give up, he urged me to persevere in getting this book published. He also put me in touch with Bonnie Porter, a freelance writer/editor for the religious market, who helped me develop the outline for the overall presentation of this material. I would like to thank Dr. William Bell of Dallas Baptist University for reading the manuscript and giving me encouragement. I appreciate all the work the people at Winepress Publishing have done in making my dreams of writing this book become a reality.

As I look back through my life, I thank God for His provision and His grace. When we first returned to Knoxville in 1977, I was thankful to God for the fact that He had saved me and was taking care of me, but I not could say, for certain, that I really loved Him. Now, after all the experiences that helped me come to know Him, caused me to better understand Him, and forced me to depend on Him, I can say, with confidence, that I do love Him.

INTRODUCTION

Many people struggle with the concept of suffering in the world, especially if they believe in a loving God. I have dealt with this problem for much of my life, but even more so since I became a physician. Sometimes I do ponder God and His relationship with His children. Throughout my life, I have seen God's guidance and direction to bring me to where I am today. I want to share with you some highlights of my life to give you a perspective of why I am writing this book and how my life has affected my viewpoints in this area.

When I was seven years old, I accepted Jesus Christ as my Savior. At the age of twelve, I attended a Children's Bible Mission camp. That summer, I learned about 1 John 5:13: "I write these things to you who believe in the name of the Son of God so that you may know that you have eternal life." During that week at camp, I received the assurance of my salvation, and at the same camp the next summer, I dedicated my life to the Lord Jesus Christ.

From an early age, a strong work ethic was instilled in me. When I was in the second grade, at my father's insistence, my brother and I started our own business, buying and selling comic books. Two years later we started working for my dad in his bookstore. At times I would resent getting on the bus after school and riding downtown to the store when my friends were out playing. But in retrospect, I realize that the experience in my dad's store helped to develop my character. I learned to listen to people and try to meet their needs.

My mother's parents had moved in with our family before I was born, and so I grew up close to my grandparents. Unfortunately, my grandfather had significant problems with arthritis. When I was twelve years old, he permanently took to his bed. This continued for about a year, until he developed acute urinary retention. He was taken to the hospital, never to return home. Health care was different in those days, and my grandfather lived at Saint Mary's Hospital in Knoxville for the last three years of his life. My grandmother would go there and sit with him every day. My grandfather had been in the hospital two and a half years when my grandmother became ill, was hospitalized, and died, all within just a few days. My grandfather was devastated when his wife of sixty-two years passed away. We had just always assumed that he would pass on before she did. Even though the minister from our church came to talk with him, he could provide no words of comfort for my grandfather. When my mother told me what had happened, my heart ached for him. I began to understand the presence of true suffering in the world.

During my first three years in high school, I was unhappy. I was overweight and socially inept. Even though I was on the football team, I spent most of my time on the bench. I was very sensitive, and this made me a source of sport for several bullies in our school. In an effort to be popular, I began to run with the wrong crowd. I strayed away from the Lord for several years, but as a high school senior, I finally began to search in earnest for God's plan for my life.

After high school, I enrolled at the University of Tennessee in Knoxville. In college I was filled with indecision, and I changed majors frequently. I remember sitting in a Greek class one day and thinking to myself, *What am I doing here?* During my junior year, I went to Bryan College, a small Christian liberal arts college in Dayton, Tennessee. When I was there, I took several classes on biblical scholarship, and it was at Bryan that I learned to trust in Christ to direct my life's course.

After completing my undergraduate studies, I attended medical school at the University of Tennessee in Memphis. Medical school was very difficult. I had had no idea that there would be so much to learn. I began to be filled with self-doubt. Would I really be able to graduate successfully? But after years of hard work, I finally graduated on a very positive note.

During my time in medical school, I also embarked on another new experience: I married my lovely wife, Barbara. Throughout our marriage, I have learned the importance of commitment. Barbara and I have learned to accept each other as we are. We have learned the true meaning of 1 Corinthians 13:5: "Love keeps no record of wrongs." As of this writing, we have been married thirty-three years.

I undertook my internship at Roanoke Memorial Hospitals in Roanoke, Virginia. I learned many things about taking responsibility and making decisions, but I also came to appreciate that my sensitive spirit was an asset. Being sensitive to patients' needs and feelings is often the first step in discovering the most appropriate solution for what is troubling them.

I never really thought much about my own death until I went to Vietnam. I was called into service, and I spent my initial six and a half months as a Battalion Surgeon with the 1/69 Armor (tanks), Fourth Infantry Division, based at Camp Radcliff in An Khe. Each evening, the battalion officers in base-camp had a meeting with the commanding officer. I remember sitting in that meeting one evening, shortly after I arrived in country. As I listened to the different men giving their reports, I thought to myself, *They're talking about killing people!* My first trip to the morgue at the 17th Field Hospital was a troubling experience. It was my responsibility to check on four men who had been killed in a firefight. Later, I was to lose friends of mine in the conflict. My last five months in country were spent at the 8th Field Hospital in Nha Trang. I was the Officer in Charge of the outpatient department and emergency room.

After I returned from Vietnam, I was fortunate enough to spend my last ten months in the army at Walter Reed Army Medical Center in Washington, D. C. I was a General Medical Officer and worked in the outpatient clinic. But I was allowed to spend Thursday afternoons in the Nephrology Clinic, and it was there that I got my first real taste of what it was like to take care of patients with kidney disease.

The rest of my training took place at the University of Tennessee Medical Units in Memphis, Tennessee. During my internal medicine training, I had a misunderstanding with one of my professors and was given a bad report. Because I was intimidated by that professor, I did not offer any of my own opinions on rounds. She reached the conclusion that I was not keeping up with the literature as I should and could not think for myself. That bad report was discouraging, but it caused me to reevaluate my methods. I began going to the hospital library after seeing the patients in consultation to read about their particular diseases. Then, on rounds with the attending physician, I would present the case and report what I had recommended to the referring physician, not asking his opinion. In the long run, that misunderstanding was one of the best things that ever happened to me professionally.

I chose Nephrology, the branch of medicine that deals with the kidney, as a medical subspecialty. In my Nephrology training there were many times when I was not sure what to do for the patients, and seeking opinions from others was not always satisfactory. I learned how to go to the library and dig out the latest information for myself. During this time, I was fortunate to be able to present a few papers at meetings and have a few published in the literature. In order to publish a paper about something in the literature, it is essential to have a thorough knowledge of what has already been written about the subject, and so those were real learning experiences.

During my residency and fellowship training, our two sons were born. Many times it was difficult to juggle my family life with my career. But I knew that it was my responsibility to maintain a relationship with my sons and nurture them spiritually. Now that they are adults, I am glad I made those efforts.

In 1975, when I first went into practice in Roanoke, Virginia, the reality of life and death decisions, both my own and my patients', began to sink in. It can be intimidating to know the depth of responsibility a physician has. I sought to help my patients and their families cope with their problems, including illness and death. I was able to pass on to them several Christian books, literature, and a list of comforting Bible verses as it seemed appropriate (Job 5:7; Matt. 5:1–12; Matt. 6:25–34; Rom. 5:3–5; Rom. 8:18–39; 1 Cor. 10:13; 2 Cor. 1:3–5, 2 Cor. 4:7–10, 2 Cor. 12:1–10; 1 Thess. 5:18; 2 Tim. 1:7; James 1:2–5; 1 Pet. 1:6, 7; Rev. 21:1–4). The Lord used that list of verses to turn around the lives of many people.

Over the years God has directed my life and placed me in situations that have helped me grow spiritually. God helped me appreciate the fact that any success I had professionally was His gift to me, and that He could take it away at any time. Experiences as a short-term missionary caused me to realize that people in the United States are very pampered and spoiled. In general they take too much for granted and do not appreciate what they have.

I and my family have had several medical issues that made me continue to deal with the problem of suffering in the world. I have had problems with my vision that required a cornea transplant. Four years ago my wife was diagnosed with breast cancer. At the time of the diagnosis she already had widespread bony metastasis. About five weeks after my wife was diagnosed with cancer, she developed severe pain in her back and left hip. Because of the pain she was unable to stand. I had to take off work to care for her. During that time, I started a more earnest search of what the Bible has to say about tribulation. The information I have discovered in the Bible has been therapeutic, both for me and for my wife. I share this information with you in this book.

The Lord has taught me many things throughout my life. I like to think they are in the category of the New Testament term, "mystery." The Greek word *musteerion* refers to the secret thoughts, plans, and dispensations of God, hidden from human reason and from all other comprehension below the divine level. Mysteries must be revealed to those for whom they are intended. They are too profound for human ingenuity.[1]

The Sovereign LORD has given me an instructed tongue,
to know the word that sustains the weary. (Isa. 50:4a)

I have spent the majority of my life dealing with people who have needs and searching for ways to help them meet those needs. Solutions are not always easy. During my life, I myself have experienced some of those needs, and because of that, I have a better understanding of what others are going through. The Lord has taught me much to help me deal with my own difficulties and in so doing, has made me better able to reach out a helping hand to others.

As a young man, Malcolm Muggeridge was a British newspaperman.[2] During the early 1930s, he was the Moscow correspondent for the *Manchester Guardian*. Muggeridge was the first journalist to tell the world about the hardship, famine, and terror in Russia under Stalin. In the early 1960s Muggeridge rediscovered Christianity. Afterwards, while working with the BBC, Muggeridge was one of the people responsible for introducing the general public to Mother Teresa. He interviewed her for the film *Something Beautiful for God* and authored a book about her that carried the same title.[3]

Many people complain because life seems to be one difficulty after another. They survive one crisis, and another comes along. They never seem to get to enjoy life. According to Muggeridge, "Any happening, great and small . . . is a parable whereby God speaks to us; and the art of life is to get the message."[4] My purpose in writing this book is to try to help people maintain spiritual stability during difficult situations and to help them profit from their experiences. My desire is to help them get the message.

PART ONE:

UNDERSTANDING TRIBULATION

1

THE REALITY OF TRIBULATION

I f we live long enough, troubles and tribulations come to all of us at some time in life. Jesus said, "In this world you will have trouble. But take heart! I have overcome the world" (John 16:33). The Greek word for tribulation is *thlipsis*. According to Bauer, Arndt, and Gingrich's *A Greek-English Lexicon of the New Testament*, the word means "pressing or pressure." The meaning also includes "oppression" or "affliction." It speaks of distress that is brought about by outward or difficult circumstances. "Affliction" in the spiritual sense embraces the ideas of "trouble" and "anguish of heart."[1]

After I completed my medical training, I went into practice in Roanoke, Virginia. I was associated with a general internist, a man who had been one of my mentors during my internship. I received several referrals from a family practitioner. On one occasion he sent me a young hockey player who, according to the patient, just "didn't feel right." My conclusion about the hockey player was that rather than a physical illness, he was dealing with a sense of meaninglessness and emptiness about life. Many people have this same trouble, this same lack of fulfillment.

When I telephoned the referring physician about the case, he agreed with my conclusion. He also recommended to me a book written by Paul Tillich entitled *The Courage To Be*.[2] When I read this book, I learned about the concept of the "anxiety of existence." Tillich said that anyone who exists has to contemplate the possibility of not existing. He divided the anxiety of existence into three categories: the anxiety of fate and death, the anxiety of meaningless and emptiness, and the anxiety of guilt. He said that all three were interrelated. After reading the book, I began to develop more of an appreciation for my own anxiety of existence.

Another resource recommended to me by a former Vietnam buddy was a book by Gail Sheehy entitled *Passages*.[3] One of my favorite lines from her book is her description of the time of a person's life between the ages of eighteen and thirty years: "The safety and security of home left behind, we begin trying on life's uniforms in search of the perfect fit."[4] The book allowed me to appreciate the anxieties that go along with just being alive, but it did not do much for me in providing solutions.

The various struggles we each face in life seem to have more or less urgency depending upon our season of life. Throughout my life I have heard a great number of testimonies. I have found that I can get a fair idea of someone's age simply by listening to his or her testimony. I can tell by listening to what tribulations are stretching that person. I can tell by listening to what it is that is getting that person's attention, the thing for which he is trusting God. If the person is trusting God to get him where he needs to be in life, he is usually a teenager or young adult. If he is trusting God to sustain him in his ministry or other vocation, then he is usually older and more established. If his life seems dominated by physical or health problems, then he is usually much older and in the declining years of life.

During the summer of 1999, my wife and I took a cruise of the Baltic Sea. Her cancer seemed to have worsened, and we wanted to "seize the day." The ship left out of Amsterdam, and, including the Netherlands, we visited nine countries in two weeks. Our first stop was Oslo, Norway. During a tour of Oslo, we visited the Vigeland sculpture park, a 79-acre park with more than 200 bronze, granite, and wrought iron statues. One large fountain especially caught my eye. In the center of the basin of the fountain were six giants, holding up a large saucer-shaped vessel. Water spilled down around the edge of the vessel. There was a lesson to be learned from this fountain. The water represented life, and the giants seemed to be caving in under the weight of the vessel, of life. The face of one of the giants was a self-portrait of the artist. The reality of our existence is that life can be hard. We have difficulties to face. We have problems to solve. Let's take a look at some of those problems which are common to the human race.

Each of Us Struggles with Hardship

For most people, surviving in this life is hard work. We have to make a living. We need food, clothing, and shelter. We also need sufficient rest if we are to keep going. God created Adam and Eve and placed them in a glorious garden, but after Adam's sin, the ground was cursed:

> To Adam he said, "Because you listened to your wife and ate from the tree about which I commanded you, 'You must not eat of it.'
> Cursed is the ground because of you; through painful toil you will eat of it all the days of your life.
> It will produce thorns and thistles for you, and you will eat the plants of the field. By the sweat of your brow you will eat your food until you return to the ground, since from it you were taken; for dust you are and to dust you will return." (Gen. 3:17–19)

Life is hard work for all of us since the fall of Adam. The earth has been cursed, and life is a struggle.

Each of Us Searches for Intimacy

The need for intimacy is apparent, even in infancy. Babies deprived of intimacy do not develop properly. God provided for Adam's need for intimacy at the time of creation:

> The Lord God said, "It is not good for the man to be alone. I will make a helper suitable for him." (Gen. 2:18)

People are created with a need for intimacy. We search for a kindred spirit. We like to be around others who have the same interests as we do. We need someone with whom to share our hopes and dreams, our triumphs, and our disappointments. We need to be able to share our feelings.

Unfortunately, some people have no one with whom to share their lives. People may be desperate for intimacy and for companionship.

EACH OF US STRUGGLES FOR INDEPENDENCE

Most of us have a desire for independence. We do not wish to be subject to or controlled by other people. We do not want to be told by other people how to think or act. This desire for independence is part of the normal process of maturing.

It is important for each of us to come to our own conclusions about spiritual matters. We are created individually, and God's grace is given individually (Eph. 4:7). We have to decide individually how we will respond to God's message.

Some people look to their family members for guidance in spiritual matters. That is appropriate up to a point. But our final decisions in spiritual matters should be based on our *own* study of the Bible (Acts 17:11; Rom. 14:5), and through communion with the Spirit of God (1 Cor. 2:9–16).

Jesus said that faith in Him would cause family disruption:

> "Do not suppose that I have come to bring peace to the earth. I did not come to bring peace, but a sword. For I have come to turn
> 'a man against his father,
> a daughter against her mother,
> a daughter-in-law against her mother-in-law—
> a man's enemies will be the members of his own household.'
> Anyone who loves his father or mother more than me is not worthy of me; anyone who loves his son or daughter more than me is not worthy of me." (Matt. 10:34–37)

EACH OF US STRIVES FOR MEANING IN LIFE

Most of us want our lives to count for something; we do not want to be here on the earth just taking up space. Existentialists would call the process of finding fulfillment in life as "authenticating our existence." There are different ways to find this fulfillment and meaning in our lives. We can seek God's will for our lives, or we can be filled with selfish ambition. We can love God, or we can love the world. Satan tempted Jesus with the things of this world (Matt. 4:1–11). But Jesus would not go against what the Father wanted Him to do.

John referred to the love of the world this way:

> Do not love the world or anything in the world. If anyone loves the world, the love of the Father is not in him. For everything in the world—the cravings of sinful man, the lust of his eyes and the boasting of what he has and does—comes not from the Father but from the world. The world and its desires pass away, but the man who does the will of God lives forever. (1 John 2:15–17)

Choosing God's way does not end our struggles. We may struggle over the sincerity of our commitment. If we decide to choose God's will for our own life's path, we may struggle to discover what that will is. If we are in God's will, we may struggle with how we may stay in His will.

EACH OF US STRUGGLES WITH GUILT

All of us have sin natures (Rom. 5:12). The Bible tells us, "All have sinned and fall short of the glory of God" (Rom. 3:23). After committing adultery with Bathsheba and murdering her husband, King David had a sense of guilt over his sins. The prophet Nathan confronted him about his sin (2 Sam. 12:1–14). David wrote Psalm 51 as an expression of his remorse:

> Have mercy on me, O God, according to your unfailing love; according to your great compassion blot out my transgressions. Wash away all my iniquity and cleanse me from my sin. (Ps. 51:1, 2)

Some people neglect their sense of guilt, sear their consciences, and purposefully continue in sin. However, a person's deliberate spiritual blindness and willful unbelief do not remove the reality of his sin. Just because someone does not admit that it exists, does not mean that it does not exist.

> They [the Gentiles, the heathen] are darkened in their understanding and separated from the life of God because of the ignorance that is in them due to the hardening of their hearts. Having lost all sensitivity, they have given themselves over to sensuality so as to indulge in every kind of impurity, with a continual lust for more. (Eph. 4:18, 19)

When we become Christians, it settles our place in eternity, but it does not remove our struggle with sin and guilt. As Paul said:

> So I find this law at work: When I want to do good, evil is right there with me. For in my inner being I delight in God's law; but I see another law at work in the members of my body, waging war against the law of my mind and making me a prisoner of the law of sin at work within my members. What a wretched man I am! Who will rescue me from this body of death? (Rom. 7:21–24)

EACH OF US STRUGGLES WITH FAMILY RESPONSIBILITIES

There are family responsibilities that most people must deal with in life. Financial obligations to keep a household running cause, many times, both husbands and wives to work outside the home. But to keep family relationships strong, vibrant, and alive, time must be spent toward that end as well. Many Christians have the feeling that they should not put their jobs or careers ahead of their families. In my opinion, there are occasionally times when it is necessary to put the job first. Throughout the years, with my job as a physician, there have been times when we had to change our family's plans because of the needs of my sick patients. The trick is to organize one's life so that adequate attention is given to both job and family.

Of course, most parents feel responsible to their children. It is important for parents to cultivate the parent-child relationship, to spend time with their children, to read to them when they are small, to nurture them spiritually, emotionally, and intellectually. It is necessary to attend their children's church and school performances and athletic events. When children want to talk, parents need to put down whatever they are doing and pay attention to what the child wants to discuss. Good parenting takes *time*!

As the years roll by, the parent-child relationship changes. As our own parents become elderly, it can cause a significant amount of stress. Decisions about care for the elderly may be difficult. Jesus experienced this situation as well. When He was on the cross, He exhibited concern for His mother, Mary, and provided for her through the person of His cousin John (John 19:25–27).

Each of Us Observes People in
Difficult Circumstances

Human suffering is all around us. There is a responsibility to meet some of the needs we observe every day. God would have us to put action to our faith and help needy people. There are times when the need is physical; at other times the need may be emotional or spiritual.

Religion that God our Father accepts as pure and faultless is this: to look after orphans and widows in their distress. (James 1:27a)

When he [Jesus] saw the crowds, he had compassion on them, because they were harassed and helpless, like sheep without a shepherd. Then he said to his disciples, "The harvest is plentiful but the workers are few. Ask the Lord of the harvest, therefore, to send out workers into his harvest field." (Matt. 9:36–38)

In 1993, I spent a week with my son Jason in Mexico. The entire time we were there, he never passed a beggar without giving that person some money. His unselfishness was a witness to me. A believer who identifies with others and their needs must feel responsible and struggle with how the Lord would have him help meet those needs.

EACH OF US STRUGGLES WITH THOSE WHO SEEK TO OVERCOME US

Our enemy, the devil, prowls around like a roaring lion looking for someone to devour (1 Pet. 5:8b). In addition to directly affecting our souls and spirits himself, the devil uses other people as secondary agents to afflict us. This can be seen in the life of Job in the Old Testament. The Sabeans and the Chaldeans stole Job's property and killed his servants (Job 1:14, 15, 17); they were secondary agents of Satan. Unfortunately, both non-Christians and Christians are sometimes used as agents of Satan to bring affliction to people. In the Corinthian church, some believers were troubling other believers with strife and lawsuits among them. Paul admonished them:

> The very fact that you have lawsuits among you means you have been completely defeated already. Why not rather be wronged? Why not rather be cheated? Instead, you yourselves cheat and do wrong, and you do this to your brothers. (1 Cor. 6:7, 8)

Throughout life, others may try to get the best of us in many different ways. In college, I was belittled for my belief in the inspiration of Scripture. In medical school, I was ridiculed because I would not accept the theory of evolution as fact.

Many times, our Lord Jesus was also on the receiving end of offensive behavior. On one occasion, the Pharisees attempted to trap Jesus in His words regarding the issue of paying taxes to Caesar (Matt. 22:15–22), but Jesus put them in their place.

Of course, the greatest offenses to Jesus occurred around the events of His trial and crucifixion. After Jesus' arrest in the Garden of Gethsemane, He was taken to the house of the high priest. While He was there, he was treated badly:

> The men who were guarding Jesus began mocking and beating him. They blindfolded him and demanded, "Prophesy! Who hit you?" And they said many other insulting things to him. (Luke 22:63–65)

Man's inhumanity to man is a fact of life. On our first trip to the former Soviet Union, we were taken to Paneriai, just outside of Vilnius, Lithuania. Paneriai is a significant place because it is where the Germans led 70,000 Jews down into holes dug in the ground and shot them in the head. The small museum exhibiting some of the personal effects of the victims made the significance of what happened there all the more real. It can be appalling how people treat one another, and we must all deal with this fact at some point in our lives.

EACH OF US DEALS WITH SICKNESS AND DISEASE

Each of us has to face the prospect of sickness, both in ourselves and in our family members. Disease entered the world when Adam was judged for his sin. It is a natural fact of life: as we get older, our body parts break down.

> Remember your creator in the days of your youth, before the days of trouble come and the years approach when you will say, 'I find no pleasure in them'—before the sun and the light and the moon and the stars grow dark, and the clouds return after the rain, when the keepers of the house tremble, and the strong men stoop, when the grinders cease because they are few, and those looking through the windows grow dim; when the doors to the street are closed and the sound of grinding fades; when men rise up at the sound of birds, but all their songs grow faint; when men are afraid of heights and of dangers in the streets; when the almond tree blossoms and the grasshopper drags himself along and desire no longer is stirred. Then man goes to his eternal home

and mourners go about the streets. Remember him—before the silver cord is severed, or the golden bowl is broken; before the pitcher is shattered at the spring, or the wheel broken at the well, and the dust returns to the ground it came from, and the spirit returns to God who gave it. (Eccles. 12:1–7)

EACH OF US FACES THE REALITY OF DEATH

For, "All men are like grass, and their glory is like the flowers of the field; the grass withers and the flowers fall, but the word of the Lord stands forever." (1 Pet. 1:24, 25a)

There is a time for everything, and a season for every activity under heaven: a time to be born and a time to die. (Eccles. 3:1, 2a)

It is better to go to a house of mourning than to go to a house of feasting, for death is the destiny of every man; the living should take this to heart. (Eccles. 7:2)

Therefore, just as sin entered the world through one man, and death through sin, and in this way death came to all men. (Rom. 5:12a)

Man is destined to die once, and after that to face judgment. (Heb. 9:27)

If the Lord tarries, each one of us will die. It is not a question of *if* we will die but of *when* we will die. The day of our death is appointed before we are born (Job 14:5; Ps. 139:16b). When we see others die, it makes us more aware of our own coming departure from this life.

Remember how fleeting is my life. For what futility you have created all men! What man can live and not see death, or save himself from the power of the grave? (Ps. 89:47, 48)

36

Some people think that if they are Christians, their lives should be free from trouble. That idea is illusionary and in my mind is not based on Scripture. Tribulation comes to each of us in different forms throughout our lives, but it is still a recurrent theme for all of us. As each of us goes through our own particular trials, we can be sure that others are troubled, in like manner as we are. For some of us, the knowledge that others are afflicted provides some consolation. For others, that knowledge provides no comfort. However, the knowledge that tribulation affects us all should help us realize that there are better and worse ways to handle the troubles that come. Understanding what is going on is the first step in dealing with it. If tribulation is universal, then God knows about it and has a plan, both collectively and individually, to help us through it.

Jesus said, "Come to me, all you who are weary and burdened, and I will give you rest" (Matt. 11:28). God grants rest from trouble, if we will learn to trust in Him.

2

HOW TRIBULATION MAY AFFECT US

There was one time in my life when I thought I had been abandoned by God. After I left my practice in Roanoke, Virginia, I was in an internal medicine practice for fourteen months in Florence, Alabama. A former medical school classmate, who was practicing in my hometown of Knoxville, Tennessee, called to tell me about a practice opportunity there, one for a nephrologist. I had a strong desire to return to my home town, but I struggled for several weeks with what to do. During this time, I could not seem to hear God's voice or sense His direction, until one morning, I came across the following passage in my Bible: "See, I have placed before you an open door that no one can shut" (Rev. 3:8). I took this verse as a sign from God that I should return home. A decision had not been made yet about a choice of someone for that practice opportunity, but we moved back to Knoxville anyway. I was able to find a position doing emergency room work, while we waited for a decision to be made.

During this time, I believed the following principle that I had heard some Christian teachers promote: If we want something to happen and we believe strongly that it has already been accomplished in heaven, it will work out as we desire. The idea was based on Mark 11:24. I concluded that if I just had enough faith, things would work out as I hoped. I had been in Knoxville two and a half months, when I was notified that another nephrologist had been chosen for the position.

Spiritually, the props were knocked out from under me. I was overwhelmed with a sense of betrayal. I thought God had mislead me, brought me to Knoxville, and then abandoned me. I was filled with uncertainty about what to do.

Within forty-eight hours, I had worked through my pain. I realized that if the Lord had shut one door, He would open another. Eventually, I started my own practice, which was God's will for my life, and things have worked out just fine. The Lord had placed an open door before me—I just had not realized which door it was.

When I was in Vietnam, I learned about the concept of a secondary explosion. A primary explosion occurs when a round of artillery lands. A secondary explosion is one that occurs at the same site, just after the primary explosion. A secondary explosion is a sign that the artillery round hit something that itself has also exploded, such as an ammunition cache. In chapter one of this book, we looked at the reality of life's struggles. For all of us, life is filled with challenges, difficulties, and painful experiences. Now we are going to examine what those painful experiences may do to us, how they may affect us, how they might injure us, how they can potentially destroy us completely. In each of our lives, there are times when the secondary explosions may be worse than the primary ones.

TRIBULATION TAKES ITS TOLL SPIRITUALLY

It is difficult to separate the effects of painful experiences into those that are spiritual and those that are mental. With regard to the spiritual effects caused by tribulation, I'll discuss those that relate to how our relationship with God is affected, those effects that may have a more eternal significance.

We May Feel Deserted by God

Our trials may cause us to feel abandoned by God. We may feel as if God has brought us to a certain point in life and then turned His back on us. God may seem silent. We may wonder if He is really there.

Feelings of abandonment are a recurrent theme in the book of Psalms.

Why, O Lord, do you stand far off? Why do you hide yourself in times of trouble? (Ps. 10:1)

Awake, O Lord! Why do you sleep? Rouse yourself! Do not reject us forever. Why do you hide your face and forget our misery and oppression? (Ps. 44:23, 24)

I am set apart with the dead, like the slain who lie in the grave, whom you remember no more, who are cut off from your care. (Ps. 88:5)

There are other passages in Scripture describing those who felt forsaken by God. Consider the case of John the Baptist. He had a significant ministry, but later he was put in a situation where he felt abandoned by God. John's ministry was anointed by God. It was prophesied in the Old Testament (Mal. 3:1; Isa. 40:3). The significance of his life was revealed to his father before he was born (Luke 1:5–17). He was to "Go on before the Lord, in the spirit and power of Elijah, to turn the hearts of the fathers to their children and the disobedient to the wisdom of the righteous—to make ready a people prepared for the Lord" (Luke 1:17). Jesus said, "among those born of women there is no one greater" (Luke 7:28).

But after Jesus' ministry began, people stopped following John the Baptist and began following Jesus (John 3:26). John lost his ministry, and eventually, he was put in prison. He must have felt deserted by God. After having proclaimed that Jesus was the Christ, he sent messengers to Jesus questioning that fact:

When John heard in prison what Christ was doing, he sent his disciples to ask him, "Are you the one who was to come, or should we expect someone else?" (Matt. 11:2, 3)

Perhaps John the Baptist had the idea that once the Messiah came, he would be in a position of influence, not incarcerated in some jail. Jesus' response is recorded in Luke 7:22, 23:

> Go back and report to John what you have seen and heard: The blind receive sight, the lame walk, those who have leprosy are cured, the deaf hear, the dead are raised, and the good news is preached to the poor. Blessed is the man who does not fall away on account of me.

I believe that Jesus was saying in that last sentence: *I may not be doing things as you thought I would. Try to keep your faith despite your situation.*

We May Feel Mistreated by God

At times, I speak with people who are perplexed by their particular set of difficulties. They feel that their calamity should be happening to someone else, someone less productive, less good, less worthy of good things, someone who is obviously making no effort to follow the Lord. They feel mistreated, as if they did not deserve the trials and tribulations that came their way.

During Job's trials, he felt that he had been wronged by God (Job 19:6, 7). He thought he had been denied justice (Job 27:2). Job was righteous in his own eyes (Job 32:1). Job sought to prove this point to his friends:

> But I desire to speak to the Almighty and to argue my case with God . . . I will surely defend my ways to his face. (Job 13:3, 15b)

He also sought to prove his point to God:

> How many wrongs and sins have I committed? Show me my offense and my sin. (Job 13:23)

Jeremiah had similar feelings of mistreatment by God. Like Job, he questioned God's justice:

You are always righteous, O Lord, when I bring a case before you. Yet I would speak to you about your justice: Why does the way of the wicked prosper? Why do all the faithless live at ease? (Jer. 12:1)

Consider the words from Jeremiah's Complaint in Chapter 20:

O LORD, you deceived me, and I was deceived; you overpowered me and prevailed. I am ridiculed all day long; everyone mocks me. (Jer. 20:7)

Consider these words of Isaiah:

Look down from heaven and see from your lofty throne, holy and glorious. Where are your zeal and your might? Your tenderness and compassion are withheld from us. (Isa. 63:15)

Consider also the words of the psalmist:

For I eat ashes as my food and mingle my drink with tears because of your great wrath, for you have taken me up and thrown me aside. (Ps. 102:9, 10)

We May Feel That Life Has No Purpose

Many individuals have a sense of meaninglessness in their lives. This sense of meaninglessness is prevalent in our society. The naturalists, beginning with Darwin have, little by little, explained away the supernatural. Determinism, another belief system of our modern society, asserts that everything is caused by something that happened previously. It ultimately denies the importance of human decisions. So, for many people, life is a bland existence that has very little importance. Consider the words of Solomon:

I have seen all things that are done under the sun; all of them are meaningless, a chasing after the wind. (Eccles. 1:14)

Many people today have the same feelings that Solomon had when he wrote this verse. This sense of despair and hopelessness may be seen in the various forms of literature and media. Many television programs and movies demonstrate this despair. Some music videos reflect this hopelessness to our young people.

A sense of meaninglessness about life is often heightened or intensified following some sort of tragedy. You may be familiar with someone who developed such feelings after the loss of a loved one. When a person loses someone close to him, such a sense of despair may develop.

We May Feel Overwhelmed with Sorrow

Circumstances may overwhelm us with sorrow. Consider the words of David:

> How long, O Lord? Will you forget me forever? How long will you hide your face from me? How long must I wrestle with my thoughts and every day have sorrow in my heart? (Ps. 13:1, 2)

Examples of sorrow abound from everyday life. Every day people get sick, people die, people have devastating things happen to them. These events do not just affect those particular people alone, but everyone associated with them, especially spouses, family members, and friends.

The story of Joseph provides us with a biblical example of such a situation. Terrible things happened to Joseph himself, but they affected his entire family, especially his father. Joseph's brothers sold him into slavery. They deceived their father into thinking Joseph was dead. The brothers brought Joseph's robe, dipped in goat's blood, to their father. Consider Jacob's response:

> He recognized it and said, "It is my son's robe! Some ferocious animal has devoured him. Joseph has surely been torn to pieces." Then Jacob tore his clothes, put on sackcloth and mourned for his son many days. All his sons and daughters came to comfort him, but he refused to be comforted. "No," he said, "In mourning will I go down to the grave to my son." So his father wept for him. (Gen. 37:33–35)

Jacob remained in a state of unresolved grief until he was told that Joseph was alive (see Gen. 42:36, 45:26–28). The length of time was almost 22 years.

Because He was a man, as well as God, Jesus was not completely immune to the effects of oppressive circumstances on His Spirit. In the Garden of Gethsemane He was in agony over His coming trial and crucifixion:

> He took Peter and the two sons of Zebedee [James and John] along with him, and he began to be sorrowful and troubled. Then he said to them, "My soul is overwhelmed with sorrow to the point of death. Stay here and keep watch with me." (Matt. 26:37, 38)

Tribulation Takes Its Toll Mentally

In addition to spiritual effects of tribulation, there are emotional repercussions as well. Emotional stress affects our minds.

We May Experience Emotional Fatigue

Emotional fatigue often accompanies prolonged stress. One example is found in the story of Samson and Delilah in the Old Testament. Delilah was offered a reward to betray Samson, to find out the source of his great strength. She kept after him until she wore him down emotionally.

> Then she said to him, "How can you say, 'I love you,' when you won't confide in me? This is the third time you have made a fool of me and haven't told me the secret of your great strength." With such nagging she prodded him day after day until he was tired to death. (Judg. 16:15, 16)

Another example is that of caregivers in the hospital setting. These caregivers experience emotional fatigue. When my wife Barbara went to Vanderbilt University for her stem cell transplant, she received excellent care, but I could not help noticing that she had a different nurse every day, for several days in a row. The nurses were scheduled that way on purpose to keep the intensity of the situation from producing emotional burnout.

We May Feel As If We Have No Friends

> Scorn has broken my heart and has left me helpless; I looked for sympathy, but there was none, for comforters, but I found none. (Ps. 69:20)

We May Experience Fear

Psalm 55 is a psalm by King David, written on the occasion of his being betrayed by a former friend. That person was someone with whom he had enjoyed sweet fellowship, but the turn of events disturbed him deeply.

> My heart is in anguish within me. The terrors of death assail me. Fear and trembling have beset me; horror has overwhelmed me. (Ps. 55:4, 5)

I am well acquainted with fear. When I was in Vietnam, I made many trips along highway 19, the highway that stretched between Qui Nhon and Pleiku. At times along that highway we were close to active combat, but that is not what frightened me. Instead, what frightened me was the possibility of hitting a land mine. When we would have to pull to the side of the road or drive over a hole in the road filled with dirt, I would uncontrollably tense up. I tried to schedule any necessary trips I had to make during the afternoons; I wanted the roads to have already seen plenty of traffic for the day before we drove on them. But nevertheless, my fear continued.

During my wife's illness, I have experienced fear: fear of losing her, fear of what she would have to endure with the treatment, fear of what my responsibilities would be. If we get a good report from the doctor, I feel good. But if we get a bad report, I experience fear.

At some point in life, each of us will encounter something to fear. The key is learning how to act despite the fear and not allowing it to paralyze you.

We May Develop a Sense of Uncertainty

After Moses died, Joshua became the leader of the Israelites. Consider God's words to Joshua:

> I will give you every place where you set your foot, as I promised Moses . . . No one will be able to stand up against you all the days of your life. As I was with Moses, so I will be with you; I will never leave you nor forsake you . . . Be careful to obey all the law my servant Moses gave you; do not turn from it to the right or to the left, that you may be successful wherever you go. Do not let this Book of the Law depart from your mouth; meditate on it day and night; so that you may be careful to do everything written in it. Then you will be prosperous and successful. Have I not commanded you? Be strong and courageous. Do not be terrified; do not be discouraged, for the Lord your God will be with you wherever you go. (Josh. 1:3–9)

Joshua confidently led the Israelites across the Jordan River and into the Promised Land. With the victory at Jericho, the conquest of Canaan had begun. But the Israelites subsequently suffered defeat at Ai. The defeat was God's punishment for Achan's sin. That defeat caused Joshua to feel uncertain:

> Then Joshua tore his clothes and fell facedown to the ground before the ark of the Lord, remaining there till evening. The elders of Israel did the same, and sprinkled dust on their heads. And Joshua said, "Ah, sovereign Lord, why did you ever bring this people across the Jordan to deliver us into the hands of the Amorites to destroy us? If only we had been content to stay on the other side of the Jordan! O Lord, what can I say, now that Israel has been routed by its enemies? The Canaanites and the other people of the country will hear about this and they will surround us and wipe out our name from the earth. What then will you do for your own great name?" (Josh. 7:6–9)

Consider these words of David:

Save me, O God, for the waters have come up to my neck. I sink in the miry depths, where there is no foothold. I have come into the deep waters; the floods engulf me. (Ps. 69:1, 2)

During my wife's illness I have felt great uncertainty. We have been uncertain about treatment options. I have been uncertain about how much to work and how much to stay home. I have experienced uncertainty about the future. Uncertainty about earthly matters is a fact of life.

We May Feel Trapped in a Difficult Situation

Many people feel trapped by their circumstances. They may feel trapped because of bad decisions made in the past. Overwhelming debt may make them feel trapped. They may feel trapped in a bad marriage. They may feel trapped in a job that they do not like, trapped because their salary is such that to change jobs would mean a significant cut in pay. They may feel trapped by someone else's illness or their own.

As a physician, I see many people in my practice who have medical problems that affect the quality of their lives. They must make significant adjustments in how they carry out their activities of daily living. For many people, their medical problems are such that they have to do many things just to stay alive.

Take, for example, the hemodialysis patients. They have to come in to the dialysis center for treatments three times a week. They must not miss an appointment. Those that skip treatments usually die. They must maintain their nutritional balance, so they must eat, but they must be careful what they eat. Too much potassium could kill them. Too much phosphorus could weaken their bones. Too little protein could affect their general level of health and make them susceptible to infection. While they are eating their food, they must not drink too much liquid. If they drink too much liquid between treatments, their lungs could fill up with fluid, and they could become very short of breath, at times short of breath to the point of death. Those who gain large amounts of fluid between treatments and survive until their next dialysis have a rough time with the treatment. Taking off a large amount of fluid during hemodialysis taxes the circulatory system. Excessive removal of fluid during dialysis could cause the blood pressure to drop. The patients could develop muscular cramps. They could vomit. After such a dialysis, patients usually feel terrible.

These patients have their physical problems, but they also have their spiritual and emotional reactions to those problems. If they are not able to sustain a fairly positive mental attitude, they are not able to do all the things they need to do just to stay alive.

In the book of Lamentations, Jeremiah wrote of feeling trapped:

> He [God] has besieged me and surrounded me with bitterness and hardship. He has made me dwell in darkness like those long dead. He has walled me in so I cannot escape; he has weighed me down with chains. (Lam. 3:5–7)

We May Feel Inadequate, Discouraged, or Unhappy

Some people feel inadequate or ordinary. They don't think they are capable of handling the challenges of life. The Lord appeared to Gideon while he was threshing wheat in a winepress and told him to rescue Israel from the hand of the Midianites. Gideon thought he was inadequate for the task: "'But Lord,' Gideon asked, 'how can I save Israel? My clan is the weakest in Manasseh, and I am the least in my family'" (Judg. 6:15).

Many men and women are discouraged about life in general. Others feel discouraged or unhappy about specific situations. In 1981, we began building our current house. Both my wife's brother and mother had cancer, and so the house was built to be a large duplex with quarters for her parents and brother. Sadly, her brother died before the house could be completed. After we moved into the house, her mother lived five more years.

Later, as Barbara's father approached the end of his life, he did not want medical treatment beyond comfort measures. He did not want to go to the hospital or to a nursing home. We promised him that we would care for him in our home. During those last few months of his life, we took turns sitting with him at night. We had to do everything for him. He was too weak to get out of bed. There were times when Barbara was not sure she was up to the task. There were times when she felt inadequate, times when she was particularly overwhelmed. She was unhappy about both his suffering and her own. At times, she would cry uncontrollably. It was an unnerving experience for me to witness such a thing. All I could do was just hold her and try to reassure her that things would get better.

TRIBULATION TAKES ITS TOLL PHYSICALLY

For each of us, life's trials may be detrimental to our ability to function in everyday life. We may become overwhelmed with fatigue. Long hours of work may predispose us to accidents. Depression may cause us to have trouble getting ourselves going in the mornings. We may have difficulty doing what we know we need to do to get through each day.

People undergoing trials may develop psychosomatic illnesses. There is a part of the nervous system that controls what is voluntary, and then there is a part of the nervous system that controls what is involuntary. The part that controls what is involuntary is called the autonomic nervous system. Our emotions affect our autonomic nervous system. Emotions may cause the head to hurt, the heart to pound, the throat to constrict, the breathing to be difficult, the stomach to ache, the bladder to feel irritated, or the back to hurt.

Anger may lead to cardiovascular disease. Middle-aged women with hostile attitudes, a high level of suppressed anger, and high levels of "public self-consciousness" had an increased risk for carotid atherosclerosis as evaluated by carotid ultrasound.[1] In a study from Finland, men with high levels of expressed anger were at increased risk for strokes.[2] In a study among veterans, a dose-response relationship was found between poor control of anger and overall risk of coronary heart disease.[3] Anger is capable of triggering heart attacks.[4]

A study about caregivers and health risk was published in the *Journal of the American Medical Association.* The authors noted an increased risk for caregivers of elderly spouses, to develop their own health problems:

1. Caregivers are less likely to be attentive to their own health needs.
2. Compared with controls, their immune systems are functionally impaired.
3. They exhibit greater cardiovascular reactivity.
4. Their wound healing is impaired.

For the purposes of the study, caregivers were defined as "individuals whose spouses had difficulty with at least one activity of daily living or instrumental activity of daily living due to physical or health problems or problems with confusion." For six activities of daily living and six instrumental activities of daily living tasks, caregivers were asked, "Do you help your spouse with this task?" Caregivers were also questioned about the level of emotional strain associated with helping their spouses. During a four-year period, spouses providing care and experiencing caregiver strain had mortality risks that were sixty-three percent higher than control subjects. The authors concluded that spousal caregiving is an independent risk factor for mortality.[5]

In an editorial about the article, published in the same issue of the journal, it was noted that marriage is the most important relationship for the majority of adults.[6] Severity of illness and frequency of death are lower for the married than the unmarried for many acute and chronic conditions, in part because of the support provided by the marriage relationship. When the spouse is ill, the primary source of support may become the major generator of stress and also limit the spouse's ability to seek support in other relationships. Although some of the data is conflicting, it does appear that death of a spouse is associated with a higher mortality in men.[7]

We all need support in one way or another. Many times, people experiencing affliction think that no one understands them or understands how they feel. We are all unique, so no one can completely understand another person's feelings; however as human beings, we do exhibit certain similarities. There are similarities in our physical makeup. In most situations, each of us has a head, two arms, a body, and two legs. In the same way, there are similarities in the nature of our spiritual and emotional makeups. There are similarities in the ways each of us may be wounded. We need to understand how tribulation affects mankind in general so that we will be able to deal with it in our own personal situation in particular. We need to understand how tribulation causes wear and tear on our makeup so that we can do what is necessary to take care of ourselves.

When I was in Vietnam, initially I was in a tank battalion. The soldiers had to keep up the tanks. It was called preventive maintenance. Preventive maintenance is necessary for every part of our being. In the middle of our own particular situation, we need to understand how our spirit is reacting. It is important to know whether or not we see the Lord as an ally or as an adversary in the situation. Christians need to understand that the Lord is our ally and is working for our ultimate good. We also need to understand how our minds and bodies are reacting to the situation so we can take care of them, and provide them with adequate nourishment, adequate rest, and adequate preventive maintenance. If we understand how our experience is similar to the experience of others and how they handled tribulation, it helps each of us to be overcomers ourselves.

3

NEGATIVE REACTIONS TO TRIBULATION

P eople experience tribulation throughout life, with more or less severity at different times in life. Negative reactions during our struggles are common; they are natural. However, what comes naturally is often not what is best. The Bible tells us, "The natural man receiveth not the things of the Spirit of God: for they are foolishness unto him: neither can he know them." (1 Cor. 2:14a KJV)

ANGER

My dear brothers, take note of this: Everyone should be quick to listen, slow to speak and slow to become angry, for man's anger does not bring about the righteous life that God desires (James 1:19, 20).

Refrain from anger and turn from wrath; do not fret—it leads only to evil. (Ps. 37:8)

The end of a matter is better than its beginning, and patience is better than pride. Do not be quickly provoked in your spirit, for anger resides in the lap of fools (Eccles. 7:8, 9).

Do not make friends with a hot-tempered man, do not associate with one easily angered, or you may learn his ways and get yourself ensnared. (Prov. 22:24, 25)

Anger Toward God

Recently several people were killed in a plane crash. Someone asked, "Where was God?" Consider Psalm 115:2, 3: "Why do the nations say, 'Where is their God?' Our God is in heaven; he does whatever pleases him." In my mind, when someone responds to tragedy by asking, "Where was God?", their response to the tragedy is one of anger. It is an initial reaction that needs to move toward resolution. Consider Jude 14–16:

> Enoch, the seventh from Adam, prophesied about these men: 'See, the Lord is coming with thousands upon thousands of his holy ones to judge everyone, and to convict all the ungodly of all the ungodly acts they have done in the ungodly way, and of all the harsh words ungodly sinners have spoken against him.' These men are grumblers and faultfinders; they follow their own evil desires; they boast about themselves and flatter others for their own advantage.

Consider also Jesus' words in Matthew 12:36, 37:

> But I tell you that men will have to give account on the day of judgment for every careless word they have spoken. For by your words you will be acquitted, and by your words you will be condemned.

Words spoken against the Lord God Almighty will later return to condemn us.

Anger Toward Others

> You have heard that it was said to the people long ago, "Do not murder, and anyone who murders will be subject to judgment." But I tell you that anyone who is angry with his brother will be subject to judgment. (Matt. 5:21, 22a)

"In your anger do not sin": Do not let the sun go down while you are still angry, and do not give the devil a foothold. (Eph. 4:26, 27)

Moses had a problem with anger. As a young man, he killed an Egyptian who had been beating a Hebrew (Exod. 2:11–15). Subsequently, Moses fled to Midian. After God spoke to Moses from the burning bush, he returned to Egypt to give Pharaoh the message from God. When Pharaoh would not accept the message, Moses became angry with Pharaoh (Exod. 11:4–10).

After the Israelites left Egypt, the people quarreled with Moses at Rephidim because they were thirsty (Exod. 17:1–7). Moses replied, "Why do you quarrel with me? Why do you put the Lord to the test?" When he struck the rock, water came out. Moses called the place *massah* which means "testing" and *meribah* which means "quarreling."

While Moses was on Mount Sinai communicating with God, the Israelites made a golden calf and worshipped it (Exod. 32). When Moses came down from the mountain and saw the calf and the dancing, his anger burned. He broke the tablets of the Ten Commandments. In his anger, he took the calf and burned it in the fire; then he ground the calf to powder, scattered it on the water, and forced the Israelites to drink it. He had 3000 of the Israelites killed.

At Kadesh, the Israelites again had no water and quarreled with Moses (Num. 20:1–13). The Lord told Moses to take the staff and speak to the rock. Moses and Aaron gathered the assembly together in front of the rock. Moses said, "Listen, you rebels, must we bring you water out of this rock?" In his anger and impatience, Moses struck the rock twice rather than speaking to it as God had instructed. Water gushed out. The Lord said to Moses, "Because you did not trust in me enough to honor me as holy in the sight of the Israelites, you will not bring this community into the land I give them." Moses' fate ought to be a lesson to us not to lose patience with those whom God has called us to serve. The other side of the coin is this: those being served should not make things too difficult for the people caring for them and push them into reacting in such a way as to sin against God.

Consider this quote from the Psalms:

> By the waters of Meribah they angered the Lord, and trouble came to Moses because of them; for they rebelled against the Spirit of God, and rash words came from Moses' lips. (Ps. 106:32, 33)

Anger occurs when our sense of justice is violated. Of course our sense of justice is often flawed by the world, the flesh, and the devil. Anger is frequently related to selfishness or pride. It often occurs if we are inconvenienced, slighted, or not *appropriately* respected. David's older brother Eliab was good-looking and tall. But he was not chosen to be king (1 Sam. 16:6, 7). The rejection probably had something to do with the taunting that Eliab later gave David when David was talking to the other soldiers about Goliath. In 1 Samuel 17:28, Eliab "burned with anger at him and asked, 'Why have you come down here? And with whom did you leave those few sheep in the desert? I know how conceited you are and how wicked your heart is; you came down only to watch the battle.'" David must have had prior experience with this type of treatment. His response was, "Now what have I done?"

When I was in practice in Roanoke, Virginia, I read *The Kink & I* by James Mallory.[1] It was then I learned some things about my relationship with my wife. I learned that how I treated my wife should not depend on how she treated me. I learned that I was responsible to God for how I treated her. If she became angry with me, I did not have to return anger for anger. If we had a conflict, it was up to me to come up with a solution that was good for both of us. I learned not to "keep score". I accepted my wife as she was, God's perfect gift to me. Gradually, I learned to do the same for my children and most of the other people around me.

The main exception to this, the people I had the most difficulty with, were those who were in authority over me. I believe that my feelings toward authority figures were rooted in an unhappy relationship with my father. I expected those in authority over me to be perfect, to be *worthy* of my allegiance. My expectations were unreasonable. I could become very resentful if decisions were not made the way that I thought they should be made. And once resentments developed, I nurtured them. I stored them away, ready to bring them out at the slightest provocation. God enlightened me about this sin when we were on a mission trip in Guatemala. We were having devotions one morning. The speaker read from 1 Corinthians 13. The phrase "It [love] keeps no record of wrongs" got my attention. I realized that I was storing up my resentments. I learned to expect less and to be more forgiving. I learned to accept those in authority over me, whether or not they always did exactly as I thought they should. Their responsibility for what they did was to God, not to me. I was responsible to God to do a good job regardless of the actions of those around me. The concept was tremendously liberating.

BITTERNESS

Bitterness is related to anger but is more deep-seated.

Why is light given to those in misery, and life to the bitter of soul, to those who long for death that does not come, who search for it more than for hidden treasure, who are filled with gladness and rejoice when they reach the grave? . . . I have no peace, no quietness; I have no rest, but only turmoil. (Job 3:20–22, 26)

Bitterness is a sin. (Acts 8:23; Rom. 3:14). Bitterness can cause our spiritual lives to deteriorate. We are to rid ourselves of bitterness (Eph. 4:31; Heb. 12:15). There are times when bitterness and hatred simply will not leave us in spite of how hard we try to make them go away. We may need God's help in reaching those places in our hearts. Perhaps we feel bitter toward a colleague, a supervisor, someone who seems to succeed in spite of his character flaws. For those who are oppressed by bitterness, I would suggest confessing those feelings as sin and seeking deliverance. The Lord is good to those whose hope is in Him. Because of the Lord's great love we are not consumed by bitterness, for His compassions never fail (Lam. 3:19–22).

SELF-PITY

The first time I thought much about self-pity was years ago when I read a book entitled *Spirit-Controlled Temperament* by Tim LaHaye.[2] Self-pity has no redeeming virtues. There is nothing it motivates us to do that is profitable.

After God rejected Saul, Samuel anointed David king over Israel (1 Sam. 16). Saul tried to kill David, pursuing him for about seven years until his death. (1 Sam. 19–30). I am sure that during those times of trial, it strengthened David to know that he would eventually become king. He received encouraging words from both Jonathan (1 Sam. 23:15–17) and Abigail (1 Sam. 25:28–31). David wrote Psalm 57 from a cave while he was on the run from Saul:

> Have mercy on me O God . . . for in you my soul takes refuge . . . I cry out to God, who fulfills his purpose for me . . . I will sing and make music . . . I will praise you, O Lord among the nations . . . For great is your love reaching to the heavens; your faithfulness reaches to the skies.

I believe that overcoming self-pity has to do with recognizing the sovereignty of God, understanding our identity in Christ, and realizing that if something bad happens to us that we did not bring on ourselves, that that occurrence is the Lord's will for our lives. We each need to be aware that God has a plan for us.

> Though I walk in the midst of trouble, you preserve my life; you stretch out your hand against the anger of my foes, with your right hand you save me. The LORD will fulfill his purpose for me; (Ps. 138:7, 8a)

There may be a time when we need to focus less on the question, "Why?" and focus more on the question, "What now?"

WORRY

Worry may affect our emotional equilibrium. It may make us ineffective in our daily tasks. It may affect our judgment. Worry can become so overwhelming that it is paralyzing. Some people are so overcome by anxiety they are unable to do anything. There are people who are afraid to come out of the house.

There are many things we may worry about. At times we may have specific fears. Other times we may have a vague, non-specific sense of dread, not related to anything in particular. Jesus spoke about those who worry:

> Therefore I tell you, do not worry about your life, what you will eat or drink; or about your body, what you will wear. Is not life more important than food, and the body more important than clothes? Look at the birds of the air; they do not sow or reap or store away in barns, and yet your heavenly Father feeds them. Are you not much more valuable than they? Who of you by worrying can add a single hour to his life? And why do you worry about clothes? See how the lilies of the field grow. They do not labor or spin. Yet I tell you that not even Solomon in all his splendor was dressed like one of these. If that is how God clothes the grass of the field, which is here today and tomorrow is thrown into the fire, will he not much more clothe you, O you of little faith? So do not worry, saying, 'What shall we eat?' or 'What shall we drink?' or 'What shall we wear?' For the pagans run after all these things, and your heavenly Father knows that you need them. But seek first his kingdom and his righteousness, and all these things will be given to you as well. Therefore do not worry about tomorrow, for tomorrow will worry about itself. Each day has enough trouble of its own." (Matt. 6:25–34)

EXCESSIVE INTROSPECTION AND SELF-CONDEMNATION

Tribulation may cause us to spend too much time looking at ourselves. There is a certain level of scrutiny that no one can stand up under. If we look hard enough, we can find something about ourselves to be displeased about. And once we find it, we can beat ourselves to death.

In my practice, I see many people who do not have good self-concepts, who do not like themselves. I know how that feels. During my first two years of college, I was filled with self-doubt. I did not like myself. I would read my Bible and then look at my life, and I felt I did not measure up. During my third year in college, at Bryan College in Dayton, Tennessee, I learned some things about my identity in Christ and how I was to view myself. I came to understand that when the Lord saved me in 1949, He knew exactly what I would be like in 1962. He also knew exactly how the rest of my life was going to turn out, and He saved me anyway. He took me just as I was. Because He accepted me, I needed to accept myself. I am someone for whom Christ died, just as you are. We are not to become bound down in self-condemnation. I learned to confess my sins and forget them. I learned to accept and even like myself. I learned that if I would turn each day over to Christ, He would help me throughout the day. If I would abide in Christ, He would work out His purpose for my life.

People may be angry with themselves for many reasons. That anger may result in endless brooding. I have some people in my practice who are overweight and unable to stop eating. They do not like the way they look in the mirror. They are not happy about the size of clothes they have to wear. But they still continue to eat. I see others who experience self-deprecation because they cannot get their work done around the house. Some are angry with themselves about their bad habits, habits that they seem powerless to break.

Expending excess emotion over a difficult situation does little to change it. Consider obesity for instance. A person who is overweight may be in anguish about it. That person can earnestly seek forgiveness; he can pray for spiritual help in the future. But the simple fact is that it is a matter of arithmetic. If we take in more calories that we burn up, then we are going to gain weight. All of the anguish and emotional self-flagellation does not change that fact. If we have trouble making ourselves do what we know we need to do, then we should get the help we need.

Many caregivers of people who are sick find excuses to feel guilty. Because I am a nephrologist, I see many patients who are very sick. I see many patients who are near the end of the road, and I see many patients who die. I have found that frequently, when someone dies, that person's caregiver finds something about which to feel guilty. The caregiver is often a spouse or offspring of the recently deceased. Perhaps the caregiver had been doing 24 hour-a-day duty for months or even years. After the person dies, the caregiver has all sorts of negative thoughts: "If only I had done this! If only I had done that!" I suspect that some of those negative thoughts may come from the fact that, at some point, the caregiver felt resentful about some of his responsibilities to the patient.

Caring for someone who is ill can be a real chore. Occasional feelings of resentment are natural. If we can learn to put those feelings behind us, and do what we know we need to do, we should not feel guilty. Perhaps we made a mistake, an error in judgment. None of us is perfect. None of us can care for a sick person perfectly. We simply need to do the best job we can and trust God for the results. When any imperfections, or deficiencies come to mind, we need to confess them and put them in the past. We need to remember that we do not have the power of life or death. That power rests in the hand of God Almighty. We should not allow the Enemy of Souls to gain a stronghold in our lives through guilt over something we could not control.

Some people worry excessively about something that might have happened. Perhaps they faced their own death and could not cope with the harsh reality. When this happens, I believe the thing to remember is that we have a Sovereign God who is in complete control. The important thing is not what might have happened but what did happen. Put the past in the past.

Our tribulation may lead to negative reactions. Understanding those negative reactions ought to help us recognize them, should they occur within our own souls and spirits. If we recognize them, it may help us in dealing with them in the way most pleasing to the Lord.

4

ADVERSE BEHAVIOR
DURING TRIBULATION

People have different responses when they face tribulation; some are positive, but some are detrimental. We are told in Romans 14:23b that, "Everything that does not come from faith is sin." In my opinion, any response to tribulation, that moves us farther away from God, should be considered sin. Such responses can be in thought, word, or deed. Improper thoughts may lead to negative speech and adverse behavior.

REBELLION

As we go through our own tribulations, we should not put the Lord our God to the test the way the Israelites did in the desert (Deut. 6:16). In the Old Testament, Moses led the Children of Israel out of Egypt, but over the next two years, while they were sojourning in the desert, the Israelites tested God no fewer than ten times (Num. 14:22). William MacDonald lists those ten occurrences in his referenced, *The Believer's Bible Commentary - Old Testament*.[1] The Hebrew word *nasa* means *to test* or *try* or *tempt*. Harris indicates that when it comes to the idea of testing God the way the Israelites did in the desert, the word *nasa* carries the idea of having a defiant attitude.[2] If we look at what the Bible says about those ten incidents, we can get a better idea of what it means to test God.

1. After the Israelites initially left Egypt, they were camped by the Red Sea. When they realized the Egyptian army was approaching, they became frightened and began complaining (Exod. 14:10–12).

2. At Marah, the Israelites grumbled about the bitter water (Exod. 15:22–24). The word *marah* actually means "bitter."

3. In the Desert of Sin, they grumbled because they were hungry (Exod. 16:1–3).

4. When God sent manna, some of the Israelites disobeyed and kept it, during the week, overnight (Exod. 16:19, 20).

5. Some of the Israelites tried to gather manna on the Sabbath (Exod. 16:22–27).

6. At Rephidim, the Israelites quarreled with Moses because they were thirsty. They tested the Lord saying, "Is the Lord among us or not?" Moses called the place *Massah* which means "testing" and *Meribah* which means "quarreling." (Exod. 17:1–7)

7. At Horeb, their impatience led to idolatry; God referred to them as a stiff-necked people. Aaron let them get out of control, and they were running wild (Exod. 32:1–35).

8. At Taberah, the Israelites complained because of hardship (Num. 11:1–3).

9. At Kibroth Hattaavah, the Israelites complained because they were not satisfied with God's provision. They craved other food besides manna. They wanted meat. They rejected the Lord (Num. 11:4–34).

10. At Kadesh, they grumbled. They lacked faith regarding God's ability to help them conquer the land of Canaan (Num. 13, 14).

Many of these occurrences were first mentioned in the historical record, but they were also cited again later in the Old Testament. There are references in books such as Exodus and Numbers but also in Psalms and Ezekiel. These verses teach us that we should not test the Lord our God the way they did. We are given examples of what we should not do.

1. Not remembering the great things the Lord has done in the past (Ps. 78:42;106:13)
2. Not being satisfied with the Lord's provision (Num. 11:4–6)
3. Lack of faith (Exod. 17:7; Ps. 78:22)
4. Becoming Impatient (Exod. 32:1)
5. Demanding what we want (Ps. 78:18)
6. Speaking out against the Lord (Ps. 78:19)
7. Complaining (Exod. 16:2, 3)
8. Quarreling (Exod. 17:2)
9. Treating God with contempt (Num. 14:23)
10. Being stubborn (Exod. 32:9, 10)
11. Rejecting the Lord (Num. 11:20)
12. Letting our behavior get out of control (Exod. 32:25)
13. Rebellion (Num. 14:9)
14. Disobedience (Num. 14:22)
15. Idolatry (Exod. 32:1)

All of these things could be considered as various forms of rebellion. We are rebelling when we refuse to put our trust in God, our Creator. Consider Samuel's words to Saul about rebellion:

> But Samuel replied: "Does the Lord delight in burnt offerings and sacrifices as much as in obeying the voice of the Lord? To obey is better than sacrifice, and to heed is better than the fat of rams. For rebellion is like the sin of divination, and arrogance like the evil of idolatry. Because you have rejected the word of the Lord, he has rejected you as king." (1 Sam. 15:22, 23)

If we rebel against God, there are consequences. One major consequence is that rebellion leads to lack of understanding (Ezekiel 12:2). It impairs our ability to comprehend God's truth.

Let us consider what is said in the New Testament about the time of testing the Israelites experienced in the desert:

> Now these things occurred as examples to keep us from setting our hearts on evil things as they did. Do not be idolaters as some of them were; as it is written: "The people sat down to eat and drink and got up to indulge in pagan revelry." We should not commit sexual immorality, as some of them did—and in one day twenty-three thousand of them died. We should not test the Lord, as some of them did—and were killed by snakes. And do not grumble, as some of them did—and were killed by the destroying angel. These things happened to them as examples and were written down as warnings for us, on whom the fulfillment of the ages has come. (1 Cor. 10:6–11)

> So, as the Holy Spirit says: "Today, if you hear his voice, do not harden your hearts as you did in the rebellion, during the time of testing in the desert, where your fathers tested and tried me and for forty years saw what I did. That is why I was angry with that generation, and I said, 'Their hearts are always going astray, and they have not known my ways.' So I declared on oath in my anger, 'They shall never enter my rest'' See to it, brothers, that none of you has a sinful, unbelieving heart that turns away from the living God. But encourage one another daily, as long as it is called Today, so that none of you may be hardened by sin's deceitfulness. We have come to share in Christ if we hold firmly till the end the confidence we had at first. As has just been said: 'Today, if you hear his voice, do not harden your hearts as you did in the rebellion.' Who were they who heard and rebelled? Were they not all those Moses led out of Egypt? And with whom was he angry for forty years? Was it not those who sinned, whose bodies fell in the desert? And to whom did God swear that they would never enter his rest if not to those who disobeyed? So we see that they were not able to enter, because of their unbelief." (Heb. 3:7–19)

During times of affliction, we are instructed to pay attention to what the Lord is doing (Jer. 6:10–17) and respond appropriately with an attitude of contrition (Jer. 2:30, 32:33). Rather than rebelling against God (Revelation 16:8–11), we are instructed to accept correction (Lev. 26:23, 24). God's discipline is a call to holiness (Heb. 12:10, 11). We are to seek the Lord (Deut. 4:25–31; Ps. 9:9, 10; Isa. 26:8, 9; Isa. 55:6, 7; Jer. 29:10–13; Hos. 5:14, 15; Zeph. 2:3). We are to acknowledge known sin, search our hearts for other sin and then confess our sins and repent (Ps. 32:3–5; Ps. 139:23, 24; Isa. 30:15; Ezek. 33:11; 1 John 1:9). We are to bow to His will and make Him Lord of our lives. I would think it would be terrible to be in the declining years of life and be filled with regret, realizing that one's whole life was spent in futility (Prov. 5:11–14). Remember, "There is no wisdom, no insight, no plan that can succeed against the Lord" (Prov. 21:30).

ADDICTIVE FORMS OF BEHAVIOR

Alcohol and substance abuse are not appropriate responses to tribulation (Prov. 20:1; 23:20, 21; 1 Cor. 5:11; 1 Cor. 6:10; Eph. 5:18). They lead to a distortion of reality.

> Who has woe? Who has sorrow? Who has strife? Who has complaints? Who has needless bruises? Who has bloodshot eyes? Those who linger over wine, who go to sample bowls of mixed wine. Do not gaze at wine when it is red, when it sparkles in the cup, when it goes down smoothly! In the end it bites like a snake and poisons like a viper. Your eyes will see strange sights and your mind imagine confusing things. You will be like one sleeping on the high seas, lying on top of the rigging. (Prov. 23:29–34)

There have been many well-known people in the entertainment industry who ended their lives prematurely because of substance abuse. Such disastrous consequences of an indulgent lifestyle are a clear-cut testimony to us of the dangers of such behavior. Many Christians are repulsed by those who cannot resist the temptation to participate in the drug scene. Although such behavior is sinful,

I feel pity for those people. Many of them are just trying to ease emotional pain in the only way they know how. They are choosing a poor response to the tribulation they have experienced.

People who use alcohol and drugs use them as a means to lift their spirits. But the reality of the situation is that regular use of such agents eventually destroys emotional stability. As such behavior becomes more compulsive, the self-concept suffers.[3] People involved in substance abuse subconsciously create defense mechanisms in an effort to maintain emotional stability. They often repress their true feelings about themselves and project their self-hatred onto others.[4] Their memory is affected, and they become unaware of the fact that they are on a downward spiral to emotional death.[5]

There are other forms of addictive behavior besides substance abuse. People may habitually eat too much. They may have a sexual addiction. They may have a problem with impulse buying or habitually spending too much money. Gambling may be an addiction. These addictive behaviors may provide relief and a temporary escape from the pain that tribulation brings. There is often a biological basis for many of these forms of behavior, but it is still wise to find a way to control them.

CODEPENDENCY

Life's difficulties may lead to codependency. Codependency was first described as a characteristic of children of alcoholics. Since that time the disorder has assumed larger proportions. This definition of codependency appears in the book, *Love Is a Choice*, by Hemfelt, Minirth, and Meier.

> "Codependency can be defined as an addiction to people, behaviors, or things. Codependency is the fallacy of trying to control interior feelings by controlling people, things, and events on the outside. To the codependent, control, or the lack of it, is central to every aspect of life. The codependent may be addicted to another person. In this interpersonal codependency, the codependent has become so elaborately enmeshed in the other person that the

sense of self—personal identity—is severely restricted, crowded out by that other person's identity and problems."[6]

If a child grows up in a home where a parent is missing or does not relate to him well, he needs to seek the Lord to fill that void. Psalm 68:5 tells us that God is a Father to the fatherless. Psalm 27:10 says, "Though my father and mother forsake me, the Lord will receive me." No one's parents are perfect. Children need to ultimately look to the Lord for their emotional support.

Years ago I read a book by Hemfelt and Warren called *Kids Who Carry Our Pain*.[7] According to those authors, parents have to be there for their children, but the children do not have to be there for the parent. It is important for parents not to put too much emotional strain on their children before they are ready to handle it.

I believe that *being there for them* refers to emotional needs, not all needs. When children reach a certain age, the parents should not continue to meet *all* the needs of the son or daughter. When my older son decided to drop out of college, I said, "That's fine, but I think you should support yourself." He said, "Okay." So on a financial level, my son supports himself, but whenever he comes around now, I make an effort to put down whatever I am doing and be available to talk to him. I still meet some of his emotional needs.

Codependency manifests in many different ways. We will discuss a few of the primary characteristics: difficulty setting or respecting boundaries, conflict avoidance, reward dependence, zero balance, and goal visualization.

Difficulty Setting or Respecting Boundaries

Codependent people have difficulty defining their own boundaries and respecting the boundaries of others. An example of a personal boundary being invaded would be the feeling someone gets when another person gets too close to him or her in the elevator. I have, at times, watched some people's reactions with amusement in elevators. People do not like to have their personal boundaries invaded.

Being able to define, set, and maintain proper boundaries helps us in our interpersonal relationships. We need to set limits on how we let people treat us, and other people need to be able to set limits on how we treat them. Moses (Exod. 18:13–26), Nehemiah (Neh. 6:1–4), Paul (Acts 15:36–41), and even Jesus (Mark 5:18, 19; Luke 12:13, 14) were able to set boundaries. When I first entered my medical practice in Roanoke, Virginia, one of my female patients wanted me to meet her one evening out, away from the office. I said, "No." Her request overstepped the appropriate boundaries of the patient-doctor relationship. If I had agreed to go, I would have overstepped appropriate boundaries myself.

When I opened my own office in Knoxville, my wife set some boundaries. One had to do with telephones. She insisted that in our home, we put in two telephone lines. There was one for regular calls with an unlisted number. The second number was known only to the exchange and the other doctors with whom I was sharing call; it was also unlisted. The first number was turned off at night. The other number was left on in case of emergencies. One night when I was off call, there was an emergency with one of my patients. The doctor covering for me had a question about the patient. He asked the dialysis nurse to ring the number of the more private line. She remembered the number. She called me at that number, a couple of days later, to ask me about another patient. I told her not to call me again on that line. If she needed to speak with me, she was to call the exchange. I was not abusive about it, just firm. If people are in the habit of setting limits, they can do so in a nice way. Codependent people have difficulty doing so.

I allow my patients to express any anger they feel toward me. If there is something that they are upset about, I want to know. I do not want any suppressed hostility. Sometimes if I perceive that they might be upset about something, I give them a call to allow them to express themselves before the situation escalates.

Other people need to be able to set limits on us. When they do that, we need to be sensitive to what they are trying to do. Parents have a tendency to try to tell their children how to run their lives even after they are grown. When it comes to such things as vocational choice, the parent needs to let the Lord tell the son or daughter what to do. There are times when children need to be able to draw boundary lines with their parents.

I allow others to set limits on my behavior. Once I tried to share with a patient a biblical resolution for some of his mental stress. From his reaction, I thought he was responding positively. On his next visit he told me he almost did not come back to see me, but he finally decided that I cared about him. He decided to continue using me as his doctor, but he wanted me to be his *doctor*, not his *minister*, and so I have complied with his request.

Related to the concept of boundaries is the concept of independence. As we grow up we need to learn to be independent from other people, not looking to them for our own opinions or for guidance in conduct. Our self worth should not be derived from other people, not our parents, not our brothers or sisters, nor our spouse. For men, much of their self worth is usually tied to their vocation. Our main source for our self worth should come from our relationship with Jesus Christ. We need to have some sense of being able to succeed with God's help. Otherwise, we would never start a business, never run for public office, never plan an evangelistic campaign, never attempt anything. I have a message for people who have difficulty becoming independent, for those who have a problem with their self worth:

1. God is interested in you.
2. He knows you by name.
3. He knows the number of hairs on your head.
4. He loves you.
5. He died for you.
6. He has a plan for your life.
7. He is able to communicate that plan to you.

Conflict Avoidance

Many codependent people enjoy controversy. They go around stirring up trouble. They need to make more of an effort to avoid conflict.

He who loves a quarrel loves sin; (Prov. 17:19a)

Warn a divisive person once, and then warn him a second time. After that, have nothing to do with him. (Titus 3:10)

In dealing with difficult people, we should overlook an offense if possible (Prov. 19:11). We are supposed to overlook the faults of others (Rom. 15:1). Overlooking the faults of others is a sign of strength. We should not fret because of evil doers (Ps. 37:1). Evil men will receive their just reward (Ps. 37:7, 8, 12, 13).

> Do not repay evil for evil. Be careful to do what is right in the eyes of everybody. If it is possible, as far as it depends on you, live at peace with everyone. Do not take revenge, my friends, but leave room for God's wrath, for it is written: "It is mine to avenge; I will repay," says the Lord. On the contrary: "If your enemy is hungry, feed him; if he is thirsty, give him something to drink," . . . Do not be overcome by evil, but overcome evil with good. (Rom. 12:17–20a, 21)

Each of us can be a witness to those who persecute us. If it becomes necessary to become confrontational, we should not do so in an angry or abusive way. As a former colleague has said, "It is more important to fix the problem than it is to fix the blame." My brother-in-law has a similar saying, "It's not *who's* right; it's *what's* right."

In the first seventy-two psalms there are several recurring themes. The psalmist often feels overwhelmed by his circumstances, which were frequently related to others giving him a hard time. Some of his responses to difficult situations are recurrent:

1. In his anger, he made an effort not to sin.
2. He talked to God about what was bothering him.
3. He worshipped God.
4. He searched his heart.
5. He repented of his sins.

6. He asked God for discipline in love rather than discipline in anger.
7. He asked God to help him be more like God wanted him to be.
8. He remembered his identity in the Lord.
9. He remembered God's past faithfulness to others.
10. He remembered God's past faithfulness to himself.
11. He asked God to hear his cry for help.
12. He asked God for deliverance and mercy.
13. He left any revenge to God.
14. He trusted in the Lord.
15. He realized that God alone was his refuge, security, and covering.

Reward Dependence

Codependent people frequently have a problem with reward dependence. They desperately need positive feedback from others, or the approval of others. They have trouble saying, "No." When someone shows up at a codependent's door selling magazine subscriptions that he does not want, he or she may be unable to refuse to buy. There are times when we need to say, "No."

I remember one especially manipulative patient in Roanoke, Virginia. I was having difficulty dealing with the things this patient wanted me to do. One colleague's suggestion was this: "If someone tries to get you to do something you do not want to do, just say, 'I can't do that.'"

When I first went into practice in Knoxville, I had to make a living. Initially I accepted primary care patients. But later on, as my nephrology practice built up, I was forced to stop taking primary care patients. One of the hardest things I had to do was to explain to friends of mine why I could not be their doctor. Occasionally, I would give in and accept a patient, but those who were the most insistent that I be their doctor were also the most demanding if I did accept them. Setting boundaries became easier.

Zero Balance

Many codependent people have the concept of "zero balance." They think that for them to gain anything in their relationship with another person, that person has to lose. Such a concept makes it hard for them to be assertive. It is possible to create a win-win resolution to conflicts.

One example would be a time, two and a half years ago, when after being bed and chair-bound for several months due to her illness, Barbara started walking again. She wanted her independence back. She wanted to resume driving. I was afraid for her to do so. I was afraid she would get stranded on the interstate. I came up with a solution that pleased both of us. We got her a new, more dependable car and purchased a cellular telephone for her so that she could call for help if necessary. The conflict was resolved favorably for both of us. Codependent persons are generally unable to negotiate in such a manner.

Goal Visualization

People need to envision their goals. We need to plan for the future and work hard to fulfill our objectives. I believe that God expects us to do the best we can at whatever we do. Ecclesiastes 9:10 says, "Whatever your hand finds to do, do it with all your might." We are told not to *worry* about tomorrow (Matt. 6:25–34), but we are still supposed to *prepare* for it.

> Go to the ant, you sluggard; consider its ways and be wise! It has no commander, no overseer or ruler, yet it stores its provisions in summer and gathers its food at harvest. (Prov. 6:6–8)

> Suppose one of you wants to build a tower. Will he not first sit down and estimate the cost to see if he has enough money to complete it? For if he lays the foundation and is not able to finish it, everyone who sees it will ridicule him. (Luke 14:28, 29)

We need to envision goals, but as we do so, we need to entrust our lives to Christ. We are supposed to commit our way unto the Lord. Proverbs 3:5, 6 says, "Trust in the Lord with all your heart and lean not on your own understanding; in all your ways acknowledge him, and he will make your paths straight." Psalm 127:1 says," Unless the LORD builds the house, its builders labor in vain. Unless the LORD watches over the city, the watchmen stand guard in vain." Philippians 1:6 says, "Being confident of this, that he who began a good work in you will carry it on to completion until the day of Christ Jesus." After each of us commits his life to Jesus Christ, he needs to believe that Jesus took it into His capable hands and that He will make it prosper. Then he needs to move on with the rest of his life. We need to abide in Christ. He will get us to where we need to be.

ABANDONING OUR RESPONSIBILITIES

In the middle of tribulation, some people abandon their responsibilities. They may abandon a spouse who is ill. In a difficult situation they may flee the scene. Abandonment can occur on a mental or spiritual level as well as a physical level. We may withdraw emotionally from someone who needs our help, though still physically present. In my view, the ultimate abandonment of the family is suicide. Some people reach such a level of mental illness that they attempt suicide as a means of escape. This is their way of coping with adverse situations.

Thank God that we do not have to reach such extremes. In the next chapter, we will examine the causes of tribulation so that we might be able to find more positive methods of dealing with it.

5

Causes of Tribulation

When people face difficult situations, they tend to ask the question, "Why did this have to happen to me?" There are many answers to this question. In this chapter we will review some of the many reasons for the tribulation we go through in this life. The first of these is *sin*.

Sin

A major cause of tribulation is sin, both Adam's sin and our own. Sin has plagued mankind since the fall.

Adam's Sin

Adam's sin led to God's judgment. When Adam sinned, the ground was cursed. Decay became part of mankind's existence. The judgment that came about because of Adam's sin brought the world disease and death.

To Adam he said, "Because you listened to your wife and ate from the tree about which I commanded you, 'You must not eat of it,' Cursed is the ground because of you; through painful toil you will eat of it all the days of your life. It will produce thorns

77

and thistles for you, and you will eat the plants of the field. By the sweat of your brow you will eat your food until you return to the ground, since from it you were taken; for dust you are and to dust you will return." (Gen. 3:17–19).

Although disease is not the only cause of death, disease and death go hand in hand. Patients with *diabetes mellitus* provide us with a common example of the entropy that came upon all creation. *Diabetes mellitus* results from a complete absence or partial deficiency of insulin. It occurs in both juvenile and adult forms. Patients with *diabetes mellitus* develop vascular disease that affects the eyes, the heart, the alimentary canal, the kidneys, the peripheral circulation, and the nervous system.

Over the years God has made provision for diabetics in many ways. Insulin is now available to keep them out of a diabetic coma and to control polyuria, large volumes of urine output associated with high blood sugars. Oral agents, such as pills to control blood sugar for diabetes, are becoming more and more effective. Drugs to control blood pressure are also more effective. We now have drugs that specifically control the pressure within the basic filtering mechanism of the kidney, and prolong the life of the kidney. Diuretics to control edema, fluid retention, are more effective. Diabetics whose kidneys fail are being dialyzed. They receive kidney transplants. Diabetics are living longer and longer, but unfortunately there is a trade-off. More and more, new and different complications are becoming prevalent. One of the hardest things for me to deal with emotionally is the diabetics who have a successful kidney transplant, but still continue to have the vascular problems associated with *diabetes mellitus*. The transplanted kidney works fine, but they still have vascular disease causing them to lose blood supply to their legs and arms. In some cases, they still require amputations. They have strokes and heart attacks. They develop strange infections. Eventually entropy takes its toll.

Adam's sin caused all sorts of disease, including *diabetes mellitus* to come upon the human race. We live in a world full of disease and sickness. Even though we live under a new covenant made possible by Jesus Christ, we still face the natural world of germs, viruses, and bacteria. People, including Christians, contract sicknesses and die. There's a purpose however, for the fallen state of our world.

> For the creation was subjected to frustration, not by its own choice, but by the will of the one who subjected it, in hope that the creation itself will be liberated from its bondage to decay and brought into the glorious freedom of the children of God. (Rom. 8:20, 21)

Our Own Sin

Our own personal sin may require God's judgment. God caused seven years of mental illness in Nebuchadnezzar because of his sin of pride (Daniel 4). King Uzziah became proud of his position. Presumptuously, he entered the temple of the Lord to burn incense, an act reserved only for the sons of Aaron. As judgment, the Lord afflicted him with leprosy. He remained leprous until the day of his death (2 Chron. 26). King Herod Agrippa I also had a problem with pride. Acts 12:23 records that an angel of the Lord struck him down, and he was eaten by worms and died. We are told that anyone who takes communion in an unworthy manner brings judgment on himself (1 Cor. 11:27–32). There is a sin that leads to death (1 Cor. 11:30, 1 John 5:16, 17).

Sin can be more directly responsible for disease and death. Tobacco abuse, drug abuse, and sexual sin can all lead to illness and an early demise. Personal sin has natural consequences. For instance, sexual sins may cause sexually transmitted disease including AIDS. Drug abuse may cause permanent mental defects or death. There are often natural consequences to a poor choice of habits.

Satan's Harrassment

Satan is the leader of the spiritual forces of evil in the heavenly realms (Eph. 6:12). The whole world is under the control of the evil one (1 John 5:19). In the gospel of John, Satan is referred to as the "prince of this world" three times (John 12:31; John 14:30; John 16:11). He is the god of this age (2 Cor. 4:4). He is even able to deceive believers (2 Cor. 11:3). He leads the whole world astray (Rev. 12:9)

Satan Has Power Over The Sick

Satan has power over the sick. Peter referred to the sick who were healed by Jesus as "under the power of the devil" (Acts 10:38). A spirit kept one Jewish woman crippled for eighteen long years until Jesus healed her. Prior to her encounter with Jesus, she was not able to stand erect (Luke 13:10–17). Satan was also responsible for Paul's "thorn in the flesh" (2 Cor. 12:7).

Satan Wants to Keep the Lost from Receiving God's Message of Salvation

Satan has power over unbelievers (Acts 26:17, 18). He wants to prevent the lost from understanding the gospel (Luke 8:12).

> And even if our gospel is veiled, it is veiled to those who are perishing. The god of this world has blinded the minds of unbelievers, so that they cannot see the light of the gospel of the glory of Christ, who is the image of God. (2 Cor. 4:3, 4).

Satan wants lost souls to continue in disobedience.

> As for you, you were dead in your transgressions and sins, in which you used to live when you followed the ways of this world and of the ruler of the kingdom of the air, the spirit who is now at work in those who are disobedient. All of us also lived among them at one time, gratifying the cravings of our sinful nature and following its desires and thoughts. (Eph. 2:1–3a)

Satan deceives those who are perishing. He wants them to have a defiant attitude toward God. In 1996, I made a trip to Ukraine with another physician, a nurse, and a lady who was from Ukraine. The lady served as our interpreter. The object of the trip was to exchange ideas and to provide medical supplies and medical literature to the people there. On the overnight train from Kiev to

Donetsk, we met an interesting man who had retired from the Soviet Army after twenty-six years of service. During the conversation he abruptly announced that he was an atheist. He was angry with God, and gave three reasons for his anger: human suffering, the fact that there are so many different religions, and the fact that Christians don't always act as they are supposed to act.

Satan Has Been Given Power to Afflict Believers

Just before He ascended into heaven, Jesus said to His disciples, "But you will receive power when the Holy Spirit comes on you; and you will be my witnesses in Jerusalem, and in all Judea and Samaria, and to the ends of the earth" (Acts 1:8). The Greek word translated "witness" is *martys*. It is the word from which we get the English word "martyr." The word "martyr" refers to someone who is a witness unto death.[1] Greek words similar to *martys* include *martyreo*, meaning to bear witness, *martyria*, meaning testimony, and *martyrio*, that which serves as testimony or proof.[2]

Each Christian, in his own way, will become a martyr, or a witness for Christ. There will be few exceptions. Believers who have made a decision to follow Christ, become subject to attacks by Satan. The question is not *if* it will happen, but *when* it will happen. We will be on the receiving end of the flaming arrows of the evil one (Eph. 6:16), the enemy of our souls. How we react to his attacks will be a witness of what the Spirit of God has done in our lives. We may either have a testimony of a mature relationship with the Father or a testimony that we are still spiritual infants. Most of us will fall somewhere in between. We will be witnesses to others of what God has done in our lives during our tribulation, both by our words and our deeds, whether we make positive statements or negative ones.

Although Satan can afflict believers, there is a limit to what he can do to us. He does not have the power to take away our salvation (John 17:12; Rom. 8:35–39; 2 Tim. 1:12b). He does have some power over life and death (Heb. 2:14), but he cannot take away our lives without God's permission (Job 2:6). Satan can try to destroy our lives in an indirect manner. He can tempt us into sin that leads to death (1 Cor. 11:29, 30; 1 John 5:16).

Satan Wants to Interfere with Believers' Relationships with the Father

Satan wants to destroy our faith (Luke 22:31, 32; 1 Tim. 1:19). He wants us to get the idea that tribulation is evidence that God is not there or that He doesn't care about us. He wants us to think that God does not love us (Rev. 3:9). He wants us to doubt God's motives (Gen. 3:4, 5). He wants us to charge God with wrongdoing (Job 1:22). He wants us to curse God (Job 1:5; 1:11; 2:5; 2:9). Satan wants to keep us from following through with God's purposes for our lives. He even tempted the Lord Jesus not to go to the cross (Matt. 16:21–28).

Satan wants us to lose our first love, the way those in the church in Ephesus lost theirs (Rev. 2:4). I believe Satan wants to destroy any intimacy we have with the Father, and to separate us from God's fellowship. Consider the result of Satan's first success with mankind, how Satan tempted the first couple to sin and came between them and God. Genesis 3:8 describes how the relationship between God and Adam and Eve was affected:

> Then the man and his wife heard the sound of the Lord God as he was walking in the garden in the cool of the day, and they hid from the Lord God among the trees of the garden.

Adam and Eve hid from God's presence because their perfect relationship with Him had been destroyed. It seems to me that Satan uses difficult situations to deceive us into acting is such a way that it destroys our relationship with God. When we sin and our conscience is defiled, it separates us from the Father. Consider how Satan was allowed to tempt Peter. Peter's denial of Jesus disrupted his relationship with the Lord. Peter was put in a difficult situation. He must have been very frightened. He responded to the situation by lying. Consider Jesus' words at the Last Supper:

> "Simon, Simon, Satan has asked to sift you as wheat. But I have prayed for you, Simon, that your faith may not fail. And when you have turned back, strengthen your brothers." But he replied, "Lord, I am ready to go with you to prison and to death." Jesus

answered, "I tell you, Peter, before the rooster crows today, you will deny three times that you know me." (Luke 22:31–34)

I believe that there were extenuating circumstances in Peter's situation. I believe that part of the reason Peter denied the Lord is that he was confused. He did not understand what was going on or what he was supposed to do. When the arresting party came to Gethsemane for Jesus, Peter rose up and cut off the right ear of Malchus, the high priest's servant (John 18:10). Jesus responded by saying, "No more of this!" Jesus touched the man's ear and healed him (Luke 22:51). It was Jesus Himself who had made certain Peter would have a sword (Luke 22:35–38). After the arrest, Peter and John followed Jesus, who was taken to the courtyard of Caiaphas, the high priest. John knew Caiaphas (John 18:15), and through John's influence, Peter was allowed inside (John 18:16). Peter was cold, and because of that, he was drawn over to the fire (John 18:18).

> But when they had kindled a fire in the middle of the courtyard and had sat down together, Peter sat down with them. A servant girl saw him seated there in the firelight. She looked closely at him and said, "This man was with him." But he denied it, "Woman, I don't know him," he said. A little later someone else saw him and said, "You also are one of them." "Man, I am not!" Peter replied. About an hour later another asserted, "Certainly this fellow was with him, for he is a Galilean." Peter replied, "Man, I don't know what you're talking about!" Just as he was speaking the rooster crowed. The Lord turned and looked straight at Peter. Then Peter remembered the word the Lord had spoken to him: "Before the rooster crows today, you will disown me three times." And he went outside and wept bitterly. (Luke 22:55–62)

After the resurrection, Jesus appeared to His disciples by the Sea of Galilee. Peter was restored to his fellowship with Christ (John 21:15–19).

A story in Numbers gives us another example of how a different kind of temptation may be used to separate us from God, but in my mind the situation is analogous. The Israelites were camped on the plains of Moab along the Jordan River across from Jericho. The Moabites and the Midianites were concerned about the great number of foreign people, the Israelites, in their territory. Balak, son of Zippor, the king of Moab, sent messengers to summon Balaam, son of Beor. Balak wanted Balaam to curse the Israelites. But the Lord would only allow Balaam to bless the Israelites (Num. 22–24),

Balaam gave the advice that the women should entice the Israelite men to sin (Num. 31:16), to turn the Israelites away from the Lord. The plan was to cause God to have to take his blessings away from the Israelites so that their advances would fail. Balaam's sin is referred to in Revelation 2:14. Unfortunately, the Israelite men did indulge in sexual immorality with the Moabite and Midianite women and sacrificed to their gods (Num. 25:1–3; 31:2a, 16). After the men of Israel sinned, the Lord's anger burned against the Israelites. He sent a plague on the Israelites, and twenty-four thousand people were killed (Num. 25:9).

It appears to me that one of the reasons Satan brings tribulation on us is for a similar purpose. He wants us to act in such a way that we will no longer be in fellowship with God. He wants to find a way to keep us from continuing to abide in Christ.

I have already mentioned that my wife has battled cancer. I spoke with one of Barbara's oncology nurses about this—how sickness can drive people away from God. Her response was, "I see that every day." She spoke of one believer in particular who had been very active in church work. Then the person was diagnosed with cancer. First he became angry with God. Then he became angry with himself for being angry with God! After that he decided that he was not such a good person and should not be so active in church.

I also spoke about this idea with the head nurse at our main dialysis unit. She concurred with the other nurse's observation. She said that when people first begin on dialysis, many of them are angry with God. They wonder why they have been stricken with such a disease and why God doesn't heal them of it.

Satan Wants to Destroy Believers' Witness in the World

Satan wants to destroy our witness in the world, to have us be unfruitful in our Christian lives. Satan wants to destroy our effectiveness as salt and light. He does not want us to have a purifying influence on the world or be a means by which others see God's truth. Satan wants us to respond to tribulation in such a way that we become unfit or disqualified as a good witness for Christ. He does not want us to receive our crown (1 Cor. 9:24–27).

GOD'S PROVISION

Tribulation may be part of God's provision, for the benefit of the person undergoing tribulation or for someone else.

For the Benefit of the Person Involved

When I started my internship, I wanted to be a surgeon. But God had other plans for me. I could not tolerate the scrubbing for surgery. I developed hand dermatitis. The hand dermatitis ended any plans I had to become a surgeon. I now realize that my personality is more suited to being in a subspecialty of internal medicine. God had his ways of arranging things. "In his heart a man plans his course, but the Lord determines his steps" (Prov. 16:9). In this case the trial that I went through with the dermatitis caused me to change my plans and turned out to be for my good.

For the Benefit of Someone Else

God may be using our tribulation to benefit the people in the world around us. Joseph was sold into Egypt (Gen. 37:12–36). He was wrongly accused and was even imprisoned (Gen. 39). When he helped Pharaoh's cupbearer, he was forgotten (Gen. 40). But by God's grace and miraculous intervention, he became the ruler of Egypt, second only to Pharaoh (Gen. 41:1–40). All these things occurred so that he could save the lives of his family members (Gen. 45:7) and thus preserve the godly Seed.

Consider also the case of Paul. For the chronology of Paul's life, I have utilized *The Narrated Bible* by F. LaGard Smith.[3] The Holy

Spirit descended upon the early church at the feast of Pentecost. It was not too long after that that Jesus appeared to Paul on the road to Damascus. For three days Paul was literally blind from the experience. The Lord sent Ananias to restore Paul's sight. But because of Paul's reputation for persecuting Christians, Ananias objected. The Lord replied, "Go! This man is my chosen instrument to carry my name before the Gentiles and their kings and before the people of Israel. I will show him how much he must suffer for my name" (Acts 9:15b, 16). The Lord spoke of Paul's coming trials only three days after the Damascus Road experience.

While Paul was on his second missionary journey, he traveled to Philippi in Macedonia. At Philippi, he and Silas were arrested, flogged, and thrown into prison. As they were in prison praying and singing hymns to God, a violent earthquake threw open the prison doors. The events got the jailer's attention. He and his family became Christians (Acts 16). This is just another example of how God's master plan may involve temporary tribulations for believers, but it works out for an ultimate good. God is in control, and we must trust Him that He knows what He is doing.

Paul made several references to suffering in 2 Corinthians: 2 Cor. 1:3–7; 2 Cor. 4:7–11; 2 Cor. 6:3–10; 2 Cor. 12:1–10. Paul also listed many of the specific calamities that had befallen him:

> Are they servants of Christ? (I am out of my mind to talk like this.) I am more. I have worked much harder, been in prison more frequently, been flogged more severely, and been exposed to death again and again. Five times I received from the Jews the forty lashes minus one. Three times I was beaten with rods, once I was stoned, three times I was shipwrecked, I spent a night and a day in the open sea, I have been constantly on the move. I have been in danger from rivers, in danger from bandits, in danger from my own countrymen, in danger from Gentiles; in danger in the city, in danger in the country, in danger at sea; and in danger from false brothers. I have labored and toiled and have often gone without sleep; I have known hunger and thirst and have often gone without food; I have been cold and naked. (2 Cor. 11:23–27).

The Holy Spirit warned Paul further about more suffering to come:

> And now, compelled by the Spirit, I am going to Jerusalem, not knowing what will happen to me there. I only know that in every city the Holy Spirit warns me that prison and hardships are facing me. However, I consider my life worth nothing to me, if only I may finish the race and complete the task the Lord Jesus has given me—the task of testifying to the gospel of God's grace. (Acts 20:22–24)

At the temple in Jerusalem, Paul was arrested (Acts 21). It was said that he was teaching all men everywhere against the Jews, their law, and the temple. Paul stood on the steps and made a defense of his faith. The next day Paul was taken before the Sanhedrin. His mention of his hope in the resurrection of the dead caused a dispute to break out between the Pharisees and the Sadducees. Paul was taken back to the barracks. The Scriptures tell us, "the following night the Lord stood near Paul and said, 'Take courage! As you have testified about me in Jerusalem, so you must also testify in Rome'" (Acts 23:11). The next morning the Jews formed a conspiracy to kill Paul. When the authorities discovered the plot, Paul was taken to Caesarea. Paul was placed on trial, but Felix, the governor of Judea, made no decision about his guilt or innocence. Paul remained in prison for two years (Acts 24). After Festus succeeded Felix, Paul was placed on trial again. Paul appealed to Caesar (Acts 25).

Paul was sent to Rome. He spent much of the rest of his life under house arrest or in prison before he was finally executed. Paul commented about his suffering in his letter to the Philippians, a letter written from prison:

> Now I want you to know, brothers, that what has happened to me has really served to advance the gospel. As a result, it has become clear throughout the whole palace guard and to everyone else that I am in chains for Christ. Because of my chains, most of the brothers in the Lord have been encouraged to speak the word of God more courageously and fearlessly . . . I eagerly expect and

hope that I will in no way be ashamed, but will have sufficient courage so that now as always Christ will be exalted in my body, whether by life or by death. (Phil. 1:12–14, 20)

Paul's last known letter was his second letter to Timothy. In this letter he also speaks of suffering:

So do not be ashamed to testify about our Lord, or ashamed of me his prisoner. But join with me in suffering for the gospel . . . And of this gospel I was appointed a herald and an apostle and a teacher. That is why I am suffering as I am. (2 Tim. 1:8–12a)

God was at work in Paul's affliction. Paul's suffering was for the purpose of bringing the light of the gospel to the Gentile world and edification to the early church. We each have a unique sphere of influence. Paul's imprisonment gave him access to witness to certain people that he otherwise would not have met. Paul's perseverance in spite of opposition and his courage in difficult situations authenticated his faith. Paul learned the secret of true contentment, that it was not based on outward circumstances (Phil. 4:12).

Paul's experiences gave him insight about suffering that he could not have gotten any other way. He was able to empathize with and encourage those he met along the road of life. Paul's behavior in difficult situations gave the early Christians an example of how they should live. Paul modeled an attitude. While Paul was sitting in prison, he had time to write letters, letters that would be instructional to all of Christendom.

GOD DEMONSTRATING SOMETHING TO THE WORLD

People may have to undergo tribulation because God is trying to demonstrate something to the world, something perhaps seemingly irrelevant to the individual's personal situation. We do not always understand His ways. Consider the events in Matthew 2. Wise men from the East came to Jerusalem asking about the birth of the Messiah. They had seen His star and had come to worship Him. King Herod the Great was disturbed. Herod called together all the people's chief priests and teachers of the law. He found out from the religious leaders that the Christ was to be born in Bethlehem. He sent the wise men to locate Jesus so that he could "go and worship him" (Matt. 2:8). The wise men found Jesus. They worshipped the Christ child and gave Him gifts. But they were warned in a dream not to go back to Herod, so they returned to their country by another route.

An angel of the Lord appeared to Joseph in a dream. He was instructed to take the child and his mother and flee to Egypt. Herod had a plan to kill the child. Herod knew about the signs from heaven heralding the Messiah. Herod knew that the events were a specific fulfillment of prophecy. He must have known that this birth was of God. Despite what he knew, he followed his own lust for power. When Herod realized that the wise men were not going to return with the information he so desperately wanted, he was furious. He gave orders to kill all the baby boys in Bethlehem and its vicinity who were two years old and under.

I can just imagine all those mothers crying over their dead children, wondering why they had to die. Why was Herod not stricken dead before he could do such a terrible thing? Jesus was spared. Why were the other baby boys not spared? What about the Holy Family, the three refugees who had to flee to a strange country with nothing but the clothes on their back and what they could carry?

Many of the events in Matthew chapter two are a specific fulfillment of prophecy. Christ was to be born in Bethlehem (Mic. 5:2). The slaughter of the young boys was prophesied in Jeremiah (Jer. 31:15). There was also a prophecy in Hosea 11:1: "Out of Egypt I called my son". I guess one answer to the question of why they had to die is that prophecy had been made and had to be fulfilled. But why had such a thing been prophesied in the first place? Perhaps part of the explanation might be that Herod was being given a chance to repent of his sins, of his pride. Perhaps the events were a witness to someone in the king's court or a religious leader, perhaps a young Nicodemus, perhaps a young Joseph of Arimathea. Perhaps someone was there who was to have an influence on Manaen (Acts 13:1), a man who grew up with Herod Antipas and was one of the leaders in the early church. Perhaps someone was present who was to be a witness to Joanna, wife of Cuza, the manager of Herod's household (Luke 8:3). She was one of the first witnesses to the resurrection of Christ (Luke 24:1–10). Someone friendly to the early church must have been present at Herod's meeting with the wise men to be able to tell the story. My only firm conclusion is that it had something to do with the purposes of God.

I am sure that there are many other causes of tribulation in which the details may be unexplainable. We may never know all of the answers in this lifetime. But we do know that things that happen do not occur by chance. God is in control.

Multiple Causes

In my judgment, most difficult situations probably have multiple causes. Consider the case of Jesus' crucifixion. Who was responsible for Jesus' death? The soldiers were the final instruments of Jesus' death, those who nailed Jesus to the cross (John 19:16b–24). They bore responsibility for His death, but they were just following orders. It was by Pilate's order that Jesus was crucified. He did not have the courage to stand up to the Jews (John 19:12; Luke 23:23, 24). Herod Antipas was also a part of the conspiracy (Acts 4:27, 28). The Jewish people exerted their influence by shouting, "Crucify him!" (John 19:15). The Jewish leaders exerted pressure on Pilate to kill Jesus. Judas was also responsible. He betrayed Jesus for thirty pieces of silver (Matt. 26:14–16). Satan had a part. He entered Judas just prior to the arrangements for the betrayal (Luke 22:3, 4). Collectively mankind bears responsibility for Jesus' death. Jesus died to save us from our sins (Rom. 5:6–11; 1 Cor. 15:3). Adam bore some responsibility. He brought sin into the world (Rom. 5:12–14). Jesus, Himself was responsible. In John 10:17, 18, His words are recorded as follows: "The reason my Father loves me is that I lay down my life–only to take it up again. No one takes it from me, but I lay it down of my own accord." John 19:30 records how Jesus commanded His own death. God the Father bears responsibility as well. It was the Lord's will to crush Him (Isa. 53:10). Jesus was crucified by the set purpose of God, the Father (Acts 2:23). The sovereign Lord's power and will had decided beforehand it should happen (Acts 4:28). The answer to who was responsible for Jesus' death is *all of the above*.

Our own tribulations are also likely the result of multiple causes. In the middle of tribulation it may be difficult to know exactly what is going on, whether it is Satan's harassment, the Lord's discipline, or multiple other possibilities. Job's three friends thought they understood Job's problem, but we are told that they did not (Job 42:7). Actually the response to all difficulty should be the same. We are supposed to endure hardship as discipline. "Endure hardship as discipline; God is treating you as sons. For what son is not disciplined by his father?" (Heb. 12:7) In my difficult situations I ask God what He is trying to teach me, and I attempt to profit from the experience.

Now that we have seen various causes or reasons for trouble and tribulation, let's now take a look at how God uses tribulation in our lives to bring about good.

6

HOW GOD USES
TRIBULATION IN OUR LIVES

I t has been said that the worst thing about going to the doctor is
that you have to take off your clothes. In this situation we tolerate something we don't like, such as taking off our clothes,
to gain something that has a more ultimate good, such as medical
care. I believe there are many causes of human suffering that God
does not *initiate*, but He *allows* them in order to ultimately bring
about a greater good in our lives. Let's look at how God uses our
difficult situations for our profit.

God uses tribulation in our lives to help each of us individually
in our own spiritual journey. God speaks to us in our afflictions
(Job 36:15b). Misery, grief, and pain are humbling experiences.
They help us realize that we are inadequate to control our own
destinies. They help us learn to trust in God for our security. Being
in a world where things decay helps us to appreciate the difference
between what is temporal and what is eternal. Life's trials test us.
Our response to them reveals our true spiritual condition. God uses
difficult circumstances to discipline us, to train us, and to call us
to Himself. God's discipline is a call to holiness.

I experienced the Lord's discipline in 1991. That year, I turned
48 years old. I thought that I had achieved all of my professional
goals, and I felt pretty good about myself. I planned to take my son
on a trip to the British Isles.

A few days before we were to leave, I hospitalized a woman who needed to start dialysis. I attempted to insert a dialysis catheter into the right internal jugular vein in her neck to get an adequate amount of blood to run through the dialysis machine. Unfortunately, in this procedure, she sustained an arterial puncture. The resulting hemorrhage and hematoma, or collection of blood in the tissues, grew so large that it pushed her trachea to the left. She required an endotracheal tube to maintain her airway.

When I realized the extent of what was going on and that it was happening right before we were supposed to leave on our trip, I said to myself, "Why did this have to happen?" I remembered how I had bragged to one of the nurses about how much better I was at that procedure than one of my younger associates.

The patient did fine overnight. The next morning we tried again to begin dialysis. But when she arrived in the dialysis unit from the intensive care unit, she looked much worse. A catheter was inserted into her left femoral vein for access. The dialysis was carried out with great difficulty. Her blood pressure was very unstable, and when she returned to the intensive care unit, she was in critical condition. Several consultants had been called in.

That afternoon, as I looked at her, I realized she was too sick for what I knew was wrong with her. I thought that perhaps she was septic, that perhaps she had an infection in her blood stream, but that her general condition was so poor that her immune system was suppressed, and she could not generate the usual fever. I ordered blood cultures and started high doses of penicillin and an aminoglycoside antibiotic, but she did not improve over the weekend.

Monday morning, I was in a real quandary. I did not know what to do about the trip. I felt I had followed the Lord's leading when I initially bought the airline tickets. And I was afraid that canceling the trip would be an admission of *guilt*, that is, that the adverse result from the procedure was more than just an "expected complication." I agonized about the decision, but finally decided we should go.

We flew out of Atlanta, to begin our trip which initially took us to London, Dublin, and Belfast. While in Belfast, I found a

copy of A. N. Wilson's biography of C. S. Lewis.[1] I bought it and
began reading it. A main theme of the book has to do with growing spiritually through life's trials. Eventually, we went on to my
brother's place in Swindon, England. My brother John has a Christian bookshop. He was to have a bookstall in association with a
concert to be given by Marilyn Baker at the Ellendune Centre in
Wroughton. Marilyn Baker is a Christian singer who is blind. She
has told her story in a book entitled *Another Way of Seeing*.[2] I went
along to the concert.

Marilyn Baker's testimony was very moving. She had a calm
assurance of acceptance by Jesus Christ. It reminded me of my days
at Children's Bible Mission Camp, where at the age of twelve years,
I received the assurance of my salvation. I realized that at the age
of forty-eight, with all I thought I had accomplished as a physician, I did not have any more to bring to my relationship with the
Lord, than I did when I was twelve. If I had accomplished anything
in life, it was the Lord's gift to me. I repented of my sin of pride.
Somehow, I knew the healing had begun. I thought of Hosea 6:1, 2
as quoted in Evie and Pelle Karlsson's album *Restoration*: "Come, let
us return to the Lord. He has torn us to pieces, but he will heal us;
he has injured us but he will bind up our wounds. After two days
he will revive us; on the third day he will restore us. That we may
live in his presence." I went up to Marilyn Baker after the concert
and thanked her for her witness.

When I got back home to Knoxville, I found that my patient had
died. Unfortunately, there was nothing I could have done. A post-
mortem examination had been performed, and the cause of death
was listed as a heart attack. I spoke with the family, and everyone
seemed satisfied that all the right things had been done.

A year later I was sued. It was alleged that I was responsible
for a wrongful death. An announcement was even made over the
radio, and one of the dialysis patients asked me about it as I was
making rounds. That lawsuit hung over my head for three years.
It caused me to look back at her chart more closely, and I found
reports of two blood cultures returned after the patient had died;
they were positive for *streptococcus pneumoniae*. The patient had

died of overwhelming infection in the bloodstream; it was not a wrongful death! After all the depositions were taken, the suit was eventually dismissed. But during those difficult three years, the Lord taught me many things about humility. Many of the verses quoted in this book were marked in my Bible during those three years. The experience I had with that patient and her family was difficult, but I would not have missed it for anything. The discipline was a step in my spiritual development.

To Humble Us

In my judgment, a primary purpose of tribulation is to humble us.

We Need to Know That We Cannot Control Our Own Fate

It is important for each of us to know that we are not in charge of our own destiny. Through tribulation, we learn that it is foolish to trust in our own strength. Deuteronomy 8 is a passage that is especially meaningful for me. God sent tribulation to the Israelites in the wilderness to humble them and to test them in order to know what was in their hearts, whether or not they would keep His commands. The Lord disciplined them as a father disciplines his son. He humbled them and tested them so that in the end it would go well with them. At times, He allowed them to be hungry and thirsty, but He also met their needs.

God blessed them in special ways to let them know He was taking care of them. He fed them with manna to teach them that man does not live by bread alone. He brought them water out of a rock. Their clothes did not wear out. Their feet did not swell. God warned the Israelites that when they came to the Promised Land and were prosperous that they should not become proud, forgetting the Lord their God. They were to remember that it was the Lord who gave them the ability to produce wealth. If they should forget the Lord, they would be destroyed.

Daniel 4 tells the story of Nebuchadnezzar. He was at home in his palace, contented and prosperous, but he had a dream that made him afraid. He dreamed about a large, fruitful tree. A messenger from heaven made an announcement. The tree was to be cut down and stripped. The stump was to be left, bound with iron and bronze.

Daniel was asked to interpret the dream. When he first heard about the dream, he was fearful, but after reassurance from Nebuchadnezzar, he interpreted the dream. Daniel told Nebuchadnezzar that Nebuchadnezzar was the tree. Nebuchadnezzar was to be driven away from people and live with wild animals. He was to be drenched with the dew of heaven. This was to occur for seven years until he acknowledged that the Most High is Sovereign over the kingdoms of men. After he acknowledged that heaven ruled, his kingdom would be restored to him. Daniel advised Nebuchadnezzar that he renounce his sins by doing what is right and his wickedness by being kind to the oppressed. He was hopeful that such a change would allow Nebuchadnezzar's prosperity to continue.

A year later Nebuchadnezzar was walking on the roof of the royal palace of Babylon. He said, "Is not this the great Babylon I have built as the royal residence, by my mighty power and for the glory of my majesty?" The words were still on his lips when he heard a voice from heaven. The predictions from his dream were immediately fulfilled.

Seven years passed before Nebuchadnezzar raised his eyes toward heaven and his sanity was restored. Then he praised God. He acknowledged God's dominion over the earth. His honor and splendor were returned to him. He was restored to his throne and became even greater than before. Verse 37 is quoted as follows: "Now, I, Nebuchadnezzar, praise and exalt and glorify the King of heaven, because everything he does is right and all his ways are just. And those who walk in pride he is able to humble."

We Need to Realize That a Time of Accountability is Coming

". . . man is destined to die once, and after that to face judgment." (Heb. 9:27)

". . . each of us will give an account of himself to God."
(Rom. 14:12)

"Nothing in all creation is hidden from God's sight. Everything is uncovered and laid bare before him to whom we must give account." (Heb. 4:13)

"For we must all appear before the judgment seat of Christ, that each one may receive what is due him for the things done while in the body, whether good or bad." (2 Cor. 5:10)

That time of reckoning may come sooner than we think. We are not promised tomorrow.

Now listen you who say, "Today or tomorrow we will go to this or that city, spend a year there, carry on business and make money." Why, you do not even know what will happen tomorrow, What is your life? You are a mist that appears for a little while and then vanishes. Instead, you ought to say, "If it is the Lord's will we will live and do this or that." As it is, you boast and brag. All such boasting is evil. Anyone then, who knows the good he ought to do and doesn't do it, sins." (James 4:13–17)

For he says, "In the time of my favor I heard you, and in the day of salvation I helped you." I tell you, now is the time of God's favor, now is the day of salvation. (2 Cor. 6:2)

All People Are Participants in the Warning of Coming Judgment

Now there were some present at that time who told Jesus about the Galileans whose blood Pilate had mixed with their sacrifices. Jesus answered, "Do you think that these Galileans were worse sinners than all the other Galileans because they suffered this way? I tell you, no! But unless you repent, you too will all perish. Or those eighteen who died when the tower of Siloam fell on them—do you think they were more guilty than all the others living in Jerusalem? I tell you, no! But unless you repent, you too will all perish." (Luke 13:1–5)

This passage suggests to me that believers and non-believers alike have to participate in the warning about the brevity of life and the coming judgment. We all experience disease and death.

For all can see that wise men die; the foolish and the senseless alike perish and leave their wealth to others. (Ps. 49:10)

So I reflected on all this and concluded that the righteous and the wise and what they do are in God's hands, but no man knows whether love or hate awaits him. All share a common destiny— the righteous and the wicked, the good and the bad, the clean and the unclean, those who offer sacrifices and those who do not.
> As it is with the good man,
> so with the sinner;
> as it is with those who take oaths,
> so with those who are afraid to take them.

This is the evil in everything that happens under the sun: The same destiny overtakes all. The hearts of men, moreover, are full of evil and there is madness in their hearts while they live, and afterward they join the dead. . . . I have seen something else under the sun:
> The race is not to the swift
> or the battle to the strong,
> nor does food come to the wise
> or wealth to the brilliant
> or favor to the learned;
> but time and chance happen to them all.

Moreover, no man knows when his hour will come:
> As fish are caught in a cruel net,
> or birds are taken in a snare,
> so men are trapped by evil times
> that fall unexpectedly upon them.
> (Eccles. 9:1–3, 11, 12)

TO HELP US APPRECIATE THE THINGS OF ETERNAL SIGNIFICANCE

Physical sickness and death are a picture of how we are spiritually without Christ. Tribulation helps us appreciate the fact that we are mortal. It helps us grasp the significance of the difference between mortality and immortality. Appreciating our own physical mortality should cause us to focus on spiritual things. We are to strive not for what is perishable but for what is imperishable.

> Do not store up for yourselves treasures on earth, where moth and rust destroy, and where thieves break in and steal, But store up for yourselves treasures in heaven, where moth and rust do not destroy, and where thieves do not break in and steal. For where your treasure is, there your heart will be also . . . No one can serve two masters. Either he will hate the one and love the other, or he will be devoted to the one and despise the other. You cannot serve both God and Money. (Matt. 6:19–21, 24)

When we were on the mission trip to Ukraine, we informed the people helping us that we were interested in cultural exposure. One night we went to the ballet *Don Quixote*. As we were walking to the theater, we passed a very nice, large city park. The park was named after a general, one of the heroes of the Bolshevik Revolution. As I looked at his representation in a large bust on a high pedestal, I thought it was impressive, but I also thought to myself, "For what shall it profit a man, if he shall gain the whole world, and lose his own soul?" (Mark 8:36 KJV)

> Then he [Jesus] said to them, "Watch out! Be on your guard against all kinds of greed: a man's life does not consist in the abundance of his possessions." And he told them this parable: "The ground of a certain rich man produced a good crop. He thought to himself, 'What shall I do? I have no place to store my crops.' Then he said, 'This is what I'll do. I will tear down my barns and build bigger ones, and there I will store all my grain and my goods. And I'll say to myself, 'You have plenty of good

things laid up for many years. Take life easy; eat, drink and be merry.' But God said to him, 'You fool! This very night your life will be demanded from you. Then who will get what you have prepared for yourself?' This is how it will be with anyone who stores up things for himself but is not rich toward God." (Luke 12:15–21)

In 2 Corinthians 4:7, Paul compares our bodies to jars of clay. As Christians, we are merely conduits for the power of God. As we bear fruit, we glorify God. The all-surpassing power is from God and not from us.

To Test Us

The Greek word for temptation is *peirasmos*. According to Strong, it means "a putting to proof (by experiment [of good], experience [of evil], solicitation, discipline or provocation); by impl. Adversity;—temptation.[3] Bauer, Arndt, and Gingrich include the meanings of "test, trial, temptation, and enticement" to sin.[4]

I know, my God, that you test the heart and are pleased with integrity. (1 Chron. 29:17a)

The crucible for silver and the furnace for gold, but the LORD tests the heart. (Prov. 17:3)

The Lord your God is testing you to find out whether you love him with all your heart and all your soul. (Deut. 13:3b)

Tribulation Tests Our Identity as Christians

Tribulation tests our identity. In the parable of the sower (Matt. 13:1–23), Jesus described several situations. The seed that landed on rocky places did not have much soil. It sprang up quickly, because the soil was shallow. When the sun came up, the plants were scorched, and they withered because they had no root. Jesus said that the one who received the seed that fell on rocky places is the man who hears the word and at once receives it with joy. Since he has no root, he lasts only a short time. When trouble or persecution comes because of the word, he quickly falls away. The one who received the seed that fell among thorns is the man who hears the word, but the worries of this life and the deceitfulness of wealth choke it, making it unfruitful. The seed that fell on good soil produced a good crop. By implication, that seed that fell on good soil stayed connected to the source of its life and was not destroyed by trouble, persecution, the worries of this life, or the deceitfulness of wealth. When we deal with tribulation as we should, it authenticates our true identity as believers.

Tribulation Tests Our Faith

These [trials] have come so that your faith—of greater worth than gold, which perishes even though refined by fire—may be proved genuine and may result in praise, glory and honor when Jesus Christ is revealed. (1 Pet. 1:7)

Tribulation Tests Our Sense of Purpose

When I was in my first year of medical school, I was about one minute late to Histology class two or three times in a row. Our professor approached me in the laboratory and notified me that my tardiness reflected on my "sense of purpose." I was never late again, because I realized how it would reflect on my character. As it says in James, "Blessed is the man who perseveres under trial, because when he has stood the test, he will receive the crown of life that God has promised to those who love him." (James 1:12)

Tribulation Tests Our Obedience

They [the nations the Lord left in Canaan] were left to test the Israelites to see whether they would obey the LORD's commands, which he had given their forefathers through Moses. (Judg. 3:4)

The reason I wrote you was to see if you would stand the test and be obedient in everything. (2 Cor. 2:9)

We Are Tested to Teach Us to Rely on God

We do not want you to be uninformed, brothers, about the hardships we suffered in the province of Asia. We were under great pressure, far beyond our ability to endure, so that we despaired even of life. Indeed, in our hearts we felt the sentence of death. But this happened that we might not rely on ourselves but on God, who raises the dead. He has delivered us from such a deadly peril, and he will deliver us. On him we have set our hope that he will continue to deliver us, as you help us by your prayers. Then many will give thanks on our behalf for the gracious favor granted us in answer to the prayers of many. (2 Cor. 1:8–11)

We Are Tested so That It will Go Well with Us

Moses said to the people, "Do not be afraid. God has come to test you, so that the fear of God will be with you to keep you from sinning." (Exod. 20:20)

He gave you manna to eat in the desert, something your fathers had never known, to humble and to test you so that in the end it might go well with you. (Deut. 8:16)

Some People Do Not Pass the Test

In the New Testament, there is a Greek word, *adokimos*, that speaks of people who are tested but do not pass the test.[5] It is used several times in the New Testament. I have included selected quotations.

No, I beat my body and make it my slave so that after I have preached to others, I myself will not be *disqualified* for the prize. (1 Cor. 9:27)

Examine yourselves to see whether you are in the faith; test yourselves. Do you not realize that Christ Jesus is in you—unless of course you *fail the test*? And I trust that you will discover that we have not *failed the test*. Now we pray to God that you will not do anything wrong. (2 Cor. 13:5–7a)

They claim to know God, but by their actions they deny him. They are detestable, disobedient and *unfit* for doing anything good. (Titus 1:16)

But land that produces thorns and thistles is *worthless* and is in danger of being cursed. In the end it will be burned. (Heb. 6:8)

Consider what 1 John 2:19 says about some who left the fellowship: "They went out from us, but they did not really belong to us. For if they had belonged to us, they would have remained with us; but their going out showed that none of them belonged to us."

As I study these concepts, I can only come to one conclusion: Salvation is a gift from God, but if your life does not show evidence of God working in it, you likely never received the gift.

To Discipline Us

God uses our difficult situations to discipline us. According to Vine, one original Greek word for discipline is *sophronismos*. Literally the word means "saving the mind." It is an "admonishing or calling to soundness of mind, or to self-control."[6] According to Bauer, Arndt, and Gingrich the word was used in secular Greek to denote "the teaching of morality, good judgment, or moderation; advice, improvement." It has to do with "moderation, self-discipline, prudence."[7] Another Greek word *paideia* has to do with "upbringing, training, instruction, . . . of the holy discipline of a fatherly God."[8] The Hebrew word *yacar* is used for "discipline" in Deuteronomy 8:5. According to Brown-Driver-Briggs-Gesenius, it means to "discipline, chasten, admonish." It also means to "instruct, correct [the moral nature, with more or less severity according to circumstances]."[9]

Know then in your heart that as a man disciplines his son, so the Lord your God disciplines you. (Deut. 8:5)

Those whom I love, I rebuke and discipline. So be earnest, and repent. (Rev. 3:19)

Blessed is the man you discipline, O Lord, the man you teach from your law; you grant him relief from days of trouble. (Ps. 94:12, 13a)

The Lord may use discipline in several different ways, depending on where we are in our spiritual walk.

Discipline Is Supposed to Restore Believers to Fellowship

After you have had children and grandchildren and have lived in the land a long time—if you then become corrupt and make any kind of idol, doing evil in the eyes of the LORD your God and provoking him to anger, I call heaven and earth as witnesses against you this day that you will quickly perish from the land that you are crossing the Jordan to possess. You will not live there long but will certainly be destroyed. The LORD will scatter you among the peoples, and only a few of you will survive among the nations to which the LORD will drive you. There you will worship man-made gods of wood and stone, which cannot see or hear or eat or smell. But if from there you seek the LORD your God, you will find him if you look for him with all your heart and with all your soul. When you are in distress and all these things have happened to you, then in later days you will return to the LORD your God and obey him. For the LORD your God is a merciful God; he will not abandon or destroy you or forget the covenant with your forefathers, which he confirmed to them by oath. (Deut. 4:25–31)

But they were disobedient and rebelled against you; they put your law behind their backs. They killed your prophets, who had admonished them in order to turn them back to you; they committed awful blasphemies. So you handed them over to their enemies, who oppressed them. But when they were oppressed they cried out to you. From heaven you heard them, and in your great compassion you gave them deliverers, who rescued them from the hand of their enemies. (Neh. 9:26, 27)

Whenever God slew them, they would seek him; they eagerly turned to him again. (Ps. 78:34)

I have surely heard Ephraim's [Israel's] moaning: "You disciplined me like an unruly calf, and I have been disciplined. Restore me, and I will return, because you are the Lord my God. After I strayed, I repented; and I came to understand, I beat my breast. I was ashamed and humiliated because I bore the disgrace of my youth." "Is not Ephraim my dear son, the child in whom I delight? Though I often speak against him, I still remember him. Therefore my heart yearns for him; I have great compassion for him," declares the Lord. (Jer. 31:18–20)

Discipline Is Supposed to Keep Us from Being Proud
Consider the apostle Paul's humility. He received visions and revelations from the Lord. But God gave him a "thorn in the flesh" to keep him humble:

To keep me from becoming conceited because of these surpassingly great revelations, there was given me a thorn in my flesh, a messenger of Satan, to torment me. Three times I pleaded with the Lord to take it away from me. But he said to me, "My grace is sufficient for you, for my power is made perfect in weakness." Therefore I will boast all the more gladly about my weaknesses, so that Christ's power may rest on me. That is why, for Christ's sake, I delight in weaknesses, in insults, in hardships, in persecutions, in difficulties. For when I am weak, then I am strong. (2 Cor. 12:7–10)

Discipline Brings Us Under Conviction
God uses discipline to bring us under conviction. God used the tribulation I discussed at the beginning of this chapter to bring me under conviction, to expose the reality of my situation to me. The

Greek word *elegcho* is used several times in the New Testament. According to Bauer, Arndt, and Gingrich, *elegcho* is defined as follows: "bring to light, expose, set forth . . . convict or convince someone of something . . . reprove, correct."[10] Consider three examples of how the word is used.

> Everyone who does evil hates the light, and will not come into the light for fear that his deeds will be *exposed.* (John 3:20)

> But everything *exposed* by the light becomes visible, for it is the light that makes everything visible. This is why it is said: 'Wake up, O sleeper, rise from the dead, and Christ will shine on you.' (Eph. 5:13, 14)

> When he [the Holy Spirit] comes, he will *convict* the world of guilt in regard to sin and righteousness and judgment. (John 16:8)

Psalm 51 was written by David after Nathan confronted him about his sin with Bathsheba. Verses 10–12 are especially meaningful to me:

> Create in me a pure heart, O God, and renew a steadfast spirit within me. Do not cast me from your presence or take your Holy Spirit from me. Restore to me the joy of your salvation and grant me a willing spirit, to sustain me.

Discipline Helps Us Submit

> Moreover, we have all had human fathers who disciplined us and we respected them for it. How much more should we submit to the Father of our spirits and live! (Heb. 12:9)

Discipline Purifies Us

> For you, O God, tested us; you refined us like silver. You brought us into prison and laid burdens on our backs. You let men ride over our heads; we went through fire and water, but you brought us to a place of abundance. (Ps. 66:10–12)

Before I was afflicted I went astray, but now I obey your word. You are good, and what you do is good; teach me your decrees. Though the arrogant have smeared me with lies, I keep your precepts with all my heart. Their hearts are callous and unfeeling, but I delight in your law. It was good for me to be afflicted so that I might learn your decrees. The law from your mouth is more precious to me than thousands of pieces of silver and gold. Your hands made me and formed me; give me understanding to learn your commands. May those who fear you rejoice when they see me, for I have put my hope in your word. I know, O Lord, that your laws are righteous, and in faithfulness you have afflicted me. May your unfailing love be my comfort, according to your promise to your servant. (Ps. 119:67–76)

Our fathers disciplined us for a little while as they thought best; but God disciplines us for our good, that we may share in his holiness. No discipline seems pleasant at the time, but painful. Later on, however, it produces a harvest of righteousness and peace for those who have been trained by it. (Heb. 12:10, 11)

Discipline Helps Us Grow in Grace and Wisdom

During a recent mission trip to Honduras we had opportunities to do street evangelism and visit patients in the hospital. I was struck by the difference in the depth of our conversation between the two groups of people. When we spoke to people on the street about having a relationship with Christ, there were several recurring themes. "I'm a good person." "I go to church." "I made a decision to accept Christ years ago, but I haven't lived it." When we were in the hospital, the conversation became very specific and was more emotional. From a farmer: "A donkey bit me, and I have a large open wound on my forearm." From a mother: "My son was in the wrong place at the wrong time and caught a stray bullet in the abdomen." From an old man: "I have prostate cancer, and I need encouragement."

Tribulation has a way of stripping the veneer of superficiality from our lives and causing us to reflect on the basic questions of life. Where did I come from? Why am I here? Where am I going? We often share a bond with those who are afflicted in like manner as we are. The common bond between patients and families of patients at a dialysis unit, at a chemotherapy center, or at a children's hospital is evident. During our difficult situations we learn things known only to those share those experiences.

Years ago, I was listening to Christian radio and heard Tony Evans say that God knows everything intellectually, but He doesn't know everything experientially. At first I wasn't too sure about what Mr. Evans said , but as I study the Bible, I'm becoming more and more convinced that he was right. Consider these passages from Hebrews:

> But we see Jesus, who was made a little lower than the Angels, now crowned with glory and honor because he suffered death, so that by the grace of God he might taste death for everyone. In bringing many sons to glory, it was fitting that God, for whom and through whom everything exists, should make the author of their salvation perfect through suffering. (Heb. 2:9, 10)

> Therefore, since we have a great high priest who has gone through the heavens, Jesus the Son of God, let us hold firmly to the faith we profess. For we do not have a high priest who is unable to sympathize with our weaknesses, but we have one who has been tempted in every way, just we are - yet was without sin. (Heb. 4:14, 15)

> During the days of Jesus' life on earth, he offered up prayers and petitions with loud cries and tears to the one who could save him from death, and he was heard because of his reverent submission. Although he was a Son, he learned obedience from what he suffered. (Heb. 5:7, 8)

> For the law appoints as high priests men who are weak; but the oath, which came after the law, appointed the Son, who has been made perfect forever. (Heb. 7:28)

As human beings, we also learn from our experiences. In retrospect, I can see that when faced with affliction, I did what many people do. I sought the Lord, and I searched the scripture for answers to my questions. This book is a product of that search. During my experiences, the Lord has taught me many things.

I have learned humility. I don't think I have any illusions about who I am. I realize that God determined where I was born, when I was born, and the parents to whom I was born. He fashioned my brain, gave me my talents and interests, and arranged my life's circumstances. God turned on the light for me to see His truth and then granted me His salvation. He caused me to grow in the faith. He arranged the course of my education and carried me through medical school. He arranged for me to open my own office in my hometown of Knoxville, TN and has given me a thriving practice within the medical community here. God has also taught me that he can take it all away at any moment He so chooses.

I have learned obedience. When my only anchor for the storm was the Lord, I wasn't about to commit any willful sin that would separate me from fellowship with Him (e.g. taking sample medication from the office that rightfully should have gone to the patients, watching an R rated movie, or not keeping check on my temper). Of course, I still have to work on these things. Now that I have written this book and gone public with my faith, I have to watch how I act out in polite society and at home.

I have learned a better understanding of personhood, and I have more respect for others, regardless of race, age, or social status. I have learned that there is a big difference in being of service to someone because it is the right thing to do as opposed to doing it because I identify with that person and feel his pain and want to bring him some relief. I have witnessed how God fits my life's experiences together to help me learn better ways to be of service to others. For example, I believe that going through the experiences of being a spousal caregiver has helped me be a better doctor.

I have learned about God's grace under pressure. That kind of grace is something I would have never understood had I never experienced the pressure. I have learned to view life's events from an eternal perspective and walk by faith and not by sight. I have seen how God has used my struggles to conform me to the image of His Son. I have been made more aware of the all-sufficiency of Christ to heal my wounded soul.

Discipline Makes Us More Fruitful

> I am the true vine, and my Father is the gardener. He cuts off every branch in me that bears no fruit, while every branch that does bear fruit he prunes [cleans] so that it will be even more fruitful. (John 15:1, 2)

God may allow tribulation in our lives for several reasons. If we are experiencing tribulation, we should examine our lives and ask the Lord how He will take the situation to turn it for our good.

PART TWO:

UNDERSTANDING GOD'S NATURE, PURPOSES, AND WORKS

7

Characteristics of God

S everal months ago I heard on a Christian radio station that we should love God because of His character. As we struggle with adversity, we need to grow in our understanding of who God is and what He is like. As we understand better who God is, we should be better able to accept what He does.

God Is Sovereign

God told us much about Himself in His response to Job's complaint (Job 38–41). My synopsis of God's response to Job is as follows:

1. My knowledge is greater than yours.
2. I created the universe.
3. I sustain the universe.
4. I am more powerful than anything in all creation.
5. I do not owe my creatures an explanation for what I do.

Consider some quotes from that passage:

Who endowed the heart with wisdom or gave understanding to the mind? (Job 38:36)

Unleash the fury of your wrath, look at every proud man and bring him low, look at every proud man and humble him, crush the wicked where they stand. Bury them all in the dust together; shroud their faces in the grave. Then I myself will admit to you that your own right hand can save you. (Job 40:11–14)

Who then is able to stand against me? Who has a claim against me that I must pay? Everything under heaven belongs to me. (Job 41:10b, 11)

Note Job's final reply:

I know that you can do all things; no plan of yours can be thwarted. You asked, "Who is this that obscures my counsel without knowledge?" Surely I spoke of things I did not understand. Things too wonderful for me to know. You said, "Listen now and I will speak; I will question you and you shall answer me." My ears had heard but now my eyes have seen you. Therefore I despise myself and repent in dust and ashes. (Job 42:2–6)

GOD IS WISE

Do you not know? Have you not heard? The LORD is the everlasting God, the Creator of the ends of the earth. He will not grow tired or weary, and his understanding no one can fathom. (Isa. 40:28)

"For my thoughts are not your thoughts, neither are your ways my ways," declares the LORD. "As the heavens are higher than the earth, so are my ways higher than your ways and my thoughts than your thoughts." (Isa. 55:8, 9)

Oh, the depth of the riches of the wisdom and knowledge of God! How unsearchable his judgments, and his paths beyond tracing out! (Rom. 11:33)

GOD IS HOLY

Exalt the Lord our God and worship at his holy mountain, for the Lord our God is holy. (Ps. 99:9)

Francis Brown's *The New Brown-Driver-Briggs-Gesenius Hebrew and English Lexicon* tells us that the original Hebrew word for "holy" also means "sacred."[1] God is separate and apart from His creation. He is separate from human infirmity, impurity, and sin.

GOD IS JUST

God is just or righteous. As a description for God, the two words mean the same thing. Vine says that the Greek word *dikaios* designates the perfect agreement between God's nature and His acts in which He is the standard for all men.[2] It signifies that God is just without prejudice or partiality.

He is the Rock, his works are perfect, and all his ways are just. A faithful God who does no wrong, upright and just is he. (Deut. 32:4)

The Lord is righteous in all his ways and loving toward all he has made. (Ps. 145:17)

There is no God apart from me, a righteous God and a Savior; there is none but me. (Isa. 45:21b)

This is what the LORD says: "Let not the wise man boast of his wisdom or the strong man boast of his strength or the rich man boast of his riches, but let him who boasts boast about this: that he understands and knows me, that I am the LORD, who exercises kindness, justice and righteousness on earth, for in these I delight," declares the LORD. (Jer. 9:23, 24)

God Is Just in His Condemnations

Job 34:17a is recorded as follows: "Can he who hates justice govern?" God does not make a law that He would be unwilling to enforce. That is the nature of true justice.

> These also are sayings of the wise: To show partiality in judgment is not good: Whoever says to the guilty, "You are innocent"—peoples will curse him and nations denounce him. But it will go well with those who convict the guilty, and rich blessing will come upon them. (Prov. 24:23–25)

In his book *The Plight of Man and the Power of God*, D. Martyn Lloyd-Jones makes the following statement: "God's wrath . . . does not mean impatience or uncontrolled anger. There is nothing arbitrary or unjust about it."[3]

Through Scripture and by what we see in creation around us God gives each one of us ample evidence for what he is supposed to do.

> The wrath of God is being revealed from heaven against all the godlessness and wickedness of men who suppress the truth by their wickedness, since what may be known about God is plain to them, because God has made it plain to them. For since the creation of the world God's invisible qualities—his eternal power and divine nature—have been clearly seen, being understood from what has been made, so that men are without excuse. (Rom. 1:18–20)

> The Lord our God did not hesitate to bring the disaster upon us, for the Lord our God is righteous in everything he does; yet we have not obeyed him. (Dan. 9:14)

> In all that has happened to us, you have been just; you have acted faithfully while we did wrong. (Neh. 9:33)

> Consider therefore the kindness and sternness of God: sternness to those who fell, but kindness to you, provided that you continue in his kindness. (Rom. 11:22a)

God Is Just in How He Provides Redemption

"But now a righteousness from God, apart from the law, has been made known, to which the Law and the Prophets testify. This righteousness from God comes through faith in Jesus Christ to all who believe. There is no difference, for all have sinned and fall short of the glory of God, and we are justified freely by his grace through the redemption that came by Christ Jesus. God presented him as a sacrifice of atonement, through faith in his blood. He did this to demonstrate his justice, because in his forbearance he had left the sins committed beforehand unpunished—he did it to demonstrate his justice at the present time, so as to be just and the one who justifies those who have faith in Jesus. (Rom. 3:21–26)

God Is Just in How He Deals with Each One of Us

I have often heard it said that life is not fair. I get tired of hearing that. If God is just, then life is fair. If we say, "Life is not fair," we are passing judgment on God. Perhaps it appears to us, at times, that life is not fair. We need to be patient. The accounts have not been settled yet. God still has many outstanding debts on his balance sheet. We haven't seen the final conclusion of the matter. Eventually we will witness the justice of the Lord.

For the Lord is righteous, he loves justice; upright men will see his face. (Ps. 11:7)

You have said, "It is futile to serve God. What did we gain by carrying out his requirements and going about like mourners before the Lord Almighty? But now we call the arrogant blessed. Certainly the evildoers prosper, and even those who challenge God escape." Then those who feared the Lord talked with each other, and the Lord listened and heard. A scroll of remembrance was written in his presence concerning those who feared the Lord and honored his name. "They will be mine," says the Lord Almighty, "in the day when I take up my treasured possession. I will spare them, just as in compassion a man spares his son who serves him. And you will again see the distinction between the righteous and the wicked, between those who serve God and those who do not." (Mal. 3:14–18)

All this [your faith, your love, your perseverance] is evidence that God's judgment is right, and as a result you will be counted worthy of the kingdom of God, for which you are suffering. God is just: He will pay back trouble to those who trouble you and give relief to you who are troubled, and to us as well. This will happen when the Lord Jesus is revealed from heaven in blazing fire with his powerful angels. He will punish those who do not know God and do not obey the gospel of our Lord Jesus. (2 Thess. 1:5–8)

GOD IS TRUE

God is true. What He says is right.

I have not spoken in secret, from somewhere in a land of darkness; I have not said to Jacob's descendants, "Seek me in vain." I, the Lord, speak the truth; I declare what is right. (Isa. 45:19)

Vine says that in the New Testament, the original Greek word for "true" is *aleethinos*. It means "real, ideal, or genuine."[4]

Now this is eternal life: that they may know you, the only true God, and Jesus Christ, whom you have sent. (John 17:3)

Yes, Lord God Almighty, true and just are your judgments. (Rev. 16:7b)

I tell you the truth, until heaven and earth disappear, not the smallest letter, not the least stroke of a pen, will by any means disappear from the Law until everything is accomplished. (Matt. 5:18)

To emphasize the truthfulness of what He was saying, Jesus used the word *ameen* 31 times in Matthew. The King James Version translates it "verily." The NIV translates it, "I tell you the truth." Bauer, Arndt, and Gingrich refer to *ameen* as an "asseverative particle beginning a solemn declaration."[5] To asseverate means "to affirm or aver positively."[6] God keeps his promises (Neh. 9:8b). God cannot lie (Heb. 6:18). God did not lie to us about tribulation. Tribulation should not come as a surprise to us. Consider Peter's words:

> Dear friends, do not be surprised at the painful trial you are suffering, as though something strange were happening to you. But rejoice that you participate in the sufferings of Christ, so that you may be overjoyed when his glory is revealed. (1 Pet. 4:12, 13)

GOD IS LOVE

God is love. According to Vine, the Greek word *agapao* is used to describe the attitude of God toward the human race. Vine says that God's love is "an exercise of the Divine will in deliberate choice, made without assignable cause save that which lies in the nature of God Himself."[7] Love expresses the essential nature of God.

> For God so loved the world that he gave his one and only Son, that whoever believes in him shall not perish but have eternal life. (John 3:16)

> But God demonstrates his own love for us in this: While we were still sinners, Christ died for us. (Rom. 5:8)

> Whoever does not love does not know God, because God is love. (1 John 4:8)

> This is love: not that we loved God, but that he loved us and sent his Son as an atoning sacrifice for our sins. (1 John 4:10)

Lack of love from others can cause intense emotional pain, especially if those who withhold that love are our own family members. Consider what David says about how the Lord's love may soothe that pain: "Even if my father and mother abandon me, the Lord will hold me close" (Ps. 27:10 NLT).

GOD IS FAITHFUL

Vine says that the Greek word for faithful, *pistos,* is a verbal adjective.[8] When used in connection with God it is used in the passive. It means "to be trusted" or "reliable."

> God, who has called you into fellowship with his Son Jesus Christ our Lord, is faithful. (1 Cor. 1:9)

> No temptation has seized you except what is common to man. And God is faithful; he will not let you be tempted beyond what you can bear. But when you are tempted, he will also provide a way out so that you can stand up under it. (1 Cor. 10:13)

GOD IS NO RESPECTER OF PERSONS

Acts 10:34 tells us that God does not show favoritism. Bauer Arndt, and Gingrich say that the Greek word *prosopoleemptees* has been found only in Christian writings. The word expresses the idea that God does not show partiality.[9] "Anyone who does wrong will be repaid for his wrong, and there is no favoritism" (Col. 3:25).

I am very interested in history, especially the history that relates to my family. Most of my ancestors were Scotch-Irish. I have learned in reading about the history of Scotland that it is necessary to understand the bias of the author of the book I am reading. Most of the stories from Scottish history have two sides. From the perspective of the English, the Scottish clan system was a bad system. Might made right. It was force of arms that decided how things were going to be. The English wanted to establish an impartial law in the Scottish highlands, one that meted out justice, regardless of the identity of the person who was involved. They wanted a certain crime to have a certain punishment. The English decided that the only way that they could establish an impartial law in Scotland was to dismantle the clan system. In the United States today, we still do not have an impartial law. When a poor man is found drunk in public, he is often taken to jail. When a rich man is found drunk in public, he is more likely to be taken home.

For the LORD your God is God of gods and Lord of lords, the great God, mighty and awesome, who shows no partiality and accepts no bribes. (Deut. 10:17)

But the Lord said to Samuel, "Do not consider his appearance or his height, for I have rejected him. The Lord does not look at things man looks at. Man looks at the outward appearance, but the Lord looks at the heart." (1 Sam. 16:7)

God does not show prejudice based on outward appearance. He does not judge a book by its cover.

GOD IS MERCIFUL

The word "merciful" means "full of mercy, compassionate or providing relief."[10] Compassion carries the idea of having a sympathetic consciousness of others' distress together with a desire to alleviate it.[11] Sympathetic has to do with showing empathy.[12] Empathy is the action of understanding, being aware of, being sensitive to, and vicariously experiencing the feelings, thoughts, and experience of another.[13] Vine says that mercy (*eleos*) "is the outward manifestation of pity; it assumes need on the part of him who receives it, and resources adequate to meet the need on the part of him who shows it."[14]

For the Lord your God is a merciful God; he will not abandon or destroy you or forget the covenant with your forefathers, which he confirmed to them by oath. (Deut. 4:31)

But because of his great love for us, God, who is rich in mercy, made us alive with Christ even when we were dead in transgressions—it is by grace you have been saved. (Eph. 2:4, 5)

GOD KNOWS OUR SORROWS AND IS CONCERNED

God knows our sorrows and is concerned (Exod. 3:7). The Lord does not willingly bring affliction or grief to the children of men (Lam. 3:33). In our distress, He too is distressed (Isa. 63:9; Jer. 8:21; Heb. 4:15).

God is trying to create in us a character similar to His own. God wants us to be holy. God disciplines us so that we may share in His holiness (Heb. 12:10). It is for our good. He wants us to be no longer part of this world. We are to be transformed by the renewing of our minds (Rom. 12:2). God wants us to be truthful (Lev. 19:11). God wants us to bear the fruits of the Spirit (Gal. 5:22). God wants us to be merciful (Matt. 5:7). Showing partiality is named as a sin (James 2:1–4).

It appears to me that the main reason to consider God's character in the middle of our tribulation is to realize that God is good. God tests us in the furnace of affliction for His own sake (Isa. 48:10, 11a). However, there is perfect agreement between God's nature and His acts. Since God is good, He can be trusted. God desires our ultimate good. In the middle of our affliction, we ought to realize that Satan, more than likely, was responsible for the situation. Satan deceives us, he accuses us, and he desires our ultimate downfall. If we turn our back on God during our times of difficulty, that is just what Satan wants. It seems to me that the appropriate response is not a difficult choice.

8

GOD'S PURPOSES

During times of tribulation many people wonder why they must go through what they are going through. God told Moses that he was to lead the Israelites out of Egypt, and then when things did not seem to be working out according to plan, Moses asked God, "Why?" In Exodus chapters 3 and 4, God spoke to Moses from the burning bush. God told him, "I am sending you to Pharaoh to bring my people, the Israelites, out of Egypt." At first Moses began making excuses and finally he said, "O Lord, please send someone else to do it." But eventually Moses returned to Egypt to do the thing that God had called him to do.

Moses was warned twice that Pharaoh would not be cooperative, while God was speaking to him from the burning bush (Exod. 3:19, 20) and while Moses was on his way back to Egypt (Exod. 4:21). Moses brought his brother, Aaron, with him, and the two of them met with the elders of Israel.

Afterward Moses and Aaron went to Pharaoh and said, "This is what the Lord, the God of Israel says: 'Let my people go, so that they may hold a festival to me in the desert'" (Exod. 5:1). Pharaoh refused. He gave the order to the people in charge of the Israelites that the Israelites should no longer be provided with straw. They would have to gather their own straw for making bricks, but their

quota for making bricks was not to be reduced. The Israelite foremen were beaten when the quota was not met. The foremen said
to Moses and Aaron, "May the Lord look upon you and judge you!
You have made us a stench to Pharaoh and his officials and have
put a sword in their hand to kill us." In frustration, Moses cried
out to the Lord:

> O Lord, why have you brought trouble upon this people? Is this
> why you sent me? Ever since I went to Pharaoh to speak in your
> name, he has brought trouble upon this people, and you have
> not rescued your people at all. (Exod. 5:22b, 23)

God had a plan for Pharaoh. His destruction of Pharaoh was
to be in a special way, in a way that would be a testimony to the
Egyptians, the Israelites, and the world. He brought ten plagues on
Egypt. The final plague struck down all the firstborn of Egypt, including Pharaoh's own son. After the Israelites left Egypt, Pharaoh's
army chased them but was destroyed in the Red Sea.

As each of us goes through his or her own particular difficult
situation, it is helpful to reflect on God and His purposes, to consider why He does what He does. God gives us some insight about
His purposes in Scripture.

GOD DOES THINGS FOR HIS OWN SAKE

In Isaiah 46:8–10 God speaks of His sovereignty and
purpose.

> Remember this, fix it in mind, take it to heart . . . Remember the
> former things, those of long ago; I am God, and there is no other;
> I am God, and there is none like me. I make known the end from
> the beginning, from ancient times, what is still to come. I say:
> My purpose will stand, and I will do all that I please.

I believe that the primary reason that God does what He does is
for His own sake. It appears to me that God acts for His own sake,
and believers reap the benefits. There were times when God saved

the Israelites in situations where they did not deserve to be saved, in situations where they deserved punishment. He did it for His own sake.

> Yet he saved them for his name's sake, to make his mighty power known. (Ps. 106:8)

> But the children rebelled against me: They did not follow my decrees, they were not careful to keep my laws—although the man who obeys them will live by them—and they desecrated my Sabbaths. So I said I would pour out my wrath on them and spend my anger against them in the desert. But I withheld my hand, and for the sake of my name I did what would keep it from being profaned in the eyes of the nations in whose sight I had brought them out. (Ezek. 20:21, 22)

Eventually God's patience ran out. God punished the Israelites and later orchestrated the return of the Jews back to the Promised Land "for His own sake."

> For my own name's sake I delay my wrath; for the sake of my praise I hold it back from you, so as not to cut you off. See I have refined you, though not as silver; I have tested you in the furnace of affliction. For my own sake, for my own sake I do this. How can I let myself be defamed? I will not yield my glory to another. (Isa. 48:9–11)

God speaks in Ezekiel of the return of the Jews from captivity:

> And wherever they went among the nations they profaned my holy name, for it was said of them, "These are the Lord's people, and yet they had to leave his land." I had concern for my holy name, which the house of Israel profaned among the nations where they had gone. Therefore say to the house of Israel, "This is what the sovereign Lord says: It is not for your sake, O house of Israel, that I am going to do these things, but for the sake of my holy name, which you have profaned among the nations where you have gone. I will show the holiness of my great name,

which has been profaned among the nations, the name you have profaned among them. Then the nations will know that I am the Lord, declares the sovereign Lord, when I show myself holy through you before their eyes. For I will take you out of the nations; I will gather you from all the countries and bring you back into your own land." (Ezek. 36:20–24)

God forgives our sins for His own sake, something we do not deserve. "I, even I, am he who blots out your transgressions, for my own sake, and remembers your sins no more" (Isa. 43:25).

It was for God's own sake that the message of salvation was extended to the nations. "Through him and for his name's sake, we received grace and apostleship to call people from among all the Gentiles to the obedience that comes from faith" (Rom. 1:5). It was for God's own purpose that we were chosen to be His children:

For he chose us in him before the creation of the world to be holy and blameless in his sight. In love he predestined us to be adopted as his sons through Jesus Christ, in accordance with his pleasure and will. (Eph. 1:4, 5)

God . . . has saved us and called us to a holy life—not because of anything we have done but because of his own purpose and grace. This grace was given us in Christ Jesus before the beginning of time. (2 Tim. 1:8b, 9)

It is for His own sake that He leads us in our daily lives. "He restores my soul. He guides me in paths of righteousness for his name's sake" (Ps. 23:3). In his commentary on the Psalms, Spurgeon quotes Sir Richard Baker in reference to this verse:

"Seeing he hath taken upon him the *name* of a '*Good Shepherd*,' he will discharge his part, whatever his sheep be. It is not their being *bad sheep* that can make him leave being a '*Good Shepherd*,' but he will be 'good' and maintain the credit of 'his name' in spite of all their badness . . . there shall glory accrue to him by it, and '*his name*' shall nevertheless be magnified and extolled."[1]

128

God works in us to will and act according to His purpose (Phil. 2:13). God works in us so that we may be conformed to the likeness of His son (Rom. 8:29). God works everything out in conformity with the purpose of His will. (Eph. 1:11)

GOD DOES THINGS FOR THE SAKE OF INDIVIDUALS OR GROUPS

There were times in the Bible when God did things for the sake of men. These are not situations that are mutually exclusive. God can do things both for His sake and ours. Isaac was blessed for the sake of Abraham (Gen. 26:24). The Egyptians were punished for the sake of the Children of Israel (Exod. 18:8). God drove the nations out from the Promised Land for the sake of the Israelites (Josh. 23:3). David was established as king over Israel, and his kingdom was exalted for the sake of the Israelites (2 Sam. 5:12). Because Solomon turned away from the Lord, the kingdom was taken away from his family. But for the sake of David, it did not occur in Solomon's lifetime (1 Kings 11:12). For the sake of David and for the sake of Jerusalem, Solomon's son retained rule over one tribe (1 Kings 11:13). A remnant was preserved out of the Jews in captivity. For their sake, God remembered the covenant with their ancestors (Lev. 26:45). Jesus Christ was made man for the sake of believers (2 Cor. 8:9). The days of tribulation will be cut short for the sake of the elect (Matt. 24:22).

GOD WANTS TO MAKE HIS NAME KNOWN

God wants to make His name known. He wants to get people's attention. "Then they will know" is a phrase used once in Jeremiah and twenty three times in Ezekiel. In Jeremiah 16, God speaks of the chastening He is about to deliver to the Children of Israel, and what that chastening will bring about. Verse 21 reads as follows: "Therefore I will teach them—this time I will teach them my power and might. Then they will know that my name is the Lord."

That thought is expressed in Ezekiel over and over again. God says that He will do something; *then they will know* that He is the Lord.

> This is what the sovereign Lord says: Strike your hands together and stamp your feet and cry out "Alas!" because of all the wicked and detestable practices of the house of Israel, for they will fall by the sword, famine and plague. He that is far away will die by the plague, and he that is near will fall by the sword, and he that survives and is spared will die of famine. So will I spend my wrath upon them. And they will know that I am the Lord, when their people lie slain among their idols around their altars, on every high hill and on all the mountaintops, under every spreading tree and every leafy oak—places where they offered fragrant incense to all their idols. And I will stretch out my hand against them and make the land a desolate waste from the desert to Diblah—wherever they live. Then they will know that I am the Lord. (Ezek. 6:11–14)

God does what He does to keep us mindful of who He is. People have a tendency to forget.

Let us return to the story of the deliverance of the Israelites at the Red Sea (Exod. 13:17–14:31). God led the people through the desert toward the Red Sea. He hardened Pharaoh's heart so that he would pursue the Israelites. Exodus 14:4b reads as follows: "But I will gain glory for myself through Pharaoh and all his army, and the Egyptians will know that I am the Lord." God could have swiftly destroyed Pharaoh. Instead, He chose to delay. He punished Pharaoh in such a way so as to demonstrate His power and make His name known in all the earth (Exod. 9:15, 16).

When the Israelites saw the Egyptians approaching, they were terrified and cried out to the Lord. They also complained to Moses. Moses responded, "Do not be afraid. Stand firm and you will see the deliverance the Lord will bring you today." Moses stretched out his hand over the sea, and the Lord drove the sea back, so that the Israelites walked through the sea on dry ground. The Egyptians followed the Israelites into the sea. God jammed the wheels of their chariots. Moses stretched his hand out over the sea, and the water flowed back and engulfed the chariots and horsemen. The entire army of Pharaoh perished. Verse 31 tells us: "And when the Israelites saw the great power the Lord displayed against the Egyptians, the people feared the Lord and put their trust in him and in Moses his servant."

Consider what Psalm 106:7–12 has to say about God's delivery of the Israelites at the Red Sea. At the time of that crisis, the Israelites were frightened and forgot about the many miracles the Lord had just performed. They did not remember His many kindnesses. They were in rebellion by the Red Sea. God did not save them because they deserved it. He saved them for His name's sake. He saved them to make His mighty power known. God was doing something for His own purposes, but the Israelites benefited from it.

After Moses died and Joshua became the leader of the Children of Israel, the Israelites were about to enter the Promised Land. Joshua sent two men to spy out the land. When they arrived in Jericho, they entered the house of Rahab and stayed there. Joshua 2:8–11 tells us that the people of Jericho knew about how God had delivered the Israelites at the Red Sea.

> Before the spies lay down for the night, she [Rahab] went up to the roof and said to them, "I know that the Lord has given this land to you and that a great fear of you has fallen on us, so that all who live in this country are melting in fear because of you. We have heard how the Lord dried up the water of the Red Sea for you when you came out of Egypt, and what you did to Sihon and Og, the two kings of the Amorites east of the Jordan, whom you completely destroyed. When we heard of it, our hearts melted and everyone's courage failed because of you, for the Lord your God is God in heaven and on the earth below."

Because of what she heard about what God had done, Rahab became a believer. She acted by faith (Heb. 11:31). She helped the spies and was considered righteous (James 2:25). When the Israelites conquered Jericho, Rahab and her family were spared (Josh. 6:25). Rahab was one of the ancestors of Christ (Matt. 1:5).

It is evident to many of God's people that His name needs to be made known. Consider what David said to Goliath in 1 Samuel 17:46:

This day the Lord will hand you over to me, and I'll strike you down and cut off your head. Today I will give the carcasses of the Philistine army to the birds of the air and the beasts of the earth, and the whole world will know that there is a God in Israel.

At Mount Carmel Elijah called down fire from heaven. Elijah's prayer is recorded in 1 Kings 18:36–37:

O Lord, God of Abraham, Isaac and Israel, let it be known today that you are God in Israel and that I am your servant and have done all these things at your command. Answer me, O Lord, answer me, so these people will know that you, O Lord, are God, and that you are turning their hearts back again.

Matthew 28:18–20 records the Great Commission; we, as believers, are supposed to take the message of Jesus to all the earth.

Then Jesus came to them and said, "All authority in heaven and on earth has been given to me. Therefore go and make disciples of all nations, baptizing them in the name of the Father and of the Son and of the Holy Spirit, and teaching them to obey everything I have commanded you. And surely I am with you always, to the very end of the age."

THE FATHER GLORIFIES THE SON; THE SON GLORIFIES THE FATHER

The Messiah came to earth to do the will of the Father, "to bring Jacob back to him and gather Israel to himself." (Isaiah 49:5) Consider Jesus' prayer for Himself in the Garden of Gethsemane, the night before His crucifixion:

Father the time has come. Glorify your Son, that your Son may glorify you. For you granted him authority over all people that he might give eternal life to all those you have given him. Now this is eternal life: that they may know you, the only true God, and Jesus Christ, whom you have sent. I have brought you glory on earth by completing the work you gave me to do. And now, Father, glorify me in your presence with the glory I had with you before the world began. (John 17:1b–5)

Jesus was obedient to the Father and this obedience brought the Father glory. Because of His obedience, the Father glorified the Son.

GOD WANTS HIS LIGHT TO SHINE IN THE WORLD

God wants His light to shine in the world. Isaiah 49:6 refers to the Messiah: "I will also make you a light for the Gentiles, that you may bring my salvation to the ends of the earth." God wants His truth to be made known. It is not good for people to do what is "right in their own eyes." They need to follow God's standard. Evil men do not want the light of the truth. They do not want their evil deeds to be exposed (John 3:19, 20). The Holy Spirit exposes the sinfulness of the world. He convicts the world in regard to sin, righteousness, and judgment (John 16:8).

Consider Ephesians 5:8–14:

For you were once darkness, but now you are the light in the Lord. Live as children of light [for the fruit of the light consists in all goodness, righteousness and truth] and find out what pleases the Lord. Have nothing to do with the fruitless deeds of darkness, but rather expose them. For it is shameful even to mention what the disobedient do in secret. But everything exposed by the light becomes visible, for it is the light that makes everything visible. This is why it is said: "Wake up, O sleeper, rise from the dead, and Christ will shine on you."

James 1:22–25 tells us the Word of God is a mirror that shows us what we are really like. By exposing the truth, the Lord gives us wisdom. He helps us understand the true nature of things.

> I [Paul] keep asking that the God of our Lord Jesus Christ, the glorious Father, may give you the Spirit of wisdom and revelation, so that you may know him better. I pray also that the eyes of your heart may be enlightened in order that you may know the hope to which he has called you, the riches of his glorious inheritance in the saints. (Eph. 1:17, 18)

Christ's followers are supposed to be the light of the world (Matt. 5:14–16).

GOD DOES NOT WANT US TO PROFANE HIS NAME

God is concerned about what kind of appearance He makes to the world. He cares about how the thoughts and actions of His people reflect on His name. We are not to profane His name. God punished Israel because they profaned His name (Ezek. 20:30–38). According to Brown, Driver, Briggs, and Gesenius the Hebrew word *halal* translated "profane" means "to pollute, defile, desecrate, violate, dishonor or treat as common."[2] In the Old Testament, priests were defiled by contact with the dead, by sexual immorality, by poor grooming, or by having some physical defect (Lev. 21). According to Laird Harris, "Halal is associated with uncleanness . . . The word may . . . be used of any action which controverts God's planned order."[3] To swear falsely by God's name profanes His name (Lev. 19:12). People defile themselves (and profane God's name) when they lust after vile images (Ezek. 20:30). Fortune telling profanes God's name (Ezek. 13:17–19). It profanes God's name when we want to be like the world (Ezek. 20:32). God wants us to glorify Him. We are to be holy, separate, apart from the world. Holy things are not to be defiled.

We are not supposed to do anything that reflects negatively on our Savior. It is a common practice for believers to pray the Lord's

Prayer in church. In my judgment, when they pray, "hallowed be Thy name," it reflects an implied commitment not to do anything that would reflect negatively on the name of the Lord. I have been told that the two sins for which the world will not forgive Christian leaders are sexual sins and the misuse of money. If a man of God is led astray, it harms God's name. There will be a price to pay. Consider 1 Corinthians 6:12–20. When we become Christians, our bodies become members of Christ Himself. Paul speaks of the body not being meant for sexual immorality. We should not unite members of Christ with a prostitute. Tribulation is supposed to purify us (Isaiah 48:10), to keep us from being profane, to make us holy. Even though salvation is not a matter of works, in our daily walk, works do matter (Matt. 7:21; James 2:14–17). Our good works are not supposed to be done in our own strength but are to be carried out in the Spirit. We are told to be holy.

> As obedient children, do not conform to the evil desires you had when you lived in ignorance. But just as he who called you is holy, so be holy in all you do; for it is written: "Be holy, because I am holy." (1 Pet. 1:14–16)

Submission is the key to holiness. Submission allows the Holy Spirit to work in our lives. It allows the Lord to create in us a clean heart. It allows God to make us into the type of person we need to be. For that to happen, our false pride has to be destroyed.

GOD WILL BRING ALL CREATION IN SUBJECTION TO CHRIST

In Luke 21, Jesus foretold future events. He predicted events related to the destruction of Jerusalem and to the end of the age. He spoke of the dismantling of the temple. He spoke of antichrists. He mentioned wars and revolutions. He predicted earthquakes, floods, famines, pestilences, fearful events, and great signs from heaven. He told of coming persecution. He mentioned hatred, betrayal, and execution. His followers were to be witnesses to their persecutors. In Luke 21:9 Jesus said, "These things must happen." My question has been, "Why must they happen?" Part of the answer is to bring judgment on the wicked (Jer. 30:23, 24). I believe another answer as to why they must happen is found in Ephesians. It is all part of the process to bring about what seems to me to be God's ultimate purpose: "To bring all things in heaven and on earth together under one head, even Christ" (Eph. 1:10b).

God wants us to worship Him (Matt. 4:10). God wants us to obey Him (Rom. 16:26). God wants us to be in fellowship with Him (1 Cor. 1:9). God wants us to be conformed to the image of His Son (Rom. 8:29). God wants to give us resurrection bodies (2 Cor. 5:1–5). God has His own agenda. We need to get our plans in line with His plans, not expect Him to get His plans in line with ours. If we do this, we will be a witness to unbelievers.

9

WHY THE WICKED PROSPER

W hy do the wicked prosper? That is an age-old question. As we consider the fact that many wicked people seem to prosper in this life, we need to realize that we have a Sovereign God, and He has His plans, both for the righteous and the unrighteous. This chapter will reveal some of the reasons the wicked may prosper, but it also emphasizes the sovereignty of God.

Consider these words of Solomon:

There is something else meaningless that occurs on earth: righteous men who get what the wicked deserve, and wicked men who get what the righteous deserve. This too, I say, is meaningless. (Eccles 8:14)

Both Job (Job 10:3) and Jeremiah (Jer. 12:1, 2) expressed similar concerns.

GOD BLESSES BOTH THE RIGHTEOUS AND
THE WICKED AS AN EXAMPLE

I see many people in the middle of tribulation who are resentful toward God. They feel that God is not just, that He should reward the faithful and punish the unfaithful. Consider Jesus' words about God's blessings to both the righteous and the unrighteous. God gives us an example of how we are supposed to treat our enemies:

> You have heard that it was said, "Love your neighbor and hate your enemy." But I tell you: Love your enemies and pray for those who persecute you, that you may be sons of your Father in heaven. He causes his sun to rise on the evil and the good, and sends rain on the righteous and the unrighteous. If you love those who love you, what reward will you get? Are not even the tax collectors doing that? And if you greet only your brothers, what are you doing more than others? Do not even pagans do that? Be perfect, therefore, as your heavenly Father is perfect." (Matt. 5:43–48)

GOD IS LONGSUFFERING, GIVING THE WICKED A CHANCE TO REPENT

Consider Peter's words regarding the longsuffering of God: "The Lord is not slow in keeping his promise, as some understand slowness. He is patient with you, not wanting anyone to perish, but everyone to come to repentance" (2 Pet. 3:9).

For the wicked who are prospering, the time of reckoning has not yet come. In Matthew 13 Jesus told a parable of a man who sowed good seed in his field. While everyone was sleeping, his enemy came and sowed weeds among the wheat. The wheat and weeds sprouted and grew together. The man told his servants to wait until the time of harvest to try to separate them.

Later Jesus explained the parable. The one who sowed the good seed was the Son of Man. The field was the world. The good seed stood for the sons of the kingdom, while the weeds were the sons of the evil one. The enemy who sowed them was the devil. The harvest will come at the end of the age, and the harvesters are the angels. The weeds will be destroyed at the end of the age, in God's own time.

God Showers the Wicked With Blessings as a Testimony of His Kindness

Consider Paul's words to the crowd in Lystra:

Yet he has not left himself without testimony: He has shown kindness by giving you rain from heaven and crops in their seasons; he provides you with plenty of food and fills your hearts with joy (Acts 14:17)

Paul expresses a similar idea in his letter to the Romans:

Or do you show contempt for the riches of his kindness, tolerance and patience, not realizing that God's kindness leads you toward repentance? (Rom. 2:4)

God Uses the Wicked to Promote His Own Agenda

There are many examples in the Bible of unrighteous people who were used by God for His purposes, and they were allowed to flourish for a time. King David even prayed for those who oppressed him: "But do not kill them, O Lord our shield, or my people will forget" (Ps. 59:11a).

Paul wrote that one of God's purposes for His patience with the wicked is to make the riches of His glory known to the believers:

For the Scripture says to Pharaoh: "I raised you up for this very purpose, that I might display my power in you and that my name might be proclaimed in all the earth." Therefore God has mercy on whom he wants to have mercy, and he hardens whom he wants to harden. One of you will say to me: "Then why does God still blame us? For who resists his will?" But who are you, O man to talk back to God? Shall what is formed say to him who formed it, "Why did you make me like this?" Does not the potter have the right to make out of the same lump of clay some pottery for noble purposes and some for common use? What if God, choosing to show his wrath and make his power known, bore with great patience the objects of his wrath—prepared for destruction? What if he did this to make the riches of his glory known to the objects of his mercy, whom he prepared in advance for glory—even us, whom he also called, not only from the Jews but also from the Gentiles? (Rom. 9:17–24)

God May Demonstrate His Power Through the Destruction of the Wicked

Consider again the story of Pharaoh. In order for God to show Himself great through the destruction of Egypt, Egypt had to be a mighty empire. The greater their prosperity was, the greater was the witness when their army was destroyed. God made His name known when He destroyed Pharaoh and the Egyptian army in the Red Sea:

> For by now I could have stretched out my hand and struck you and your people with a plague that would have wiped you off the earth. But I have raised you up [or *have spared you*] for this very purpose, that I might show you my power and that my name might be proclaimed in all the earth. (Exod. 9:15, 16)

God said He would cause the Egyptians to be swallowed up by the Red Sea while pursuing the Israelites:

> I will harden the hearts of the Egyptians so that they will go in after them. And I will gain glory through Pharaoh and all his army, through his chariots and his horsemen. The Egyptians will know that I am the Lord. (Exod. 14:17, 18a)

> And when the Israelites saw the great power the Lord displayed against the Egyptians, the people feared the Lord and put their trust in him and in Moses his servant. (Exod. 14:31)

God May Use the Wicked to Test His People

Consider the situation in Israel after Joshua died:

> Whenever the Lord raised up a judge for them, he was with them and saved them out of the hands of their enemies as long as the judge lived; for the Lord had compassion on them as they

groaned under those who oppressed and afflicted them. But when the judge died, the people returned to ways even more corrupt than those of their fathers, following other gods and serving and worshipping them. They refused to give up their evil practices and stubborn ways. Therefore the Lord was very angry with Israel and said, "Because this nation has violated the covenant that I laid down for their forefathers and has not listened to me, I will no longer drive out before them any of the nations Joshua left when he died. I will use them to test Israel and see whether they will keep the way of the Lord and walk in it as their forefathers did." (Judg. 2:18–22)

God May Use the Wicked to Punish His People

God may cause the wicked to afflict His children for punitive purposes, not for any redemptive effect of the affliction. During the time of the kings of Israel, the majority of the people rejected the true God. The kingdom was united under Saul, David, and Solomon. But after Solomon's death, Israel was divided. The ten northern tribes of Israel were separated from Judah in 931 B. C. Jeroboam I became their king (1 Kings 12:20). Jeroboam I led his subjects into idolatry (1 Kings 12:25–33). Fortunately those people in the northern kingdom who feared the Lord were able to migrate to Jerusalem. They strengthened the kingdom of Judah (2 Chron. 11:13–17). The northern kingdom had nine different dynasties and nineteen different kings. All their kings were evil. There is a reference to Jehoahaz that is a typical of a recurrent theme about those kings: "He did evil in the eyes of the Lord by following the sins of Jeroboam son of Nebat, which he had caused Israel to commit, and he did not turn away from them." (2 Kings 13:2)

God used the Assyrians to punish the ten tribes of Israel. The Assyrians prospered for a time. Assyria vanquished the northern kingdom (723–721 B.C.).[1] Although God used the Assyrians, He was not happy with them: "I will punish the king of Assyria for the willful pride of his heart and the haughty look in his eyes" (Isaiah. 10:12b). The Babylonians eventually defeated the Assyrians. Nineveh fell in 612 B.C.[2]

Consider Assyria, once a cedar in Lebanon, with beautiful branches overshadowing the forest; it towered on high, its top above the thick foliage . . . It was majestic in beauty, with its spreading boughs, for its roots went down to abundant waters . . . Therefore this is what the sovereign Lord says: Because it towered on high, lifting its top above the thick foliage, and because it was proud of its height, I handed it over to the ruler of the nations . . . I cast it aside . . . I made the nations tremble at the sound of its fall when I brought it down to the grave with those who go down to the pit. (Ezek. 31:3–16a)

God May Use the Wicked to Train His People

God may use the wicked to create a climate for the spiritual growth of His children. The kingdom of Babylon prospered for a time. God used Babylon to discipline the kingdom of Judah, by taking it into captivity. Consider the description of the strength of the Babylonians in Habakkuk:

I am raising up the Babylonians, that ruthless and impetuous people, who sweep across the whole earth to seize dwelling places not their own. They are a feared and dreaded people; they are a law to themselves and promote their own honor. Their horses are swifter than leopards, fiercer than wolves at dusk. Their cavalry gallops headlong; their horsemen come from afar. They fly like a vulture swooping to devour; they all come bent on violence. Their hordes advance like a desert wind and gather prisoners like sand. They deride kings and scoff at rulers. They laugh at all fortified cities; they build earthen ramps and capture them. Then they sweep past like the wind and go on—guilty men, whose own strength is their god. (Hab. 1:6–11)

The book of Jeremiah quotes the Lord as follows:

I will hand all Judah over to the king of Babylon, who will carry them away to Babylon or put them to the sword. I will hand over to their enemies all the wealth of this city—all its products, all its valuables and all the treasures of the kings of Judah. They will take it away as plunder and carry it off to Babylon. (Jer. 20:4b, 5).

The Babylonians were an effective tool in God's hands. *The Narrated Bible* quotes ten psalms written during the Babylonian exile (44, 74, 79, 80, 85, 89, 102, 106, 123, and 137).[3] Consider the sadness, the humility, the contrition, and the supplication:

> By the rivers of Babylon we sat and wept
> > when we remembered Zion.
> There on the poplars
> > we hung our harps
> for there our captors asked us for songs,
> > our tormentors demanded songs of joy;
> > they said, "Sing us one of the songs of Zion!"
> How can we sing the songs of the Lord
> > while in a foreign land? (Ps. 137:1–4)

> I lift up my eyes to you,
> > to you whose throne is in heaven.
> As the eyes of slaves look to the hand of their master,
> > as the eyes of a maid look to the hand of her mistress,
> so our eyes look to the Lord our God,
> > till he shows us his mercy. (Ps. 123:1, 2)

> We have sinned, even as our fathers did;
> > we have done wrong and acted wickedly. (Ps. 106:6)

> Save us, O Lord our God,
> > and gather us from the nations,
> that we may give thanks to your holy name
> > and glory in your praise. (Ps. 106:47)

After God used the Babylonians to discipline Judah, He destroyed Babylon. Jeremiah 50 and 51 are a prophecy against Babylon. Babylon would become a wasteland:

> A destroyer will come against Babylon; her warriors will be captured, and their bows will be broken. For the Lord is a God of retribution; he will repay in full. (Jer. 51:56)

So desert creatures and hyena will live there, and there the owl will dwell. It will never again be inhabited or lived in from generation to generation. (Jer. 50:39)

God May Use the Wicked to Rescue or Preserve His People

Cyrus, king of Persia, was appointed by God to conquer Babylon and set the Israelites free:

This is what the Lord says to his anointed,
    to Cyrus whose right hand I take hold of
    to subdue nations before him
    and to strip kings of their armor,
    to open doors before him
    so that gates will not be shut . . .

I will give you the treasures of darkness,
    riches stored in secret places,
    so that you may know that I am the Lord,
    the God of Israel, who summons you by name.

For the sake of Jacob my servant,
    of Israel my chosen,
    I summon you by name
    and bestow on you a title of honor,
    though you do not acknowledge me.

I am the Lord, and there is no other;
    apart from me there is no God.
    I will strengthen you,
    though you have not acknowledged me, . . . (Isa. 45:1–5)

This is what the Lord says—
    the Holy One of Israel and its Maker:
    Concerning things to come,
    do you question me about my children,
    or give orders about the work of my hands?

It is I who made the earth
    and created mankind upon it.

My own hands stretched out the heavens;
    I marshaled their starry hosts.

I will raise up Cyrus in my righteousness:
    I will make all his ways straight.
    He will rebuild my city
    and set my exiles free. (Isaiah 45:11–13b)

God May Use the Wicked to Make His Name Known

ALEXANDER THE GREAT

Babylon conquered Judah. Persia conquered Babylon. The armies of Alexander the Great conquered Persia. All these powers prospered in their time. A prophecy of Alexander's conquests was written in Daniel, two centuries before the events actually took place:

> As I was thinking about this, suddenly a goat with a prominent horn between his eyes came from the west, crossing the whole earth without touching the ground. He came toward the two-horned ram I had seen standing beside the canal and charged at him in great rage. I saw him attack the ram furiously, striking the ram and shattering his two horns. The ram was powerless to stand against him; the goat knocked him to the ground and trampled on him, and none could rescue the ram from his power. The goat became very great, but at the height of his power his large horn was broken off, and in its place four prominent horns grew up toward the four winds of heaven. (Dan. 8:5–8)

> The two-horned ram that you saw represents the kings of Media and Persia. The shaggy goat is the king of Greece, and the large horn between his eyes is the first king. The four horns that replaced the one that was broken off represent four kingdoms that will emerge from his nation but will not have the same power. (Dan. 8:20–22)

God used Alexander to promote His own agenda. Many of the events surrounding Alexander's approach to Jerusalem are recorded by Josephus.[4] Alexander was carrying out God's mission. After Alexander had taken Damascus and while he was laying siege to Tyre, he sent a letter to Jaddua, the Jewish high priest in Jerusalem, asking him for aid. Alexander wanted the high priest to switch his allegiance from Persia to Alexander. Jaddua replied that he had given his word to Darius, the ruler of Persia, to not bear arms against him and he could not break his oath. Alexander became angry and decided to teach Jaddua a lesson. After his conquest of Tyre and then Gaza, Alexander headed for Jerusalem. Jaddua was terrified. He knew that Alexander was angry because he had not complied with Alexander's request. Jaddua had the people join him in offering prayers to God, seeking protection. By means of a dream, God told Jaddua what to do. Jaddua was instructed to decorate the city and open the city's gates to Alexander. Jaddua and the priests were to dress in their priestly garments, and the rest of the people were to be dressed in white. When Jaddua awoke, he was encouraged. The Jews did what they were instructed to do in the dream and waited for the coming of Alexander.

When Jaddua was informed that Alexander's forces were approaching Jerusalem, he, the priests, and the people went out to meet them. Alexander approached the Jews by himself, adored the name of God printed on the high priest's head band, and saluted the high priest. The Jews saluted Alexander. Alexander was asked why he adored the high priest of the Jews. He replied, "I did not adore him, but that God who hath honored him with his high priesthood; for I saw this very person in a dream, in this very habit, when I was at Dios in Macedonia, who, when I was considering with myself how I might obtain the dominion of Asia, exhorted me to make no delay, but boldly to pass over the sea thither, for that he would conduct my army, and give me the dominion over the Persians; whence it is, that having seen no other in that habit, and now seeing this person in it, and remembering that vision, and the exhortation which I had in my dream, I believe that I bring this army under the divine conduct, and shall therewith conquer Darius, and destroy the power of the Persians, and that all things will succeed according to what is in my own mind."

Through his conquests, Alexander created a single world from Spain to India. He opened trade and social exchange and established a common language.[5] Alexander continued to be friendly to the Jews. He encouraged Jews to settle in Alexandria, Egypt, a city he founded. Alexander died in 323 B. C., nine years after he marched through Palestine. Following Alexander's death, his empire was divided into four parts, each controlled by a different general. The Jews in Egypt built synagogues in all their settlements.[6]

It did not take long for the influence of the Jews to be felt by the Greeks and the influence of the Greeks to be felt by the Jews. The Septuagint is a Greek version of the Old Testament and Apocrypha. According to tradition, the Septuagint was translated from the Hebrew by Jewish scholars in Alexandria, Egypt during the reign of Ptolemy Philadelphus (285–247 B. C.). There are a large number of manuscript copies of the original. The Septuagint reflects the common language of the period and became the "Bible" of those Jews who spoke Greek and then later of the early Christians.[7] It provided a vehicle through which the sacred books of the Jews could be made known to the Greek population.[8] From Alexandria, the Septuagint spread to the Jews of the dispersion.[9] The New Testament was originally written in Greek. The majority of the Old Testament quotations in the New Testament are taken directly from the Septuagint.[10]

Acts chapter 2 gives some evidence of how widely the Jews were dispersed and how well they had done in reaching converts. The feast of Pentecost was celebrated by the Jews on the 50th day after the Passover.[11] Consider the account of the first Pentecost after the resurrection. Jews from all over the world had gathered in Jerusalem for the celebration.

> Now there were staying in Jerusalem God-fearing Jews from every nation under heaven. When they heard this sound [the blowing of a violent wind], a crowd came together in bewilderment, because each one heard them [the believers] speaking in his own language. Utterly amazed, they asked : "Are not all these men who are speaking Galileans? Then how is it that each of us hears them in his own native language? Parthians, Medes and Elamites;

residents of Mesopotamia, Judea and Cappadocia, Pontus and Asia, Phyygia and Pamphylia, Egypt and the parts of Libya near Cyrene; visitors from Rome [both Jews and converts to Judaism]; Cretans and Arabs—we hear them declaring the wonders of God in our own tongues!" (Acts 2:5–11)

Paul wanted to preach the gospel where Christ was not known; he did not want to build on someone else's foundation (Romans 15:20). Wherever he went however, his style was to first visit the synagogue (e.g. Acts 13:14). In many of the places Paul traveled, the Jews had already been there, with the word of God, sowing the seed.

It is said that Alexander was quick to anger. He was merciless and was not concerned about the wishes of others. He had no hesitation in executing men in whom he had lost trust.[12] I find no record that he ever became a true believer. However, Alexander's great achievement played a major role in the spread of Christianity as a world religion.[13]

THE HEROD FAMILY

Consider also how God used Herod the Great and his family. Herod the Great ruled from 37 B.C. through 4 B.C., during the time Jesus was born. The Herods were very wicked. Herod the Great sought to destroy Jesus. He killed numerous baby boys in Bethlehem and its vicinity, those two years old and under (Matt. 2:16). The reputation of Herod Archaleus caused Joseph to return to Galilee from Egypt rather than live in Judea (Matt. 2:22, 23). Herod Antipas married Herodias, the former wife of his brother Herod Philip. She was also the daughter of Aristobulus. He, Antipas, and Philip were sons of Herod the Great by three different wives. So when Antipas married his brother's wife, he was also marrying his niece.[14] Because John the Baptist condemned the union between Herod Antipas and Herodias, he was imprisoned and beheaded (Matt. 14:3–11). Herod Agrippa I tried to crush the early Christian church.[15] He was responsible for the execution of James, son of Zebedee, and for the arrest of Peter (Acts 12:1–3). Because of his pride, an angel of the Lord struck down Herod Agrippa I. He was eaten by worms and died (Acts 12:19b–23).

Although the family of the Herods was wicked, these rulers were used to fulfill God's plan. As the power of the Greeks faded, the Romans had taken control of the known world. Pompey invaded Palestine in 63 B. C. Herod the Great became ruler of Judea in 37 B. C. When Octavian became emperor in 31 B. C., he realized that Herod was the one man to rule Palestine as he wanted it ruled. Herod the Great established a necessary linkage between Judea and Rome.[16] Jerusalem was destroyed in A. D. 70. By God's grace, the Herods were used to make a connection between Judea and Rome during a critical period. Because of that connection, the Jewish remnant was preserved in Palestine until Christianity could be established. God's hand, through the Roman empire, provided a common language and good transportation, to spread Christianity to all the earth. Even the persecution of Christians by the Herod family caused members of the new Christian sect to leave Jerusalem and propagate the gospel on a wider scale.

The latter four world powers referred to above are also those mentioned in Daniel 2 in Nebuchadnezzar's dream. Nebuchadnezzar, king of Babylon, was the head of gold. Medo-Persia was the chest and arms of silver. Greece was the belly and thighs of bronze. Rome was the legs of iron with feet partly of iron, partly of baked clay. These four world powers were brought to prosperity between the time of Solomon and the time of Christ.

God's prophecy proved true. Daniel 2:44 states: "In the time of those kings, the God of heaven will set up a kingdom that will never be destroyed, nor will it be left to another people. It will crush all those kingdoms and bring them to an end, but it will itself endure forever."

HOW THINGS MIGHT HAVE BEEN

God had plans for the Children of Israel that were never fulfilled (Isaiah 26:17, 18). God created the nation of Israel to be a light to the Gentiles. He promised Abraham that through his seed, all the nations of the earth would be blessed. He desired that those who came after him should keep the way of the Lord, so that the Lord could fulfill His promises (Gen. 12:1–3; 18:18, 19). In Genesis 15 God made a covenant with Abraham and made promises about his descendants' sojourn in Egypt and their delivery. God repeated His promise of blessing to Abraham in Genesis 22:17, 18. God made similar promises to Isaac (Gen. 26:4) and Jacob (Gen. 28:14).

Egypt was used by God to forge the Children of Israel into a nation (Gen. 15:13, 14). They were in Egypt for 430 years and then were miraculously delivered from slavery (Exodus 12:40, 41). God wanted to make Israel His treasured possession. The Israelites were to become a kingdom of priests. The Israelites made a covenant with God to obey Him (Exod. 19:1–8). In Deuteronomy 28 the Israelites were reminded that if they fully obeyed the Lord, He would set them high above all the nations on earth. God would establish them as His holy people. They were told that they would lend to many nations, but would borrow from none. They would be made the head and not the tail. When it was time for the Israelites to cross the Jordan River and enter Canaan, God held back the waters, a witness to all the peoples of the earth (Josh. 4:23, 24).

Centuries later, David understood that Israel was supposed to be a witness to the nations (1 Sam. 17:46; 2 Sam. 7:22–26; 1 Chron. 16:8, 24, 28; 17:20–24). During the reign of Solomon, Israel had her best chance to fulfill God's purpose for her. The prayer of Solomon at the dedication of the temple, tells us that he understood that purpose:

> As for the foreigner who does not belong to your people Israel but has come from a distant land because of your name—for men will hear of your great name and your mighty hand and your outstretched arm—when he comes and prays toward this temple, then hear from heaven, your dwelling place, and do whatever the foreigner asks of you, so that all the peoples of the earth may know your name and fear you, as do your own people Israel, and may know that this house I have built bears your Name. (1 Kings 8:41–43)

After his prayer to the Lord, Solomon blessed the whole assembly of Israel saying:

> Praise be to the Lord, who has given rest to his people Israel just as he promised. Not one word has failed of all the good promises he gave through his servant Moses. May the Lord our God be with us as he was with our fathers; may he never leave us nor forsake us. May he turn our hearts to him, to walk in all his ways and to keep the commands, decrees and regulations he gave our fathers. And may these words of mine, which I have prayed before the Lord, be near to the Lord our God day and night, that he may uphold the cause of his servant and the cause of his people Israel according to each day's need, so that all the peoples of the earth may know that the Lord is God and that there is no other. But your hearts must be fully committed to the Lord our God, to live by his decrees and obey his commands, as at this time. (1 Kings 8:56–61)

During Solomon's reign, people from all over the world came to him with gifts, seeking advice (1 Kings 4:34; 1 Kings 10:23–25). Solomon ruled over all the kings from the Euphrates River to the land of the Philistines, as far as the border of Egypt (2 Chron. 9:26).

God gave this promise to Solomon:

> As for you, if you walk before me as David your father did, and do all I command, and observe my decrees and laws, I will establish your royal throne, as I covenanted with David your father when I said, "You shall never fail to have a man to rule over Israel." But if you turn away and forsake the decrees and commands I have given you and go off to serve other gods and worship them, then I will uproot Israel from my land, which I have given them, and will reject this temple I have consecrated for my Name. I will make it a byword and an object of ridicule among all peoples. (2 Chron. 7:17–20)

Solomon knew that God's promises were conditional. Solomon let a golden opportunity slip through his fingers because he was more interested in God's blessings (created things) than he was in God Himself. When the Israelites rejected the truth, God put another world system in place to prepare the world for the coming of Jesus.

God's plan for the Children of Israel was that their nation be a theocracy, a nation ruled by Him. The Israelites rejected that concept and demanded a king (1 Sam. 8). The kings led them astray. The King of kings came to the Jews, and they rejected him. God went to the Gentiles. The Gentiles have also failed. They do not love God with all their heart. The present world system is the way it is because of the failures of the generations that have gone before us. They have not maintained standards of holiness.

Why do the wicked prosper? In most cases we cannot be sure of a specific answer. We do know with certainty that we have a Sovereign God. God uses the wicked to compensate for the disobedience of His own children. God uses the wicked to promote His own agenda. He uses them to do things that His own people will not do, cannot do, or should not do. In His own time, God will punish the wicked (Ps. 37:7–9; Prov. 14:14; Hos. 10:10; Nah. 1:3).

10

GOD'S PROVIDENCE

S ometimes it is possible to get an idea of what someone is like by looking at his or her name. This was especially true in biblical days, for names held special significance at that time. One of the Old Testament names for God is Jehovah Jireh (Gen. 22:14 KJV), translated "the Lord will provide" (NIV). The second portion of the name means "to see, perceive, understand, or see to it.[1] God knows what is going on, and He will "see to it" as He determines is appropriate.

God's provision is also known as His providence. God takes care of what He has created according to His own will. In doing so, God is not arbitrary in what He does, but carries out His plans based on His own infinite knowledge of what is best.[2] *Merriam Webster's Collegiate Dictionary* defines providence as "divine guidance or care," or "God conceived as the power sustaining and guiding human destiny."[3] The Greek word for providence is *pronoia*. The word carries the idea of forethought.[4]

Consider some quotes from John Calvin:

"We are not afflicted by chance, but through the infallible providence of God."

"Let us . . . learn to see . . . by the eyes of faith, both in accidental circumstances (as they are called) and in the evil designs of men, that secret providence of God, which directs all events to a result predetermined by himself."

"We can form no judgment of God's providence, except by the light of celestial truth."

"Nothing can more effectively preserve us in a straight and un-deviating course, than a firm persuasion that all events are in the hand of God, and that he is as merciful as he is mighty."

"The necessary consequences of this knowledge are, gratitude in prosperity, patience in adversity, and a wonderful security respecting the future."[5]

GOD'S PROVISION EXTENDS TO THE WHOLE OF CREATION

God's providence extends to all creation, the physical universe, the animals, the nations, and to us as individuals.

God Provides for the Physical Universe

The Son is the radiance of God's glory and the exact representation of his being, sustaining all things by his powerful word. (Heb. 1:3a).

He spreads the snow like wool and scatters the frost like ashes. He hurls down his hail like pebbles. Who can withstand his icy blast? He sends his word and melts them; he stirs up his breezes, and the waters flow. (Ps. 147:16–18)

Yet he has not left himself without testimony: He has shown kindness by giving you rain from heaven and crops in their seasons; he provides you with plenty of food and fills your hearts with joy. (Acts 14:17)

God Takes Care of the Animals

How many are your works, O Lord! In wisdom you made them all; the earth is full of your creatures . . . These all look to you to give them their food at the proper time. When you give it to them, they gather it up; when you open your hand, they are satisfied with good things. When you hide your face, they are terrified; when you take away their breath, they die and return to the dust. When you send your Spirit, they are created, and you renew the face of the earth. (Ps. 104:24, 27–30)

He provides food for the cattle and for the young ravens when they call. (Ps. 147:9)

God Determines the Course of the Nations

For dominion belongs to the Lord and he rules over the nations. (Ps. 22:28)

The decision is announced by messengers, the holy ones declare the verdict, so that the living may know that the Most High is sovereign over the kingdoms of men and gives them to anyone he wishes. (Dan. 4:17a)

The king's heart is in the hand of the LORD; he directs it like a watercourse wherever he pleases. (Prov. 21:1)

Everyone must submit himself to the governing authorities, for there is no authority except that which God has established. The authorities that exist have been established by God. (Rom. 13:1)

God Provides for Individual People

Before I formed you in the womb I knew you, before you were born I set you apart; I appointed you as a prophet to the nations. (Jer. 1:5)

For you created my inmost being; you knit me together in my mother's womb. I praise you because I am fearfully and wonderfully made; your works are wonderful, I know that full well. My frame was not hidden from you when I was made in the secret place. When I was woven together in the depths of the earth, your eyes saw my unformed body. All the days ordained for me were written in your book before one of them came to be. (Ps. 139:13–16)

The Lord brings death and makes alive; he brings down to the grave and raises up. The Lord sends poverty and wealth; he humbles and he exalts. He raises the poor from the dust and lifts the needy from the ash heap; he seats them with princes and has them inherit a throne of honor. (1 Sam. 2:6–8a)

God is concerned about each one of us. He will work out the details of His purpose for our individual lives. As it says in Proverbs 16:9, "In his heart a man plans his course, but the Lord determines his steps." There are many other passages of Scripture that carry the same idea.

Although the Lord gives you the bread of adversity and the water of affliction, your teachers will be hidden no more; with your own eyes you will see them. Whether you turn to the right or to the left, your ears will hear a voice behind you, saying, "This is the way; walk in it." (Isa. 30:20, 21)

I know, O Lord, that a man's life is not his own; it is not for man to direct his steps. Correct me, Lord, but only with justice—not in your anger, lest you reduce me to nothing. (Jer. 10:23, 24)

Being confident of this, that he who began a good work in you will carry it on to completion until the day of Christ Jesus. (Phil. 1:6)

God's provision may not be what *we* have in mind, but we need to understand that His provision is the best for us and we should receive it with an attitude of thankfulness. One example of His physical provision is the reparative process He has built into each of our bodies that helps us deal with illness. Without that innate reparative process, our cuts and scrapes would never heal. Illnesses would wreak havoc on each of our bodies, and there would be very little the doctors could do for us.

Soon after I began my specialty training in internal medicine, I went to the repair shop with one of my mentors to pick up his lawn mower. As the repairman was putting the mower into the trunk of the car, he said, "That'll be thirty-five dollars. If anything goes wrong with it, bring it back, and I'll make it right. I guarantee my work. I'm not like you doctors!" There was a lot of truth in what the repairman said. Physicians may be in charge of patients' medical care, but God is in charge of their bodies, their innate reparative processes.

My wife was forced to depend on her innate reparative processes when she had her stem cell transplant. In September 1997, Barbara was diagnosed with breast cancer. She had widespread bony metastasis and five vertebral compression fractures. She lost five inches in height between her shoulders and her hips. Five weeks after starting treatment, she suddenly developed severe pain in her left hip and was unable to stand. Chemotherapy was begun, and in all, she received eight of the usual chemotherapy treatments. Regular visits by a home physical therapist helped her walk again, and in June 1998 we went to Vanderbilt Medical Center in Nashville, Tennessee for the stem cell procedure.

Before we left home, I started giving Barbara injections that were designed to stimulate the white blood cells in her own bone marrow. As they multiplied, they spilled over into her circulation. After we arrived in Nashville, she had a large catheter inserted under her right collarbone. We remained in the motel. On two successive days, she had leukophoresis to remove the immature bone marrow cells from her blood stream. When the medical team was satisfied that the harvest was adequate, Barbara was admitted to the hospital.

In an effort to eradicate the cancer, Barbara was given six days of intensive chemotherapy. That chemotherapy also destroyed her bone marrow. Two days after the chemotherapy was complete the team reinfused her stem cells. The day of reinfusion was day zero. The normal white count is 4-11 thousand/ml. On day two her white count was 0.2 (200/ml.). One day it was 0.0. During the time her white count was down, she developed high fevers. She was on three antibiotics, an anti-viral drug, and an anti-fungal agent. It appeared that one of the antibiotics was giving her a severe rash, but the doctors were afraid to stop that antibiotic for fear of infection. Her appetite was poor. Food had no taste. She had large, painful ulcers in her mouth. Whenever she would try to eat, she would develop esophageal spasms, producing severe chest pain. I finally convinced her to accept the offer of a morphine pump. Eventually she was given more injections of medicine to stimulate her white blood cells. On day eight her white count was 0.1. On day nine it was 0.3. Day ten white count was 0.8; day eleven 3.5; day twelve 11. We went home on day twelve. Those reparative processes that God built in to her body finally brought restoration, and the stem cells finally engrafted.

At this time, Barbara's condition is improved. God is making provision for Barbara. She has had the prayers of hundreds of people. She was blessed with a good constitution combined with a strong will to overcome the illness. She had good health care. Friends brought in nutritional food. I was able to take off time from my practice and care for her.

I had my own transplant experience. In August 1998 I had a cornea transplant for Fuchs' Dystrophy. That procedure would have been worthless had it not been for the processes of healing that God built into my body. I also had to learn to use those processes. The day after my transplant, the ophthalmologist was satisfied with the appearance of my eye. For some reason, I did not understand that I needed to rest my eye. Over the next several days, I spent long hours at the computer. I returned to work in the office. When I went back to the ophthalmologist on day eight, I did not get a good report. There was a fifty percent defect in the epithelialization over the graft. I went home. I did not read. I did not write. I did not work. I shaded my eyes. I rested several times a day. I began to cooperate with those processes that would help my eye heal. By day ten the defect was down to ten percent. I rested three more days and then went back to work. At my visit on day fifteen, I was told that the epithelialization was complete.

There are many situations in which people who are sick need to work *with* their bodies. One situation that comes to mind is when people who are chronically ill lose their appetite. Many dialysis patients lose their ability to eat. But when they stop eating, they deprive their bodies of what they need to survive. If we do not find a way to help them take in life-sustaining nutrition, the patients will die. Sometimes the solution is as simple as liberalizing their diet. Sometimes nutritional supplements are effective in reversing the situation. There are also some drugs that sometimes work.

Certain reparative processes are innate within our mental faculty. We can become overloaded mentally with work or stress. At times such a situation is referred to as "burn-out." With rest or a change in our situation, the reparative processes provide recuperation.

God has also made provision for our spirits. Paul spoke of that provision in referring to his troubles in Philippians 1:19: "For I know that through your prayers and the help given by the Spirit of Jesus Christ, what has happened to me will turn out for my deliverance." Peter also wrote about God's provision for our spirits: "His divine power has given us everything we need for life and godliness through our knowledge of him who called us by his own glory and goodness" (2 Pet. 1:3).

GOD'S PROVISION MAY BE DEATH

Death is a part of life. It has its time and place. There is a saying in medicine that carries the same idea: "Pneumonia is the old man's friend."

There is a time for everything, and a season for every activity under heaven:
a time to be born and a time to die,
a time to plant and a time to uproot,
a time to kill and a time to heal,
a time to tear down and a time to build,
a time to weep and a time to laugh,
a time to mourn and a time to dance,

> a time to scatter stones and a time to gather them,
> a time to embrace and a time to refrain,
> a time to search and a time to give up,
> a time to keep and a time to throw away,
> a time to tear and a time to mend,
> a time to be silent and a time to speak,
> a time to love and a time to hate,
> a time for war and a time for peace.

What does the worker gain from his toil? I have seen the burden God has laid on men. He has made everything beautiful in its time. He has also set eternity in the hearts of men; yet they cannot fathom what God has done from beginning to end. I know that there is nothing better for men than to be happy and do good while they live. That everyone may eat and drink, and find satisfaction in all his toil—this is the gift of God. I know that everything God does will endure forever; nothing can be added to it and nothing taken from it. God does it so that men will revere him (Eccles. 3:1–14).

Notice that God does what He does so that men will revere Him.

We do not have to fear death. God provides for us in life, and He provides for us in death. "Even though I walk through the valley of the shadow of death, I will fear no evil, for you are with me; your rod and your staff, they comfort me" (Ps. 23:4).

A Young Person May Be Taken to Spare Him from Trouble

We do not always understand the purposes of God, but God does give an explanation for some of the things that happen. A young person may be taken because God wants to spare him from evil.

> The righteous perish, and no one ponders it in his heart; devout men are taken away, and no one understands that the righteous are taken away to be spared from evil. Those who walk uprightly enter into peace; they find rest as they lie in death. (Isaiah 57:1, 2)

Jeroboam's son, Abijah, became ill. The prophet said that the boy would die. Israel would mourn for him and bury him. He was to be the only one in Jeroboam's household who would be buried peacefully. He was the only one in the house of Jeroboam in whom the Lord found anything good. The rest of Jeroboam's family died violently (1 Kings 14:1–18; 15:25–30).

Consider also King Josiah who lived only thirty-nine years. He was taken to be with the Lord and was buried in peace so that his eyes would not see all the disaster the Lord would bring on the Kingdom of Judah (2 Kings 22:18–20). He reigned for thirty-one years and died in 608 B. C., two years before Babylon conquered Judah and began the deportation of the Children of Israel into captivity.

On the other hand, the Lord may keep us alive to test us as he did King Hezekiah (2 Chron. 32:31). He may also keep us alive, past any apparent usefulness, to test our family members. Hezekiah did not pass the test. According to J. Vernon McGee, three things happened demonstrating that things would likely have been better had Hezekiah gone ahead and died. He became filled with pride, not responding to the kindness shown him by the Lord (2 Chron. 32:25, 26). He showed off all his treasures to the envoys from Babylon (2 Kings 20:12–19), a decision that was a contributing factor in the subsequent Babylonian invasion, He fathered Manasseh, one of the most wicked kings who ever ruled in Judah.[6]

Precious in the Sight of the Lord Is the Death of His Saints

"Precious in the sight of the Lord is the death of his saints." (Ps. 116:15)

Spurgeon's commentary on the Psalms includes several thoughts about this verse: "They [his saints] shall not die prematurely; they shall be immortal till their work is done . . . The Lord watches over their dying beds . . . sustains their hearts, and receives their souls . . . . We need not fear to die before him when the hour of our departure is at hand."[7]

Consider also Revelation 14:13:

> Then I heard a voice from heaven say, "Write: Blessed are the dead who die in the Lord from now on." "Yes," says the Spirit, "they will rest from their labor, for their deeds will follow them."

In death the righteous have a refuge (Prov. 14:32). The Hebrew word for "refuge" in this verse is the same as the one in Psalm 57:1.[8] Psalm 57:1 reads as follows: "Have mercy on me, O God, have mercy on me, for in you my soul takes refuge. I will take refuge in the shadow of your wings until the disaster is passed." The word "refuge" means "shelter or protection."[9] Consider Ecclesiastes 7:1–2:

> A good name is better than fine perfume, and the day of death better than the day of birth. It is better to go to a house of mourning than to go to a house of feasting, for death is the destiny of every man; the living should take this to heart.

Death Finishes Our State of Labor and Puts Us in Possession of the Prize

For believers, their existence in the afterlife is better than their existence in this life. Isaac Watts authored a book of sermons in 1811. The eleventh sermon was entitled "Death a Blessing to the Saints." He outlined several reasons why death, for the believer, brings "a rich variety of blessings." Consider some quotes from his sermon:

"Death finishes our state of labor and trial, and puts us in possession of the crown and the prize."[10] "So the soldier rejoices in the last field of battle; he fights with the prize of glory in his eye, and ends the war with courage, pleasure, and victory."[11]

Second Timothy was Paul's last known letter. Consider how he summed up what he had done, in his own words:

> The time has come for my departure. I have fought the good fight, I have finished the race, I have kept the faith. Now there is in store for me a crown of righteousness, which the Lord, the righteous Judge, will award to me on that day. (2 Tim. 4:6b–8a)

Death Frees Us from All Our Errors and Mistakes

"Death frees us forever from all our errors and mistakes, and brings us into a world of glorious knowledge and illumination."[12]

> Now we see but a poor reflection as in a mirror; then we shall see face to face. Now I know in part; then I shall know fully, even as I am fully known. (1 Cor. 13:12)

"Death makes an utter end of sin, it delivers us from a state of temptation, and conveys us into a state of perfect holiness, safety, and peace."[13]

> Christ loved the church and gave himself up for her to make her holy, cleansing her by the washing with water through the word . . . to present her to himself as a radiant church, without stain or wrinkle or any other blemish, but holy and blameless. (Eph. 5:25b–27)

There are several passages that help us to understand the contrast of life in our earthly bodies with life in the world to come:

> Jesus said to her, "I am the resurrection and the life. He who believes in me will live, even though he dies; and whoever lives and believes in me will never die." (John 11:25, 26a)

Consider the contrast of the earthly and the heavenly in 1 Corinthians 15:35–53. Christians, upon our death, will undergo the following transformations:

1. Earthly bodies will become heavenly bodies
2. Perishable bodies will become imperishable bodies
3. Dishonor will change to glory
4. Weakness will change to power
5. Natural bodies will become spiritual bodies
6. We will move from Earth to heaven

7. The likeness of earthly man will become the likeness of the man from heaven
8. Mortality will become immortality

> We know that if the earthly tent we live in is destroyed, we have a building from God, an eternal house in heaven, not built by human hands. Meanwhile we groan, longing to be clothed with our heavenly dwelling . . . For while we are in this tent, we groan and are burdened, because we do not wish to be unclothed but to be clothed with our heavenly dwelling, so that what is mortal may be swallowed up by life . . . Therefore we are always confident and know that as long as we are at home in the body we are away from the Lord. (2 Cor. 5:1, 2, 4, 6)

> For to me to live is Christ and to die is gain. If I am to go on living in the body, this will mean fruitful labor for me. Yet what shall I choose? I do not know! I am torn between the two: I desire to depart and be with Christ, which is better by far; but it is more necessary for you that I remain in the body. (Phil. 1:21–24)

While it is true that the families of those departed feel a sense of loss, for the believer, death is not an occasion for sorrow. Christ has conquered the power of death, and if the loved one was a believer as well, we shall see him again.

> For I am convinced that neither death nor life, neither angels nor demons, neither the present nor the future, nor any powers, neither height nor depth, nor anything else in all creation, will be able to separate us from the love of God that is in Christ Jesus our Lord. (Rom. 8:38, 39)

> On this mountain he will destroy the shroud that enfolds all peoples, the sheet that covers all nations; he will swallow up death forever. The sovereign Lord will wipe away the tears from all faces; he will remove the disgrace of his people from all the earth. The Lord has spoken. (Isa. 25:7, 8)

"I will ransom them from the power of the grave; I will redeem them from death. Where, O death, are your plagues? Where, O grave, is your destruction? (Hos. 13:14a)

But your dead will live; their bodies will rise. You who dwell in the dust, wake up and shout for joy. Your dew is like the dew of the morning; the earth will give birth to her dead. (Isa. 26:19)

If we have been united with him like this in his death, we will certainly also be united with him in his resurrection. (Rom. 6:5)

When the perishable has been clothed with the imperishable, and the mortal with immortality, Then the saying that is written will come true: "Death has been swallowed up in victory." (1 Cor. 15:54)

He will wipe every tear from their eyes. There will be no more death or mourning or crying or pain, for the old order of things has passed away. (Rev. 21:4)

11

GOD'S GRACE

In the last chapter we looked at God's provision. We have focused on His majesty and power. As we consider God's grace, our emphasis is on His love and the way He nurtures His children. God provides for the universe, and that provision extends down to individual people. God extends His grace to individuals and they can themselves become conduits of that grace. From individuals, God's grace extends outward to their families, their friends, their communities, their countries, and the whole world. Consider an example from the family unit. It has been said that the foundation of a godly nation is godly mothers. Godly mothers train up godly sons and daughters to become godly citizens, and consequently, the nation becomes blessed.

The Greek word translated "grace" is *charis*. Strong says that the word refers to "the divine influence upon the heart and its reflection in the life."[1] Other meanings of the word "grace" include benefit, favor, gift, joy, and pleasure. According to Vine, divine grace is given freely and is set in contrast with debt, with works, and with the law.[2] *Merriam Webster's Collegiate Dictionary* includes the following definition for grace: "Unmerited divine assistance given man for his regeneration or sanctification."[3]

There is not always a clear distinction between God's provision and His grace. But there does seem to be a difference in emphasis. Grace seems to be a product of the work of the Holy Spirit. God's provision is available to all. However, it is only through the work of the Holy Spirit, or God's grace, that we are able to utilize what is provided, to receive His gifts the way they should be received. For example, consider the Holy Bible. The Scriptures have been provided to the majority of the people in this world. But it is only through the work of the Holy Spirit that people can understand them. It is by God's grace that He makes His plans personal to us as individuals.

> No one can come to me [Jesus] unless the Father who sent me draws him, and I will raise him up at the last day. (John 6:44)

> But I [Jesus] tell you the truth: It is for your good that I am going away. Unless I go away, the Counselor will not come to you; but if I go, I will send him to you. When he comes, he will convict the world of guilt in regard to sin and righteousness and judgment. (John 16:7, 8)

> When the Counselor comes, whom I [Jesus] will send to you from the Father, the Spirit of truth who goes out from the Father, he will testify about me. (John 15:26)

> But the Counselor, the Holy Spirit, whom the Father will send in my name, will teach you all things. (John 14:26a)

We can be recipients of God's grace in two ways. When God touches our hearts, enlightening us with a glimpse of spiritual truth, of wisdom, that is His gift of grace in a direct form. That grace should spill out from our hearts to people around us. If He speaks to others and causes them to be of some service to us, in either a spiritual or even in a more temporal way, we are secondary recipients of His grace.

When Barbara became ill, we were on the receiving end of both God's provision and His grace. In my mind, God's provision was money we had in the bank, money that allowed me to be away from work to take care of her. An example of God's grace in a *direct* form, is how He worked with our spirits to accept the situation and take positive steps to deal with it. An example of God's grace, given in its *secondary* form, was the support we received from other believers. In particular there were three ladies from church who brought us food twice a week. They brought us so much that we did not have to cook an evening meal for over a year.

GOD IS GRACIOUS

God is gracious. Brown, Driver, Briggs, and Gesenius tell us that the Hebrew word for gracious, *channuwn* is "only used as an attribute of God, as hearing the cry of the vexed debtor."[4]

If you return to the Lord, then your brothers and your children will be shown compassion by their captors and will come back to this land, for the Lord your God is gracious and compassion-ate. He will not turn his face from you if you return to him. (2 Chron. 30:9)

The Lord is gracious and righteous; our God is full of compassion. (Ps. 116:5)

GOD'S GRACE IS GIVEN TO THE HUMBLE

Being the recipient of God's grace in its direct form starts with having the right attitude.

The sacrifices of God are a broken spirit; A broken and contrite heart, O God, you will not despise. (Ps. 51:17)

"Has not my hand made all these things, and so they came into be-ing?" declares the Lord. "This is the one I esteem: he who is humble and contrite in spirit, and trembles at my word." (Isa. 66:2)

All of you, clothe yourselves with humility toward one another, because, "God opposes the proud but gives grace to the humble." Humble yourselves, therefore, under God's mighty hand, that he may lift you up in due time. (1 Pet. 5:5b, 6)

IT IS BY GOD'S GRACE THAT SALVATION IS EXTENDED

It is only by God's grace that we are able to take that first step, the one to enter into a relationship with Him.

For it is by grace you have been saved, through faith—and this not from yourselves, it is the gift of God—not by works so that no one can boast. For we are God's workmanship, created in Christ Jesus to do good works, which God prepared in advance for us to do. (Eph. 2:8–10)

Therefore, since we have been justified through faith, we have peace with God through our Lord Jesus Christ, through whom we have gained access by faith into this grace in which we now stand. (Rom. 5:1, 2a)

IT IS BY GOD'S GRACE THAT WE CAN LIVE THE CHRISTIAN LIFE

God's grace does not just provide the salvation that initiates someone into the family of God, but grace is necessary for us to live the kind of life that we are supposed to live as Christians. The grace of God frees us from bondage to sin. We are told that sin shall not be our master (Rom. 6:11–18). It is because of God's grace that we are able to overcome the power of sin. Paul listed several things the Corinthians had received because of God's grace.

I always thank God for you because of his grace given you in Christ Jesus. For in him you have been enriched in every way— in all your speaking and in all your knowledge—because our testimony about Christ was confirmed in you. Therefore you do not lack any spiritual gift as you eagerly wait for our Lord Jesus

Christ to be revealed. He will keep you strong to the end, so that you will be blameless on the day of our Lord Jesus Christ. (1 Cor. 1:4–8)

As noted in this passage, God's grace provides us with knowledge, strength, and a good character. If we have a witness for God, it is because of His gifts to us.

Now this is our boast: Our conscience testifies that we have conducted ourselves in the world, and especially in our relations with you, in holiness and sincerity that are from God. We have done so not according to worldly wisdom but according to God's grace. (2 Cor. 1:12)

Consider what Paul and Timothy prayed for in the Colossian people (Col. 1:9–11), things to be provided by God's grace. They asked God to fill the people with the knowledge of His will through all spiritual wisdom and understanding. The request was made in order that the people might live a life worthy of the Lord and please Him in every way, bearing fruit in every good work, growing in the knowledge of God. They wanted the people to be strengthened with all power according to God's glorious might so that they could have great endurance and patience.

Paul knew that through the grace of God he had been called to be an apostle and that he had been fitted out with the powers and capabilities required for that office.[5] We ought to have that same feeling about what God has called each of us to do.

Everything we are, have, or expect to become comes to us by God's grace:

And God is able to make all grace abound to you, so that in all things at all times, having all that you need, you will abound in every good work. (2 Cor. 9:8)

It is by God's grace that we are allowed to participate in what He is doing, to be involved in any sort of meaningful activity for the kingdom of God (1 Cor. 3:10; Eph. 3:7). If someone has an ability to do something successfully, it is God's gift to him. What-ever God wants you to do, He will provide you with what you need to do it.

> LORD, you establish peace for us; all that we have accomplished you have done for us. (Isa. 26:12)

I have been blessed with material things. I thank God for them. There are times when I have a certain amount of guilt about all God has given me. One morning I was reading my Bible, and I came across the following passage:

> Command those who are rich in this present world not to be ar-rogant nor to put their hope in wealth, which is so uncertain, but to put their hope in God, who richly provides us with everything for our enjoyment. (1 Tim. 6:17)

I was glad to see that I did not have to feel guilty about all God had given me. There was more:

> Command them to do good, to be rich in good deeds, and to be generous and willing to share. In this way they will lay up treasure for themselves as a firm foundation for the coming age, so that they may take hold of the life that is truly life. (1 Tim. 6:18, 19)

It is by God's grace that we receive help in time of need (Heb. 4:16). In 2 Cor. 12, Paul discussed his "thorn in the flesh." Three times he pleaded with the Lord to take it away. God's response is noted in verse 9: "My grace is sufficient for you, for my power is made perfect in weakness." God promised Paul that he would give him the strength to endure. God would enable Paul to fulfill his heavenly Father's plan for the rest of his life in spite of, and prob-ably because of, that limitation, that thorn.

IT IS BY GOD'S GRACE THAT SPIRITUAL GIFTS ARE GIVEN

The word *charisma* is a word related to *charis*, which means grace. Strong says that the word *charisma* means "a [divine] *gratuity,* i.e. *deliverance* [from danger or passion] . . . a [spiritual] *endowment,* i.e. [subjectively] religious *qualification,* or [objectively] miraculous *faculty:*—[free] gift."[6] Vine says that the word refers to a gift of grace involving God as the donor and is used both of his free gifts given to sinners and of his endowments upon believers by the operation of the Holy Spirit in the churches.[7]

By God's grace He gives us spiritual gifts. Some of those gifts are listed in Romans 12:6–8 and include prophecy, service, teaching, encouraging, governing, and showing mercy. Another list of spiritual gifts appears in Ephesians 4:11.

Each one should use whatever gift he has received to serve others, faithfully administering God's grace in its various forms. If anyone speaks, he should do it as one speaking the very words of God. If anyone serves, he should do it with the strength God provides, so that in all things God may be praised through Jesus Christ. (1 Pet. 4:10, 11a)

Although I am less than the least of all God's people, this grace was given me: to preach to the Gentiles the unsearchable riches of Christ, . . . (Eph. 3:8)

Each one of us has his or her own gifts from God (1 Cor. 7:7). Each of us should use his own gift to serve others and build them up in the faith. If we understand that all we are or have is by God's grace, we should be more willing to extend that grace to others. We should not neglect our gifts but should cultivate them (1 Tim. 4:14). It is through the grace of God that we are able to function in the body of Christ, each having different uses in the church. God uses gifts to individual believers to provide for the church in general.

For by the grace given me I say to every one of you: Do not think of yourself more highly than you ought, but rather think of yourself with sober judgment, in accordance with the measure of faith God has given you. Just as each of us has one body with many members, and these members do not all have the same function, so in Christ we who are many form one body, and each member belongs to all the others. We have different gifts, according to the grace given us. If a man's gift is prophesying, let him use it in proportion to his faith. If it is serving, let him serve; if it is teaching, let him teach; if it is encouraging, let him encourage; if it is contributing to the needs of others, let him give generously; if it is leadership, let him govern diligently; if it is showing mercy, let him do it cheerfully. (Rom. 12:3–8)

The idea that we are individually different, but still all parts of one body is further expressed in 1 Corinthians 12:12–31a. Verse 18 says, "But in fact God has arranged the parts in the body, every one of them, just as he wanted them to be." Each part needs the other parts. Verses 24b and 25 read as follows: "God has combined the members of the body and has given greater honor to the parts that lacked it, so that there should be no division in the body, but that its parts should have equal concern for each other." The alternate translation for verse 31a is "But you are eagerly desiring the greater gifts." It seems to me that the people given *lesser* gifts were envying those with *greater* gifts. Each of us should be proud of the gift God gave us, because God gave it to us. David comments on the subject in Psalm 16:5a: "Lord, you have assigned me my portion and my cup." We should be content and do our assigned job well. The hand should not be resentful because it cannot see, and the eye should not become disheartened because it cannot grasp. If we become dissatisfied with our role in the body of Christ, that is just what Satan wants.

My first mission trip to Guatemala was in 1993. It was at that time that I was given a graphic picture of how the body of Christ should function. The people in our group plus those in base camp numbered perhaps 20–25 people. There were several groups within our group from different ministries: family blessing clinic, school ministry, medical clinic, vacation Bible school for the children, and evangelistic services. In the medical clinic we had intake people, interpreters, a physician, people to dispense medicine, and those to explain directions for taking the medicine. All of us had to be fed, and arrangements had to be made for our sleeping. There were all of these people down there doing different jobs; most of them were doing jobs the others could not have done, but yet, together we functioned as a well-oiled machine. The body of Christ should function in the same way, each member an important person with an important and unique task to perform.

> It was he who gave some to be apostles, some to be prophets, some to be evangelists, and some to be pastors and teachers, to prepare God's people for works of service, so that the body of Christ may be built up until we all reach unity in the faith and in the knowledge of the Son of God and become mature, attaining to the whole measure of the fullness of Christ. (Eph. 4:11–13)

> Each one should use whatever gift he has received to serve others, faithfully administering God's grace in its various forms. (1 Pet. 4:10)

SPIRITUAL GIFTS NEED TO BE CHANNELED WITH LOVE

First Corinthians 12:7–10 lists manifestations of the Spirit for the common good: wisdom, knowledge, faith, gifts of healing, miraculous powers, prophecy, distinguishing between spirits, speaking in different kinds of tongues, and the interpretation of tongues. Several of those manifestations are listed again in 1 Corinthians 13: tongues, prophecy (being able to fathom all mysteries and all knowledge), faith, and service. The issue in 1 Corinthians 13 is that love in itself is greater than all other individual gifts. First Corinthians 13:2 says "If I . . . have not love, I am nothing."

In my mind what we are being told in 1 Corinthians 12–14 is that we are to be a channel of God's grace to the people in the world around us. We do it through our spiritual gifts. However, ministering to people with love is more important than which particular spiritual gift we actually have. As Medicare has gotten more involved in the practice of medicine and telling the health care industry what to do, diseases are categorized. Certain diagnoses "require" certain numbers of days of hospitalization. After that number of days, if the person is still sick, the compassion factor in many health care workers rapidly begins to fade. I recently overheard one case manager speaking about a patient on the telephone. It was her job to come up with an extended care facility to which to send the patient. She said, referring to the patient, "She has overstayed her welcome here by four days." Patients still need an advocate. Even if there is a limit to what we can do for someone, we still need to do what we *can* do with love. As individuals, if we are not a conduit of God's love to others, we are nothing.

Sometimes the best thing we can do for people is to affirm them. Many years ago I read a book called *Hide or Seek* by James Dobson.[8] In the book he mentioned that the two most important things that determine how people are treated are looks and intelligence. His point was that there are a lot of people who are not necessarily beautiful or smart, but who are working hard and need to be appreciated for what they do. I thought about it and realized that at the hospital, my tendency was to interact more with the nurses who were younger and prettier. It was not hard as they were used to it and were more outgoing. I decided to observe and see if that were true for other doctors. I noticed that frequently it was true. One day I was sitting at a nursing station and observed one doctor carrying on a particularly spirited conservation with an attractive nurse. There were three nurses, older and heavier, who were standing in the corner watching. They noticed! I really felt bad for them. I decided that rather than decrease my interactions with the young, pretty ones, I would interact more with the other ones as well.

Each of us should please his neighbor for his good, to build him up. (Rom. 15:2)

WE NEED TO BE SENSITIVE TO GOD'S MESSAGE OF GRACE

William Hendricks wrote a book entitled *Exit Interviews*.[9] In that book he spoke of several people who committed their lives to the Lord for full-time Christian service, but in each person's life, something happened that pulled him out of the ministry, and he developed a spiritual malaise. Spiritually, he was defeated. I expect that there are many readers who have some bad feelings related to previous decisions they have made. Perhaps they promised God that they would go into full-time Christian work and then did not, or maybe they were in the ministry but were unable to persevere. They may be struggling with past decisions, commitments they made that were not carried out. They may think that God views them as failures. It may have caused them to not be able to do anything for the Lord.

I would like to give some personal testimony about the grace of God in my life. As with others, my life has been a curious mixture of positive and negative influences. When I was twelve years old, by God's grace, I received the assurance of my salvation at Bible camp. A few days later, there was a call for each of us to commit our lives to become missionaries. My emotions told me that I wanted to be of great service for God. Being a missionary seemed to be a wonderful way to do that. Everyone else was going forward, so I did too. The same thing happened the next two summers. The summer before my senior year in high school, I recommitted my life to Christ. But in college I was under great stress about the future; I did not know what I was going to do with my life.

One of my problems with going into full-time Christian work was my father. When I was a teenager, there were times when I expressed an interest in becoming a minister. His response was always the same: "You can't do that. Ministers have to be an example for people in the community, and you're not good enough." It was not until many years later, after my father died, that I learned the truth about what he was doing. My uncle told me that my father once said, "I don't want my boys to be ministers. If they do, they will have to live a life of poverty."

God starts developing us for His service before we are born. He builds in us certain characteristics present when we emerge from the womb. In choosing how to serve Him, we need to pay attention to what our talent is, what we like to do, what we are really interested in. Then we need to pay attention to the influences God sends our way. Over the years the Lord used many different influences to get me where I needed to be as a physician. I remember in the ninth grade, one of my friends said, "You know while I am here at Central High School, I am going to take all the math and science that I can." The idea sounded good to me, so I did the same thing. That prepared me for the appropriate courses in college.

In college, I changed majors frequently. After I changed to a major that had seemed like a good one, then it did not look so good. My third year, I went to Bryan College, a small Christian school. At the beginning of my year at Bryan, I trusted God to get me where I needed to be in life. It was during my year there that my perspective began to change with regard to my service for God. One of the chapel speakers was from a foreign country. She had come as a missionary to America. The reason she became a missionary to America was because she knew that the United States was the primary source for the world's missionaries. She had a sense that the spirituality of this country was slipping, and she wanted to try to reinforce it. She wanted the United States to continue to be a source for missionaries. I came to realize that being a positive influence right here, in this culture, would still support the Great Commission: "Go into all the world and preach the good news to all creation" (Mark 16:15). During another one of the chapels a Scripture passage about sending out missionaries was emphasized:

> "Everyone who calls on the name of the Lord will be saved." How, then, can they call on the one they have not believed in? And how can they believe in one of whom they have not heard? And how can they hear without someone preaching to them? And how can they preach unless they are sent? (Rom. 10:13b–15a)

It was a further affirmation that missionaries could not go to the mission field without support. There needed to be a strong home base from which to send them.

During the fall quarter of my fourth year in college, I was back at the University of Tennessee and majoring in physics. Another friend of mine said, "You need to go back into pre-med. What are you going to do, have fun or help people?" Those words pierced my heart. I began the application process for medical school that same day. Within three weeks I was accepted. For a while, I had thoughts of becoming a medical missionary. But I can remember three specific influences during that time in my life that turned my heart away from becoming a missionary:

1. I saw a motion picture named *The Sand Pebbles*, starring Steve McQueen. As I remember, the Chinese revolutionaries shot and killed the white Christian missionaries. The revolutionaries were rejecting the influence of the foreign culture.
2. There was a couple from our church who went to the foreign field to be missionaries. They had a grand and glorious send-off. But after about six months, they had come back home. They could not survive the rigors of the mission field.
3. When I was in Vietnam, I was initially assigned to a tank battalion. After 6 1/2 months, I was transferred to 8th Field Hospital in Nha Trang. We were responsible for some local missionaries. One day I was seeing a lady missionary who was most upset. She and her husband and children had spent the night before in a bunker at Ban Me Thuot. They had to spend the night in the bunker because of incoming, hostile artillery fire. I thought, "How could they do that to their children?" Something came up in our conservation about Hanoi. She exploded, "I hope they bomb them off the map!" I thought that her attitude was far removed from what it had been when she first made her decision to go to the mission field. I developed the impression that missionary life was not all it was cracked up to be.

Those three things might not have been able to influence me at a different time in life, but at that particular time they did.

In my development as a physician, God used many influences to guide me toward a more specific focus. God used hand dermatitis to help me choose the specialty of internal medicine over surgery. He used my experience in the Nephrology Clinic at Walter Reed Army Medical Center and other things to help me pick a subspecialty. He helped me through the rough spots in my training. He used the influence of a wife to leave Roanoke, Virginia and a mother to return home to Knoxville from Florence, Alabama. By faith, I believe that he got me where I needed to be.

I believe that God wanted me to be a physician in my own hometown. I do not have the gift of evangelism. When I share the gospel with people, generally they do not make decisions for Christ. There are of course some exceptions. I have had the privilege to be a participant when both of our sons made their decisions to become Christians. Even though I do not have the gift of evangelism, I still have an obligation to share my faith. I may be sowing the seed for others to harvest, influencing someone to prepare his heart so that later, someone else may lead him to Christ. As an aside and as an encouragement to others, let me share with you a story about a patient and sowing the seed. The man was often anxious and upset. On one occasion, soon after I met him, I tried to share with him the peace available through a relationship with Jesus Christ. He said he already knew about such things and did not want to discuss the issue any further. I put him on my prayer list and prayed for him, virtually every day, for years. There were times when he could become very difficult. On many occasions I had the urge to tell him to find another doctor, but something inside me would not let me do it. I tried to love him with Christ's love, even when I didn't feel like doing so. Eventually, his kidneys failed. He had multiple other problems and did not tolerate dialysis well. After he died, I wondered what had happened to his soul. Several days later, one of the dialysis nurses, just happened to mention to me that during the terminal phase of his illness, she had developed a relationship with him and had begun to tell him about Jesus. He said to her, "You really believe that stuff, don't you?" With her help, a couple of weeks before he died, he had prayed to receive Christ as his Savior. The circumstances of his life illustrate the principle that each of us has an incomplete understanding of how our actions fit in with God's overall plan. The Bible tells us to, "Sow your seed in the morning, and at evening let not your hands be idle, for you do not know which will succeed, whether this or that, or whether both will do equally well" (Ecclesiastes 11:6).

Consider these words of Jesus:

> He also said, "This is what the kingdom of God is like. A man scatters seed on the ground. Night and day, whether he sleeps or gets up, the seed sprouts and grows, though he does not know how. All by itself the soil produces grain—first the stalk, then the head, then the full kernel in the head. As soon as the grain is ripe, he puts the sickle to it, because the harvest has come." (Mark 4:26–29)

Even though I don't have the gift of evangelism, according to the feedback I receive, by the grace of God I am a good doctor. I believe that I have the gifts of mercy, service, healing, and encouragement. I have enough things to do that I can do. I do not need to be upset about the things that I cannot do. Even so, at times I have this lingering doubt, the feeling that since I did not become a missionary in a foreign land, I may have missed God's first and best vocational choice for my life.

My message to the reader who has similar feelings is that perhaps that "calling" you received for a full-time Christian vocation was an urge to be of service for the Lord, not God's calling for a commitment to a specific full time Christian work. Perhaps, at the time, you were too young and had an insufficient data base from which to make an informed decision. Of all the career choices individuals fantasize about, they can really only choose one (at least only one at a time that is full-time). They have to reject the rest. In your situation, that impulse you may not have followed through on may have been God's specific calling or it may not.

David had it in his heart to build a temple for the Lord but was not permitted to do so. (1 Kings 8:17–19) There were times when Peter had emotional impulses to do things for the Lord, things he was not permitted to carry out. On the Mount of Transfiguration, he wanted to build three shelters—one for Jesus, one for Moses, and one for Elijah (Matt. 17:4). That did not happen. When Jesus was arrested in the Garden of Gethsemane, Peter tried to defend him. Peter drew his sword and cut off Malchus' right ear (John 18:10). Jesus told him, "No more of this!" (Luke 22:51). He also said, "Put your sword away!" (John 18:11). Jesus touched the man's ear and healed him.

I believe that God does not want us to love Him for what He can do for us. I believe He wants us to love him for Himself, for who He is. I have come to believe that God does not love us for what we can do for Him. He loves each of us for who we are as a person. Our own individual ministry, full-time Christian work or something else, is a vehicle by which we can turn on the light for others to see, but I believe the primary reason for us to be involved in our own special ministry is that it helps us develop our relationship with the Lord. In my opinion, obedience is a means to an end. That end is a more intimate relationship with the Father. Compared to knowing Him, everything else is rubbish (Phil. 3:7–11).

As I think about whether or not I should have done something different with my life, I realize that right now it doesn't make any difference. Any past failures are confessed and forgiven. The slate is wiped clean. Life is a journey. What I need to be concerned about is what I need to do next. I do know what I am supposed to do today. There is no doubt about that. I know what I am supposed to do to serve. I know how I am supposed to be an influence in the world around me.

In evaluating your own situation, look at the events in your life. Has God led you and blessed you? Ask God for help in sorting through your feelings. If you decide that you did not have a specific calling from God in that past situation, put your anxiety behind you. If it was a specific calling and you rejected it, confess your sin to the Lord and then forget it. Put the past in the past and move forward. Perhaps now you are tied up with sick parents, debt, or other situations from which it is difficult to remove yourself. You thought earlier that you were supposed to go into full-time Christian work, but now you cannot. Do what you can to be of service to the Lord where you are now. Bloom where you are planted. There is no way to make up for lost time, but you can make the most of the time you have left (For some words of encouragement please see Matthew 20:1–14). There is time to start over.

I would like to develop another thought about God taking me where I needed to be. I believe that God put me back here in my hometown because of His grace, because that is the place where my relationship with Him would grow best. Living here, I have had to be more involved with family problems, problems with elderly or sick parents, problems with other family members. Those problems have been part of God's crucible for my purification which is still an ongoing process. I do not have resentment about those problems; I glory in them, for they have helped me have a fuller knowledge of God.

At a meeting in Boston, I met a physician who practiced in a large city. He lived there so that he could practice an immoral lifestyle and not be discovered by his coworkers or patients. Practicing here in my hometown, I have to be concerned about the kind of image I project. I can hardly go anywhere without seeing someone I know. That helps keep me in line. It makes me less likely to do things that would separate me from fellowship with the Father. In my hometown I am less likely to yield to the many temptations that are all around me.

GOD'S GRACE IS THE SOURCE OF ALL THAT WE HAVE IN THIS LIFE

All that we have in this life is given to us by God's grace. We Christians are channels of that grace, sending God's blessings out to the world by what we say, how we act, and how we serve others. We cannot be very good channels if we do not have some understanding of God's grace. We learn about God's grace in Scripture and through our fellowship with other Christians. We also learn about His grace through personal experiences, those that are pleasant and those that are not so pleasant. We cannot be truly effective channels unless we are striving for a life of holiness, unless we maintain a relationship with the Father.

I am old enough to have seen life from both ends. I understand that any successes we have in this life are God's gifts to us. After God shows me something, my tendency is to share it with others. I was sharing the thought about God being responsible for our success with a lady at a Christian bookstore in another city. Sadly, she indicated that the owners of that bookstore had forgotten the fact. The store was doing well, and the owners were puffed up with pride. My point is this: If you trusted God to get you where you needed to be, and He got you there, be thankful. Realize that *He* got you there. Do not take too much credit for your own ingenuity. The other side of that coin is this: If you trusted in God to get you where you needed to be and you abided in Christ, be satisfied with where He got you.

12

The Man of Sorrows

W hen we are faced with tribulation, we are instructed to remember Jesus and His suffering: "Consider him [Jesus] who endured such opposition from sinful men, so that you will not grow weary and lose heart" (Heb. 12:3).

Jesus Was Destined for Suffering

A suffering Messiah is described in Isaiah 53:

He was despised and rejected by men, a man of sorrows, and familiar with suffering, . . . he was despised, and we esteemed him not. Surely he took up our infirmities and carried our sorrows, yet we considered him stricken by God, smitten by him, and afflicted. But he was pierced for our transgressions, he was crushed for our iniquities; the punishment that brought us peace was upon him, and by his wounds we are healed . . . He was oppressed and afflicted, yet he did not open his mouth; he was led like a lamb to the slaughter, as a sheep before her shearers is silent, so he did not open his mouth . . . it was the Lord's will to crush him and cause him to suffer . . . by his knowledge my righteous servant will justify many.

A picture of the crucifixion is presented in Psalm 22:

My God, my God why have you forsaken me? . . . All who see me mock me; they hurl insults, shaking their heads . . . I am poured out like water, and all my bones are out of joint. My heart has turned to wax; it has melted away within me. My strength is dried up like a potsherd (pottery fragment), and my tongue sticks to the roof of my mouth; you lay me in the dust of death. Dogs have surrounded me; a band of evil men has encircled me, they have pierced my hands and my feet. I can count all my bones; people stare and gloat over me. They divide my garments among them and cast lots for my clothing.

The Father appointed Jesus to represent us, to become our high priest. Christ did not take that honor or glory upon Himself but was called by the Father to offer a sacrifice for sin (Heb. 5:1–5). Jesus offered Himself. He was faithful to the one who appointed Him (Heb. 3:2). God the Father appointed Jesus with a job to do, and He did it.

The word "cup" is used metaphorically in both the Old and New Testaments. According to Strong, the Hebrew word *kowc* is from a root meaning "to *hold* together." It can refer to a "cup" as a container or it may be used figuratively referring to someone's lot, fate, or destiny.[1] The word may also refer to a cup of judgment from which the nations or Israel must drink.[2]

Awake, awake! Rise up, O Jerusalem, you have drunk from the hand of the Lord the cup of his wrath, you who have drained to its dregs the goblet that makes men stagger. (Isa. 51:17)

The word "cup" may also metaphorically refer to a cup of blessing: "You prepare a table before me in the presence of my enemies. You anoint my head with oil; my cup overflows" (Ps. 23:5).

The corresponding Greek word for "cup" used in the New Testament is *poteerion*. According to Bauer, Arndt, and Gingrich, *poteerion* may be an expression for destiny in both good and bad senses.[3] If our cup refers to our destiny, then the word must refer to God's plan for our individual lives. Jesus spoke of His own cup of destiny at the time of His arrest in Gethsemane: "Shall I not drink the cup the Father has given me?" (John 18:11b).

JESUS BECAME A MAN SO HE COULD DIE IN OUR PLACE

In bringing many sons to glory, it was fitting that God, for whom and through whom everything exists, should make the author of their salvation perfect through suffering. Both the one who makes men holy and those who are made holy are of the same family. So Jesus is not ashamed to call them brothers. He says, "I will declare your name to my brothers; in the presence of the congregation I will sing your praises." And again, "I will put my trust in him." And again he says, "Here am I, and the children God has given me." Since the children have flesh and blood, he too shared in their humanity so that by his death he might destroy him who holds the power of death—that is, the devil—and free those who all their lives were held in slavery by their fear of death . . . For this reason he had to be made like his brothers in every way, in order that he might become a merciful and faithful high priest in service to God, and that he might make atonement for the sins of the people. Because he himself suffered when he was tempted, he is able to help those who are being tempted. (Heb. 2:10–18)

JESUS EXPERIENCED THE DISTRESS OF HUMAN WEAKNESS

Jesus lived as a man on this earth for thirty-three years. The gospel narrative indicates that during Jesus' life, He experienced physical distress. He knew hunger (Matt. 4:2; Mark 11:12). He knew thirst (John 4:7). He must also have known fatigue and other types of physical discomfort.

Jesus had emotional feelings. He experienced mental distress. Jesus became angry (Mark 3:5; John 2:13–16). He experienced frustration (Matt. 8:26; Matt. 17:17; John 6:26; John 14:9). He experienced grief (John 11:33–35). His brothers ridiculed Him

(John 7:2–5). The Pharisees ridiculed Him (Luke 16:14). The people ridiculed Him (Matt. 9:24). Jesus was rejected by many of His disciples (John 6:60–66), by the people in His hometown (Mark 6:1–6), and by His generation (Matt. 11:16–19; John 12:37). Jesus was hated by others (John 15:23–25).

Jesus experienced spiritual distress (Mark 9:19). He was tested by Satan (Matt. 4:1–11), by Peter (Matt. 16:21–23), and by the Pharisees (Mark 8:11, 12; Mark 10:2; Matt. 22:15). Mark 8:12 tells us that He sighed deeply. His authority was questioned (Mark 11:27–33). The source of His power was questioned (Matt. 12:22–30). He was distressed because of all the need he saw around him (Mark 6:34). Jesus needed communion with the Father (Mark 1:35). I suspect that He needed help just to get through the daily grind of His life. On one occasion during Jesus' ministry, He made the following comment: "But I have a baptism to undergo, and how distressed I am until it is completed!" (Luke 12:50) Jesus was touched with the feeling of our infirmities.

THE FINAL YEAR OF JESUS' LIFE WAS ESPECIALLY DIFFICULT

Jesus' three years of ministry have been divided into the Year of Inauguration, the Year of Popularity, and the Year of Opposition.[4] Early on in the final year of Jesus' life, He was transfigured on Mount Hermon. That experience marked a turning point. After that, Jesus' ministry was less public and more private. He spent more time with His disciples.[5] He was preparing them for the end of His ministry on earth.[6] Jesus was in a hostile environment. He was aware that He would be separated from the Father, and the significance of what was going to happen was bearing down on Him. Beginning with the transfiguration, the New Testament contains many references to the weight of coming events on Jesus:

On the Mount of Transfiguration

Two men, Moses and Elijah, appeared in glorious splendor, talking with Jesus. They spoke about his departure. Which he was about to bring to fulfillment at Jerusalem (Luke 9:30, 31).

Ministry in Galilee

As they were coming down the mountain, Jesus instructed them, "Don't tell anyone what you have seen, until the Son of Man has been raised from the dead." The disciples asked him, "Why then do the teachers of the law say that Elijah must come first?" Jesus replied, "To be sure, Elijah comes and will restore all things, But I tell you, Elijah has already come, and they did not recognize him, but they have done to him everything they wished. In the same way the Son of Man is going to suffer at their hands." Then the disciples understood that he was talking to them about John the Baptist. (Matt. 17:9–13)

When they came together in Galilee, he said to them, "The Son of Man is going to be betrayed into the hands of men. They will kill him, and on the third day he will be raised to life." And the disciples were filled with grief. (Matt. 17:22, 23)

To Judea for the Feast of Tabernacles

Jesus eventually traveled to Judea for the Feast of Tabernacles. This occurred in October, the year prior to His crucifixion.

After this, Jesus went around in Galilee, purposely staying away from Judea because the Jews there were waiting to take his life. But when the Jewish Feast of Tabernacles was near, Jesus' brothers said to him, "You ought to leave here and go to Judea, so that your disciples may see the miracles you do. No one who wants to become a public figure acts in secret. Since you are doing these things, show yourself to the world." For even his own brothers did not believe in him. Therefore Jesus told them, "The right time for me has not yet come; for you any time is right. The world cannot hate you, but it hates me because I testify that what it does is evil. You go to the Feast. I am not yet going up to this Feast, because for me the right time has not yet come." Having said this, he stayed in Galilee. However, after his brothers had left for the Feast, he went also, not publicly, but in secret. Now at the Feast the Jews were watching for him and asking, "Where is that man?" Among the crowds there was widespread whispering about him. Some said, "He is a good man." Others replied, "No, he deceives the people." But no one would say anything publicly about him for fear of the Jews. (John 7:1–13)

Not until halfway through the Feast did Jesus go up to the temple courts and begin to teach. The Jews were amazed and asked, "How did this man get such learning without having studied?" Jesus answered, "My teaching is not my own. It comes from him who sent me. If anyone chooses to do God's will, he will find out whether my teaching comes from God or whether I speak on my own. He who speaks on his own does so to gain honor for himself, but he who works for the honor of the one who sent him is a man of truth; there is nothing false about him. Has not Moses given you the law? Yet not one of you keeps the law. Why are you trying to kill me?" (John 7:14–19)

At that point some of the people of Jerusalem began to ask, "Isn't this the man they are trying to kill? Here he is, speaking publicly, and they are not saying a word to him. Have the authorities really concluded that he is the Christ? But we know where this man is from; when the Christ comes, no one will know where he is from." Then Jesus, still teaching in the temple courts, cried out, "Yes, you know me, and you know where I am from. I am not here on my own, but he who sent me is true. You do not know him, but I know him because I am from him and he sent me." At this they tried to seize him, but no one laid a hand on him, because his time was not yet come. (John 7:25–30)

So Jesus said, "When you have lifted up the Son of Man, then you will know that I am [the one I claim to be] and that I do nothing on my own but speak just what the Father has taught me." (John 8:28)

As he went along, he saw a man blind from birth. His disciples asked him, "Rabbi, who sinned, this man or his parents, that he was born blind?" "Neither this man nor his parents sinned," said Jesus, "but this happened so that the work of God might be displayed in his life. As long as it is day, we must do the work of him who sent me. Night is coming, when no one can work. While I am in the world, I am the light of the world." (John 9:1–5)

His [the blind man's] parents said this because they were afraid of the Jews, for already the Jews had decided that anyone who acknowledged that Jesus was the Christ would be put out of the synagogue. (John 9:22)

The reason my Father loves me is that I lay down my life—only to take it up again. No one takes it from me, but I lay it down of my own accord. I have authority to lay it down and authority to take it up again. (John 10:17, 18a)

During the Perean Ministry

But first he [the Son of Man] must suffer many things and be rejected by this generation. (Luke 17:25)

The Raising of Lazarus

Jesus received word that Lazarus, the brother of Mary and Martha, was sick. He waited two days and then said to his disciples: "'Let us go back to Judea.' 'But Rabbi,' they said, 'a short while ago the Jews tried to stone you, and yet you are going back there?'" (John 11:7b, 8).

After Jesus raised Lazarus from the dead, the chief priests and the Pharisees called a meeting of the Sanhedrin. They were concerned about Jesus' miracles and that everyone would believe in Him. They were concerned that the Romans would come and take away their positions of power. Consider the results of the meeting:

So from that day on they plotted to take his life. Therefore Jesus no longer moved about publicly among the Jews. Instead he withdrew to a region near the desert, to a village called Ephraim, where he stayed with his disciples. (John 11:53, 54)

Six days before the Passover, Jesus went to Bethany, the home of Lazarus, Martha, and Mary. A dinner was given in Jesus' honor. Mary poured expensive perfume on Jesus' feet, and wiped them with her hair. Judas Iscariot complained about the waste of money.

"Leave her alone," Jesus replied, "It was intended that she should save this perfume for the day of my burial." (John 12:7)

The Final Week of Jesus' Life on Earth

Now as Jesus was going up to Jerusalem, he took the twelve disciples aside and said to them, "We are going up to Jerusalem, and the Son of Man will be betrayed to the chief priests and the teachers of the law. They will condemn him to death and will turn him over to the Gentiles to be mocked and flogged and crucified. On the third day he will be raised to life." (Matt. 20:17–19)

But the chief priests and Pharisees had given orders that if anyone found out where Jesus was, he should report it so that they might arrest him. (John 11:57)

As he approached Jerusalem and saw the city, he wept over it and said, "If you, even you, had only known on this day what would bring you peace—and now it is hidden from your eyes. The days will come upon you when your enemies will build an embankment against you and encircle you and hem you in on every side, They will dash you to the ground, you and the children within your walls. They will not leave one stone on another, because you did not recognize the time of God's coming to you." (Luke 19:41–44)

Jesus warned the chief priests and Pharisees about the consequences that would befall them after they had carried out their plan to kill him (Matt. 21:33–41). Thereafter He spoke directly to them. Consider His words and their understanding of what was said:

"Have you never read the Scriptures: 'The stone the builders rejected has become the capstone, the Lord has done this, and it is marvelous in our eyes'? Therefore I tell you that the kingdom of God will be taken away from you and given to a people who will produce its fruit. He who falls on this stone will be broken to pieces, but he on whom it falls will be crushed." When the chief priests and the Pharisees heard Jesus' parables, they knew he was talking about them. (Matt. 21:42b–45)

When Jesus had finished saying all these things, he said to his disciples, "As you know, the Passover is two days away—and the Son of Man will be handed over to be crucified." (Matt. 26:1, 2)

When she poured this perfume on my body, she did it to prepare me for burial. I tell you the truth, wherever this gospel is preached throughout the world, what she has done will also be told, in memory of her." (Matthew 26:12, 13)

Jesus replied, "The hour has come for the Son of Man to be glorified. I tell you the truth, unless a kernel of wheat falls to the ground and dies, it remains only a single seed. But if it dies, it produces many seeds . . . Now my heart is troubled, and what shall I say? 'Father, save me from this hour'? No, it was for this very reason I came to this hour. Father, glorify your name! . . . Now is the time for judgment on this world; now the prince of this world will be driven out. But I, when I am lifted up from the earth, will draw all men to myself." He said this to show the kind of death he was going to die. (John 12:23–33)

The Last Supper

It was just before the Passover Feast. Jesus knew that the time had come for him to leave this world and go to the Father. Having loved his own who were in the world, he now showed them the full extent of his love. (John 13:1)

And he said to them, "I have eagerly desired to eat this Passover with you before I suffer. For I tell you, I will not eat it again until it finds fulfillment in the kingdom of God." . . . And he took the bread, gave thanks and broke it, and gave it to them, saying, "This is my body given for you; do this in remembrance of me." In the same way, after the supper he took the cup, saying, "This cup is the new covenant in my blood, which is poured out for you." (Luke 22:15–20)

Jesus was troubled in spirit and testified, "I tell you the truth, one of you is going to betray me." (John 13:21b)

The Son of Man will go just as it is written about him. But woe to that man who betrays the Son of Man! It would be better for him if he had not been born. (Matt. 26:24)

My children, I will be with you only a little longer. You will look for me, and just as I told the Jews, so I tell you now: where I am going, you cannot come. (John 13:33)

Simon Peter asked him, "Lord, where are you going?" Jesus replied, "Where I am going, you can not follow now, but you will follow later." (John 13:36)

Then Jesus told them, "This very night you will all fall away on account of me, for it is written: 'I will strike the shepherd, and the sheep of the flock will be scattered.' But after I have risen, I will go ahead of you into Galilee." (Matt. 26:31, 32)

It is written: "And he was numbered with the transgressors"; and I tell you that this must be fulfilled in me. Yes, what is written about me is reaching its fulfillment. (Luke 22:37)

I tell you the truth, anyone who has faith in me will do what I have been doing. He will do even greater things than these, because I am going to the Father. (John 14:12)

Before long, the world will not see me anymore, but you will see me. Because I live, you also will live. (John 14:19)

Peace I leave with you; my peace I give you. I do not give to you as the world gives. Do not let your hearts be troubled and do not be afraid. You heard me say, "I am going away and I am coming back to you." If you loved me, you would be glad that I am going to the Father, for the Father is greater than I. I have told you now before it happens, so that when it does happen you will believe. I will not speak with you much longer, for the prince of this world is coming. He has no hold on me, but the world must learn that I love the Father and that I do exactly what my Father has commanded me. (John 14:27–31a)

Greater love has no one than this, that he lay down his life for his friends. You are my friends if you do what I command. (John 15:13, 14)

If the world hates you, keep in mind that it hated me first. (John 15:18)

"Remember the words I spoke to you: "No servant is greater than his master." If they persecuted me, they will persecute you also. (John 15:20a)

But this is to fulfill what is written in the law: "They hated me without reason." (John 15:25)

I tell you the truth, you will weep and mourn while the world rejoices. You will grieve, but your grief will turn to joy. A woman giving birth to a child has pain because her time has come; but when her baby is born she forgets the anguish because of her joy that a child is born into the world. So with you: Now is your time of grief, but I will see you again and you will rejoice, and no one will take away your joy. (John 16:20–22)

But a time is coming, and has come, when you will be scattered, each to his own home. You will leave me all alone. Yet I am not alone, for my Father is with me. I have told you these things so that in me you may have peace. In this world you will have trouble. But take heart! I have overcome the world. (John 16:32, 33)

After Jesus said this, he looked toward heaven and prayed: "Father, the time has come. Glorify your son, that your son may glorify you . . . I have brought you glory on earth by completing the work you gave me to do." (John 17:1, 4)

THE BIBLE GRAPHICALLY DESCRIBES THE EVENTS SURROUNDING THE CRUCIFIXION

In Gethsemane, Jesus Was Overwhelmed with Sorrow

Then Jesus went with his disciples to a place called Gethsemane, and he said to them, "Sit here while I go over there and pray." He took Peter and the two sons of Zebedee [James and John] along with him, and he began to be sorrowful and troubled. Then he said to them, "My soul is overwhelmed with sorrow to the point of death. Stay here and keep watch with me." Going a little farther, he fell with his face to the ground and prayed, "My Father, if it is possible, may this cup be taken from me. Yet not as I will, but as you will." (Matt. 26:36–39)

One of His Own Disciples Betrayed Jesus with a Kiss

Just as he was speaking, Judas, one of the Twelve, appeared. With him was a crowd armed with swords and clubs, sent from the chief priests, the teachers of the law, and the elders. Now the betrayer had arranged a signal with them: "The one I kiss is the man; arrest him and lead him away under guard." Going at once to Jesus, Judas said, "Rabbi!" and kissed him. The men seized Jesus and arrested him. (Mark 14:43–46)

The Other Disciples Abandoned Jesus

Then all the disciples deserted him and fled. (Matt. 26:56b)

Peter Denied Jesus

Simon Peter and another disciple [John] were following Jesus. Because this disciple was known to the high priest, he went with Jesus into the high priest's courtyard, but Peter had to wait outside at the door. The other disciple, who was known to the high priest, came back, spoke to the girl on duty there and brought Peter in. "You are not one of this man's disciples, are you?" the girl at the door asked Peter. He replied, "I am not." It was cold, and the servants and officials stood around a fire they had made to keep warm. Peter also was standing with them, warming himself . . . As Simon Peter stood warming himself, he was asked, "You are not one of his disciples, are you?" He denied it saying, "I am not." One of the high priest's servants, a relative of the man whose ear Peter had cut off, challenged him, "Didn't I see you with him in the olive grove?" Again Peter denied it, and at that moment a rooster began to crow. (John 18:15–27)

One of the Jewish Officials Hit Jesus in the Face

Meanwhile, the high priest questioned Jesus about his disciples and his teaching. "I have spoken openly to the world," Jesus replied. "I always taught in synagogues or at the temple, where all the Jews come together. I said nothing in secret. Why question me? Ask those who heard me. Surely they know what I said." When Jesus said this, one of the officials nearby struck him in the face. "Is this the way you answer the high priest?" he demanded. (John 18:19–22)

The Guards of the Sanhedrin Physically and Verbally Abused Jesus

The men who were guarding Jesus began mocking and beating him. They blindfolded him and demanded, "Prophesy! Who hit you?" And they said many other insulting things to him. (Luke 22:63–65)

The Guards of the Sanhedrin Took Jesus to Pilate

They bound him, led him away and handed him over to Pilate, the governor. (Matt. 27:2)

Pilate Sent Him to Herod and Herod's Soldiers Ridiculed and Mocked Jesus

Then Herod and his soldiers ridiculed and mocked him. Dressing him in an elegant robe, they sent him back to Pilate. (Luke 23:11)

Pilate's Soldiers Physically Abused Jesus and Crucified Him

Then he released Barabbas to them. But he had Jesus flogged, and handed him over to be crucified. Then the governor's soldiers took Jesus to the Praetorium and gathered the whole company of soldiers around him. They stripped him and put a scarlet robe on him, and then twisted together a crown of thorns and set it on his head. They put a staff in his right hand and knelt in front of him and mocked him. "Hail, king of the Jews!" they said. They spit on him, and took the staff and struck him on the head again and again. (Matt. 27:26–30)

When they came to the place called the Skull, there they crucified him, along with the criminals—one on his right, the other on his left. (Luke 23:33)

Onlookers at the Cross Insulted and Mocked Jesus

Those who passed by hurled insults at him, shaking their heads and saying, "So! You who are going to destroy the temple and build it in three days, come down from the cross and save yourself!" In the same way the chief priests and the teachers of the law mocked him among themselves. "He saved others," they said, "but he can't save himself! Let this Christ, this King of Israel, come down from the cross, that we may see and believe." Those crucified with him also heaped insults on him. (Mark 15:29–32)

Jesus Felt Forsaken by the Father, the Worst Pain of All

About the ninth hour Jesus cried out in a loud voice, "*Eloi, Eloi, lama sabachthani?*"—which means, "My God, my God, why have you forsaken me?" (Matt. 27:46)

Can you imagine all this being done to the Lord God Almighty? Can you imagine Him letting it happen?

Jesus Helps Us in Our Suffering

Jesus was made perfect (complete) through suffering. He shared in our humanity so that by His death He might destroy him who holds the power of death and free us who are held in slavery by the fear of death. He had to be made like us in every way, in order that He might become a merciful and faithful high priest in service to God, and that He might make atonement for our sins. Because He suffered when He was tested, He is able to help us when we are being tested (Heb. 2:10–18).

Jesus was crowned with glory and honor because He suffered death (Heb. 2:9). Since we have Jesus as our great high priest, we need to hold firmly to the faith we profess. He is able to sympathize with our weaknesses. He has been tested in every way, just as we are. We should approach the throne of grace with confidence, to receive mercy and find grace to help us in our time of need (Heb. 4:14–16).

Everything Jesus learned from His Father, He made known to His disciples (John 15:15). Jesus showed reverent submission to the Father. One thing He learned from what he suffered was obedience. Once made perfect, He became the source of eternal salvation for all who obey Him (Heb. 5:7–10). We will all be tested, for a servant is not greater than his Master (Matt. 10:17–39; John 13:16; John 15:18–16:4).

We Need to Emulate Jesus

Jesus endured the cross. He remained instead of fleeing. He did not turn away. Christians undergoing tribulation have been given an opportunity by God to profit spiritually and be a witness to others of God's grace. What about the cup you have been given? Are you faithful in whatever you have been given to do? Are you able to drink that cup willingly for the sake of your Lord?

PART THREE:

UNDERSTANDING OUR APPROPRIATE RESPONSE TO TRIBULATION

13

A Personal Assessment

There have been times in my life when I realized I needed a change of direction. When I started high school, I began losing interest in spiritual things. I was more interested in trying to be popular than in obeying God. I stopped reading my Bible, and I developed some bad habits.

I decided to learn to dance. For me, learning to dance was part of loving the world, rather than loving God. During my junior year in high school, I joined Hi-Y, a service club sponsored by the YMCA. That spring, we had a statewide convention in Nashville. The object of the meeting was for us to learn what it was like to run the state government. For that meeting, I was a member of the state legislature. One evening during the convention we had a dance. I noticed a girl from Elizabethton, Tennessee who I had known from years before at Children's Bible Mission Camp. When I asked her for a dance, she replied, almost angrily, "I don't dance." Her words cut through me like a knife, and I realized my life was headed in the wrong direction, a direction that needed to change. The next summer, I went back to CBM for Youth Camp, and I re-committed my life to Christ. My senior year in high school was a whole different experience. I was reading my Bible again. I had a new focus. I ran with a different crowd.

Much later in my life, my own older son, Jason was born in March 1971, about a week after I started my internal medicine residency. That first year, I worked at the city hospital in Memphis every third night. I also moonlighted for extra money eight or ten other nights a month in area emergency rooms. I was hardly ever home, and when I was home, I was usually asleep. The next year, the call schedule was not so demanding. I tried to develop more of a relationship with my son, but it seemed there was nothing I could do to please him. Not knowing what to do, I withdrew from my child.

In July 1973 my father died. Our whole family was at home, in Knoxville, for the funeral. My two sisters' husbands each independently noticed that Jason would have nothing to do with me and spoke to me about it. They were concerned about the long term consequences of this sort of relationship with my son. I decided two things Jason needed every night were a bath and a bedtime story. I made up my mind I was going to provide those for him. The first night he really pitched a fit. It was so bad that Barbara could not stand it, and she had to leave the house. The second night was almost as bad as the first. But eventually, I wore him down. He began to prefer me for those tasks. I had established a relationship with him.

This chapter is an attempt to help people, whose lives need to take a new direction, come to grips with the fact and develop more of a resolve to bring about the change. Life is a journey. In order to move effectively along life's road, we need to know where we have been, where we are now, and where we should be headed. I have been on automobile trips when I was not sure where I needed to go. Before I could use a map to help me figure out which route to take, I needed to know my precise starting point, my current location.

When a person is made weary by misery and grief and pain, he needs some assessment of where he is so that he can plan a strategy to move to where he needs to be. It is wise to have some assessment of how many of our problems we are responsible for creating ourselves. We need to recognize which aspects of the situation are caused by ourselves and for which aspects we can be part of the solution. In order for each of us to plan an effective strategy for making things better, we need to assess where we are spiritually, mentally, and physically.

STATUS BEFORE GOD

Have You Ever Had an Initial Salvation Experience?

The Bible tells us how to enter into a relationship with God. Initially we need to understand that we all have a debt to God because of our sin. The payment for that sin is death.

> For all have sinned and fall short of the glory of God. (Rom. 3:23)

> For the wages of sin is death. (Rom. 6:23a)

Jesus Christ paid that debt for you and for me.

> He himself bore our sins in his body on the tree, so that we might die to sins and live for righteousness; by his wounds you have been healed. (1 Pet. 2:24)

In order to be justified before God, we must receive the gift that is freely offered.

> That if you confess with your mouth, "Jesus is Lord," and believe in your heart that God raised him from the dead, you will be saved. For it is with your heart you believe and are justified, and it is with your mouth that you confess and are saved. (Rom. 10:9, 10)

True wisdom is being able to see things as they really are, as God sees them. We are told that the fear of the Lord is the beginning of wisdom (Prov. 9:10a). Any sense of spiritual health apart from a solid relationship with Jesus Christ is mere illusion.

Have You Rejected the Christian Faith?

I have been told that one of the reasons individuals become agnostics or atheists is that they do not want to bow their knee to God. Their thinking is faulty. Eventually everyone will bow their knee to Jesus, and they will confess that Jesus Christ is Lord (Phil. 2:10, 11). The only question is how soon it will happen. There is a scriptural passage that speaks to such an attitude: "In his pride the wicked does not seek him; in all his thoughts there is no room for God" (Ps. 10:4).

Some people are indifferent to God, while others are openly hostile. Consider this passage from Isaiah:

Distressed and hungry, they will roam through the land; When they are famished, they will become enraged and, looking upward, will curse . . . their God. Then they will look toward the earth and see only distress and darkness and fearful gloom, and they will be thrust into utter darkness. (Isa. 8:21, 22)

Consider also this passage from Revelation:

They were seared by the intense heat and they cursed the name of God, who had control over these plagues, but they refused to repent and glorify him. The fifth angel poured out his bowl on the throne of the beast, and his kingdom was plunged into darkness. Men gnawed their tongues in agony and cursed the God of heaven because of their pains and their sores, but they refused to repent of what they had done. (Revelation 16:9–11)

People with such an attitude are destined for judgment.

. . . the Lord knows how . . . to hold the unrighteous for the day of judgment . . . This is especially true of those who follow the corrupt desire of the sinful nature and despise authority. Bold and arrogant . . . these men blaspheme in matters they do not understand. They are like brute beasts, creatures of instinct, born only to be caught and destroyed, and like beasts they too will perish. (2 Pet. 2:9–12).

As Robert Burns put it in *Epistle to a Young Friend,* "An atheist-laugh's a poor exchange for deity offended!"[1]

Have You Made a Profession of Faith and Then Renounced It?

If you made a profession of faith and then renounced it, there are two possibilities for what happened: either your profession was genuine and the Lord is giving you a chance to return to fellowship with Him or your profession of faith was just an emotional experience and meant nothing. Consider what John the apostle had to say about the latter situation:

> They [men who deny that Jesus is the Christ] went out from us, but they did not really belong to us. For if they had belonged to us, they would have remained with us; but their going showed that none of them belonged to us. (1 John 2:19)

Consider also Peter's words:

> It would have been better for them [followers of false teachers] not to have known the way of righteousness, than to have known it and then to turn their backs on the sacred command that was passed on to them. (2 Pet. 2:21)

Regardless of which of the above two situations is true for you, God loves you and wants to have a relationship with you. If you are able to read these words, you still have time to straighten things out with your Maker and Redeemer.

Have You Fallen Out of Fellowship with the Lord?

Are you a Christian but out of fellowship with God? Do you have a rebellious spirit? Do you have a habit that you continue in, even though you know it is wrong? Are you troubled by sins that you have not confessed? Do you have unresolved guilt? Do you have any regrets about things you have done in the past for which you cannot forgive yourself?

If you are interested, there is a way out of your dilemma. You can seek the Lord's face, ask His forgiveness, and pray for the Holy Spirit to empower you in your struggle for victory. One way to get started again is to begin reading your Bible every day.

If we confess our sins, he is faithful and just and will forgive us our sins and purify us from all unrighteousness. (1 John 1:9)

His divine power has given us everything we need for life and godliness. (2 Pet. 1:3a)

If you have sinned against other people, and you need to seek forgiveness from them, do so. Once you have confessed your sin to God, and made things right with others, forget your mistakes. Let go of those oppressive thoughts. Isaiah promised the Children of Israel that they would forget the shame of their youth (Isa. 54:4). In the third chapter of Paul's letter to the Philippians Paul wrote about his struggle to become like Christ. In verse 13 he wrote that he was forgetting what was behind and straining toward what was ahead.

Are You a Lukewarm Christian?

Jesus had the following message for the Church in Laodicea:

I know your deeds, that you are neither cold nor hot. I wish you were either one or the other. So, because you are lukewarm— neither hot nor cold—I am about to spit you out of my mouth. (Rev. 3:15, 16)

Is nothing really very wrong with your spiritual life but nothing really very right? Perhaps the Lord is speaking to you.

Are You Fairly Certain that Your Spiritual Life Is All It Should Be?

If you are involved in a crisis and are fairly certain that your spiritual life is all it should be, I offer some other thoughts for consideration.

Status of Your Spiritual Health

For those of us who already have a relationship with Jesus Christ as our Savior, it is important to understand what our spiritual condition is before the Lord. If we are having problems, it is a good time for a spiritual assessment.

What Are Your Priorities and Purposes?

Entering into a relationship with the Lord is just the beginning of a Christian's spiritual adventure. Most of us have a long way to go before reaching spiritual maturity. It is a goal that few of us, if any, will ever completely attain on this earth.

A good way to get an idea of where you are spiritually is to examine what is important to you, what you are interested in. In what do you trust? In what is your security placed? Do you love God with all your heart? Do you worship created things more than you do the Creator? What gives you satisfaction? What is your passion? What makes you happy? Unhappy? How do you spend your time? Around what is your social life centered? Do you have a regular quiet time every day, a time set aside to spend with the Lord?

Do you ever go to the devil's agents for advice? Do you seek advice from clairvoyants? Consult astrologers? Patronize spiritual mediums? Fool around with Ouija boards or tarot cards?

How do you spend your talents? What are your vocational objectives? What do you strive for? What are your career goals? Is it just to make money so that you can buy things? Are you more interested in treasures on earth than treasures in heaven? As you carry out your daily tasks, are you trying to please the Lord, or do you seek the praise of men? Is your work just a job to you?

Are you honest? Do you tell the truth? Is your speech always appropriate? Do you curse? Do you tell dirty jokes? Do you like to make people laugh with words that have double, perhaps off-color meanings? Do you gossip or spread malicious rumors? Are you mean-spirited? Do you like to put other people in their place?

Are you self-centered? How hard is it for you to be a servant? Do you love your neighbor as yourself? How do you spend your money? Do you give adequately to support the Lord's work? Do you honestly seek to cultivate the relationship with your spouse and children?

What do you do for relief when you are down emotionally? Is the way you spend that time sinful? Do you have any regular pastimes that you know are displeasing to the Lord? Do you need to repent and change your behavior?

Each one of us has to determine in his own mind what the Lord wants him to do.

> Now the Bereans were of more noble character than the Thessalonians, for they received the message with great eagerness and examined the Scriptures every day to see if what Paul said was true. (Acts 17:11)

> Your word is a lamp to my feet and a light for my path. (Ps. 119:105)

> Do your best to present yourself to God as one approved, a workman who does not need to be ashamed and who correctly handles the word of truth. (2 Tim. 2:15)

> I will instruct you and teach you in the way you should go; I will counsel you and watch over you. (Ps. 32:8)

> Therefore, my dear friends, as you have always obeyed—not only in my presence, but now much more in my absence—continue to work out your salvation with fear and trembling, for it is God who works in you to will and to act according to his good purpose. (Phil. 2:12, 13)

> And this water symbolizes baptism that now saves you also—not the removal of dirt from the body but the pledge of a good conscience toward God. It saves you by the resurrection of Jesus Christ. (1 Pet. 3:21)

What does your own conscience tell you? Read the Bible for yourself and make your own decisions. It is important to remember that we can not really see things as they are without the help of the Holy Spirit.

Do You Have Obsessive Feelings?

Are you troubled by the persistence of unwanted thoughts? Are you excessively preoccupied by negative feelings from which you wish you could escape? Are you jealous or envious of anyone? Do you have an unforgiving spirit? Are there certain people you go out of your way to avoid? Do you have any bitter, deep-seated ill will toward anyone? Is there someone for whom you have a desire to cause pain, to see suffer? Do you have an inappropriate level of fear? Are you obsessed by unresolved grief?

Is there something in this world that you see, that you want, that you would do anything to get? Are you obsessed by thoughts of attaining power or riches? Are you obsessed by sexual thoughts? Do you have an obsession with gambling? Having obsessive thoughts can ruin a person's perspective on life.

Are You Prideful?

Do you have any false pride? In my thinking, pride is similar to prejudice in that everyone has at least a little in one form or another. The question is, how much false pride do you have? Are you trying to overcome it? Do you insist on being the center of attention? Do you feel that your accomplishments in life are due to your own cleverness, or do you acknowledge God for bringing you success? Are you thankful for God's blessings, or do you give yourself more credit than you deserve?

Status of Your Mental Health

It is important to understand our mental condition.

Do You Have the Right Attitude?

How is your disposition? What is your mood? What is your point of view toward the world around you? Are you mean and grouchy? Are you resentful? Are you worried about things for which you are not responsible? Do you feel guilty about something over which you had no control? Are you able to accept things you cannot change? Do you feel sorry for yourself?

Elijah felt sorry for himself. During the reign of King Ahab in Israel, Elijah had a confrontation with the priests of Baal on Mount Carmel (1 Kings 18:16–46). God used Elijah to demonstrate His power to the Israelites. A great victory was won. But when Queen Jezebel was told of what had happened, she started looking for Elijah. She vowed to kill him (1 Kings 19:1, 2). Elijah was afraid and ran for his life (1 Kings 19:3). On Mount Horeb he spoke to God expressing his feelings. He experienced self-pity.

> . . . I have been very zealous for the Lord God Almighty. The Israelites have rejected your covenant, broken down your altars, and put your prophets to death with the sword. I am the only one left, and now they are trying to kill me too. (1 Kings 19:10)

Are You Anxious or Depressed?

Are you anxious? Can you relax? Are you coping with the situations in your life? Could you have masked depression? Do you feel like doing things you ordinarily like to do? Do you have trouble making yourself do the work you know you need to do? Do you wake up in the early morning hours and have trouble going back to sleep? Have you noticed a change in your eating habits?

One of the situations that is most difficult for me is when my patients have excessive symptoms that are out of proportion to what I know is physically wrong with them. These symptoms can be the result of several things. There may be something else wrong with them, something that has not been diagnosed yet. At times the cause of an obscure symptom may an unusual drug reaction. The solution for some patients may lie in getting an opinion from another physician, one with a different perspective. But many times, patients are affected by an emotional problem that is making them feel worse than they should for what is physically wrong with them.

Some of my patients are receptive to discussing emotional issues, and some are not. Some of my patients, I am convinced, have physical symptoms caused by their emotional problems.

Do You Need Time Apart or Do You Need Counsel?

Do you feel burned out emotionally? Do you plan your schedule so that you periodically get some relief from mental stress? Do you plan periods of recreation? Do you need time apart? After he learned of the death of John the Baptist, Jesus needed time by Himself.

When Jesus heard what had happened, he withdrew by boat privately to a solitary place. (Matt. 14:13a)

Are you ashamed to get help for your emotional problems? Emotional problems deserve attention just as physical problems do.

STATUS OF PHYSICAL HEALTH

It is important to understand our physical condition.

Do You Have Undiagnosed Problems?

Do you avoid seeing the doctor because you are afraid you might hear bad news? Are you a caregiver who is not taking the time to see your own doctor? Are your immunizations current? Has your blood pressure been checked recently? Are you up to date on your pap smear, your mammogram, your rectal exam, your colonoscopy?

Are You Working with Your Body?

People who are ill need to work with the processes of repair that God built in to their bodies. We all need to make informed decisions about our health. Are you following your doctor's instructions? Are you taking your medicine? Is your lifestyle appropriate for you? Are you getting enough exercise, enough rest? Do you eat too much? Do you eat enough? Are you hurting yourself with too much caffeine? Could caffeine be giving you headaches, making your head spin, or keeping you awake at night? Are you subject to tobacco or alcohol abuse?

Do You Need More Periods of Rest?

Are you working too hard because you have the feeling that there are certain things nobody else can do? Are you working too hard because you are seeking the praise of men? Are you depriving yourself of rest because of guilt? If you are to survive over the long haul, you must pace yourself. You must have some margin.

SPECIAL SITUATIONS

Caregiver Burdens

Are you an informal caregiver experiencing emotional stress? Do you feel adequate to deal with your many duties? Are you resentful about any of your caregiving responsibilities? Do you have the feeling they are interfering with your life? Are you having difficulty dealing with a disrupted schedule? Are you taking care of a patient who refuses to recognize the limitations caused by his infirmity, and does that refusal cause you undue burden? Is the patient's illness causing financial problems? Do you feel your current responsibilities are cheating you out of something better in life? Do you have any guilt over negative feelings about the patient? Do you plan time away from the patient to give your mind a rest? Do you have any harmful coping strategies? Are you abusing alcohol or drugs? Are you dealing with any codependency issues that may exist in the relationship?

Are you satisfied with the level of support you are receiving from the patient's doctors and others in the health care field? Are you satisfied with the level of help you are receiving from other family members? Are you connecting with friends who have been through similar experiences? Have you been able to develop self-esteem from caregiving? Do you need counseling to improve your coping skills?

Are you a caregiver who is overwhelmed by physical demands attendant with your responsibilities? Have you learned to plan ahead and use your resources efficiently? Have you been able to reduce your level of physical strain by learning proper patient-care techniques? For example, do you have the right equipment? Do you need a wheelchair? Do you need a hospital bed? Do you know about using a Hoyer lift to get someone out of the floor? Does your home need ramps or safety rails? If you have questions about what to do or what you need, help is available. You could start by talking to the patient's doctor, your own doctor, a nurse, friends who have been through similar experiences, a social worker, a hospital chaplain, or your pastor. You could also call the main number of your local hospital and seek counsel. Help is also available at the library and over the Internet.

Unresolved Grief

In his book, *Grief Counseling and Grief Therapy*, J. William Worden refers to normal or uncomplicated grief and abnormal or complicated bereavement. The former includes those feelings and behaviors that are common after a loss.[2] The latter is described as, "The intensification of grief to a level where the person is overwhelmed, resorts to maladaptive behavior, or remains interminably in the state of grief without progression of the mourning process towards completion."[3] Psychiatric illness is often an expression of such pathological mourning.[4]

I came away from Vietnam with painful feelings that would not go away. I had entered military service in 1969, right out of my internship. The Army put some Captain's bars on my collar, gave me five weeks of orientation at the Medical Field Service School in San Antonio, and sent me to Vietnam. I was assigned to the 1/69 Armor (tanks) Battalion as its Battalion Surgeon. I was responsible for such things as conducting a medical clinic each morning, providing immunizations, and inspecting latrines. Of all the difficult situations I encountered in Vietnam, there were two in particular that affected me the most.

While I was with the 1/69 Armor, there was an endocrinologist who held teaching rounds for an hour on Fridays at the 67th Evacuation Hospital in Qui Nhon. I made it down there every Friday I could. I became acquainted with the battalion surgeon from one of the infantry units in our area. One week, I invited him to go with me. He called me on the telephone early the morning we were to leave and told me he had better not try to go. His commanding officer was giving him a hard time, and there were some things he needed to stay and do. At the meeting with our commanding officer that evening, I learned he was dead. He had been out checking on some wounded men and had been killed by a land mine. I remember the feeling I had as my spirit dropped with a thud.

Most of the time I was with the 1/69 Armor, our responsibility was to protect Highway 19 between the An Khe Pass and the Mang Yang Pass. For about two months, we ran operations out in the open terrain. I spent several weeks at LZ Hard Times. One day there was an explosion in the Mortar Platoon's trash dump. A man had a second-degree burn that covered 85% of his body. He was afraid he was going to die. I tried to reassure the man and told him I thought he was going to be okay. A few days later, I went to the 67th Evacuation Hospital in Qui Nhon to check on him. I was told he had already been moved out to Japan. It was not long until we received word he was dead. My heart was broken.

I began the practice of medicine in 1975. During the 1980's and 1990's I didn't think much about Vietnam. The few times I did think about that time in life, I realized I had painful feelings that had not resolved, but I was unable to conceptualize anything to do about them. One of the things that especially troubled me was the sound of whirling helicopter blades. It reminded me of death.

My wife and I attended the 69th Armor Association reunion in Arlington, Virginia in July 2000. During the wreath-laying ceremony at the Korean War Memorial in Washington, I was touched by the prayer offered by the chaplain. I spoke with him briefly as we made our way to the Vietnam War Memorial. After the wreath laying ceremony at the Vietnam War Memorial, one man began reading the names of those men from our battalion who had been killed in Vietnam. As he read the names, another man went to the wall and placed a carnation below each name, standing it up against the wall. Their expressions of bereavement and respect tore my heart out. The chaplain could see I was having a hard time. He quietly suggested that I pray the following prayer: "Jesus, I can't handle this, but you can, and I choose to let you do so." After I prayed that prayer, a weight lifted from my shoulders. I was free from the burden I had been carrying around for over thirty years.

Unresolved grief may result in undesirable consequences both for the person involved and for the whole family. In the motion picture, *The Sound of Music*, unresolved grief was the problem in the Von Trapp household prior to the arrival of Maria. The Captain could not tolerate anything that reminded him of his deceased wife. He shut up the room where they had given parties. He stifled all singing and laughter. The Von Trapp children did not play; they marched. Because of his grief, the Captain was unable to give his children the love they so desperately needed.

For a biblical example consider Jacob. After he was tricked into believing Joseph was dead, he had unresolved grief for twenty-two years (Gen. 37:31–35; 42:36, 38; 44:29, 31; 45:27b) For people whose continued grief is affecting their families, realizing what they are doing to their families should help them assume a more proactive role in seeking resolution.

Many of the recent studies in the area of grief and mourning have been with spouses of those recently deceased. After the death of a mate, certain situations place the surviving spouse at increased risk for difficulty during the mourning period. For example, a young widow, with children living at home and no close relatives nearby to help form a support network, is likely to have an especially difficult time.[5] In a highly ambivalent relationship, the survivor's mourning is likely to be complicated by feelings of guilt, along with those of intense anger.[6] Accidental or suicidal death may also be especially difficult.[7]

Worden analyzed the process of mourning based on the concept of tasks.[8] In his mind the mourner needs to take action and do something. Worden's tasks of mourning are listed as follows:

1. To accept the reality of the loss—Talking about a loss often helps a person accept the reality of that loss. It may also be helpful for the mourner to visit places that remind him of his painful experiences.
2. To work through the pain of grief—Identifying and expressing feelings is therapeutic.

3. To adjust to an environment in which the deceased is missing.
4. To emotionally relocate the deceased and move on with life. To take the emotional energy tied up in what was lost and invest it in existing or new relationships.

Rather than looking for ways to avoid the pain of grief, the mourner needs to experience the pain in order to bring the grief to resolution. It is often helpful for the bereaved to seek emotional support from others. The Bible tells us that we are to encourage one another. Sharing experiences with others, and finding out how they handled similar situations may guide the mourner toward a more effective course of action. There are different kinds of help to suit different people's needs. That help can range from conversations with trusted individuals of like-minded faith to group therapy to formal psychiatric help. God sends His grace through many different channels. People experiencing unresolved grief do not have to stay in that situation. If they are willing to take the initiative, they can find the help they need.

We began this chapter with a discussion about assessing where we are on the road of life so we can plan an effective strategy to move to where we need to be. People have many needs that are outside the scope of this book. However, I hope this chapter will be helpful in assisting people to assess their needs and come up with a plan to deal with them. All this discussion is based on the assumption that individuals, headed in the wrong direction, would be willing to change their course in order to achieve the most effective results from their lives. Some people might not be willing to try to change their approach to life, especially those who are too proud or those who are so overwhelmed with a sense of failure that they are unwilling to make the effort. The Bible tells us that God is able to humble the proud and give hope to the discouraged. It is only by the Spirit of God that we can see ourselves as we really are and plan the most effective strategy to deal with our problems. He is our source of everything we need to come out in victory.

14

Our Proper Response to Tribulation: Love God

From my perspective, the key to successfully moving through difficult circumstances lies within the human spirit (Prov. 18:14). There is nothing that quite satisfies the longings of our spirits like the God who created them (Prov. 18:24). In this life, we may never completely understand why we are undergoing tribulation, but we have ample evidence of how we are to handle it. Jesus is our example, and we are supposed to walk as He did (1 John 2:6); we are to follow in His steps (1 Pet 2:21).

Our first responsibility in life is to love God. Consider the words of Jesus:

> Hearing that Jesus had silenced the Sadducees, the Pharisees got together. One of them, an expert in the law, tested him with this question: "Teacher, which is the greatest commandment in the law?" Jesus replied: "Love the Lord your God with all your heart and with all your soul and with all your mind. This is the first and greatest commandment. (Matt. 22:34–38)

The process of loving God encompasses many things. We will discuss some of them in this chapter.

HUMILITY

It is my perception that tribulation will either bring us closer to the Lord or drive us farther away from Him. As I see it, which it will be depends on our level of humility. During difficult times, we need to humble ourselves before Almighty God.

In *A Plain Account of Christian Perfection,* John Wesley wrote these words:

"Humility alone unites patience with love; without which it is impossible to draw profit from suffering . . . True humility in a kind of self annihilation, and this is the center of all virtues."[1]

Consider these words from Isaiah:

For this is what the high and lofty one says—he who lives forever, whose name is holy: "I live in a high and lofty place, but also with him who is contrite and lowly in spirit, to revive the spirit of the lowly and to revive the heart of the contrite." (Isa. 57:15)

Consider these words to Daniel, spoken by a messenger from heaven:

Since the first day that you set your mind to gain understanding and to humble yourself before your God, your words were heard, and I have come in response to them. (Dan. 10:12b)

There are other passages that carry the same idea.

The fear of the LORD teaches a man wisdom, and humility comes before honor. (Prov. 15:33)

Be completely humble and gentle; be patient, bearing with one another in love. (Eph. 4:2)

Consider Jesus' example:

Your attitude should be the same as that of Christ Jesus: Who, being in very nature God, did not consider equality with God something to be grasped, but made himself nothing, taking the very nature of a servant, being made in human likeness. And being found in appearance as a man, he humbled himself and became obedient to death—even death on a cross! (Phil. 2:5–8)

SUBMISSION

We have a sovereign God. We are not able to change events God has ordained, but we can determine how we respond to them. I was submissive when Barbara was diagnosed with cancer. From my perspective, I didn't have any other choice.

Samuel Rutherford was a seventeenth century Scottish theologian who lived during times of religious persecution. A large number of his letters have been published, many of them written from prison. Some of the letters speak to the idea of being submissive to God's will. Consider a couple of quotes from those letters:

"TO MISTRESS CRAIG [On the death of her son] . . . There is no way of quieting the mind, and of silencing the heart of a mother, but godly submission."[2]

"When the Lord's blessed will bloweth across your desires, it is best, in humility, to strike sail to him, and to be willing to be led any way our Lord pleaseth."[3]

During times of tribulation, the issue is not whether or not we will submit to something. The issue is *to what* we will submit. We can submit to our heavenly Father, or we can submit to the alternatives, which lead to disillusionment, isolation, and hopelessness.

Consider Jesus' words from John 8:34:

"Every one who sins is a slave to sin."

Consider also these two passages from the epistles:

Don't you know that when you offer yourselves to someone to obey him as slaves, you are slaves to one whom you obey—whether you are slaves to sin, which leads to death, or to obedience, which leads to righteousness? (Rom. 6:16)

Endure hardship as discipline; God is treating you as sons. For what son is not disciplined by his father? If you are not disciplined [and everyone undergoes discipline], then you are illegitimate children and not true sons. Moreover, we have all had human fathers who disciplined us and we respected them for it. How much more should we submit to the Father of our spirits and live!" (Heb. 12:7–9)

While in Gethsemane the night before He was crucified, Jesus was in anguish over his coming crucifixion, but He remained submissive. "And being in anguish, he prayed more earnestly, and his sweat was like drops of blood falling to the ground" (Luke 22:44). "My Father, if it is not possible for this cup to be taken away unless I drink it, may your will be done" (Matt. 26:42).

During the days of Jesus' life on earth, he offered up prayers and petitions with loud cries and tears to the one who could save him from death, and he was heard because of his reverent submission. (Heb. 5:7)

COMMUNION WITH GOD

By the grace of God, I learned as a teenager to set aside time every day to spend with the Lord. It's amazing to me, the number of Christians I speak with, who have not grasped the reality of the need for such a commitment. Spending time with the Lord, in Bible reading and prayer, helps me get through the day.

In times of affliction, those who are prudent will turn to the Lord. God reveals His thoughts to man (Amos 4:13). We should not go to the Lord's enemies for advice in spiritual matters (2 Kings 1:2–17).

Communion with God Is an End in Itself

As I have mentioned before, my first mission trip was to Guatemala in 1993. Since that time, I have been to Central America seven times, the former Soviet Union five times, Africa three times, and have gone on one trip to an Indian reservation in South Dakota. I have souvenirs from most of the places I've been, and they fill a curio cabinet in our home. I'm quite proud of some of them.

I've been to a couple of conferences for physicians at the Billy Graham Training Center in Asheville, North Carolina. Many of Billy Graham's memorabilia are on display in the lower level of the building. Built-in display cases line the halls. There are pictures of him preaching to hundreds of thousands of people, gifts from heads of state, impressive art objects, curios that, by comparison, dwarfed my meager collection. It makes a story I heard about him all the more impressive. Someone asked Billy what the most exciting thing was that had happened during his career. I'm told his response was as follows: "Time I've spent alone with the Lord."

> As the deer pants for streams of water, so my soul pants for you, O God. My soul thirsts for God, for the living God . . . My tears have been my food day and night . . . Deep calls to deep in the roar of your waterfalls; all your waves and breakers have swept over me . . . I say to God my Rock, "Why have you forgotten me? Why must I go about mourning?" . . . Put your hope in God, for I will yet praise him, my Savior and my God. (Ps. 42)

> One thing I ask of the LORD, this is what I seek: that I may dwell in the house of the LORD all the days of my life, to gaze upon the beauty of the LORD and to seek him in his temple. (Ps. 27:4)

> How lovely is your dwelling place, O Lord Almighty! My soul yearns, even faints, for the courts of the Lord; my heart and my flesh cry out for the living God. (Ps. 84:1, 2)

> I meditate on your precepts and consider your ways. I delight in your decrees; I will not neglect your word. (Ps. 119:15, 16)

How precious to me are your thoughts, O God! How vast is the sum of them! Were I to count them, they would outnumber the grains of sand. (Ps. 139:17–18a)

Yes, Lord walking in the way of your laws, we wait for you; your name and renown are the desire of our hearts. My soul yearns for you in the night; in the morning my spirit longs for you. (Isa. 26:8, 9a)

Communion with God Is to Be with a Spirit of Thankfulness

Do not be anxious about anything, but in everything, by prayer and petition, with thanksgiving, present your requests to God. And the peace of God, which transcends all understanding, will guard your hearts and your minds in Christ Jesus. (Phil. 4:6, 7)

Give thanks in all circumstances, for this is God's will for you in Christ Jesus. (1 Thess. 5:18)

Communion with God Gives Us Wisdom

In Bible study and prayer we develop wisdom. We see things as they really are.

The law of the LORD is perfect, reviving the soul. The statutes of the LORD are trustworthy, making wise the simple. The precepts of the LORD are right, giving joy to the heart. The commands of the LORD are radiant, giving light to the eyes. (Ps. 19:7, 8)

We do, however, speak a message of wisdom among the mature . . . we speak of God's secret wisdom, a wisdom that has been hidden and that God destined for our glory before time began . . . as it is written "no eye has seen, no ear has heard, no mind has conceived what God has prepared for those who love him"—but God has revealed it to us by his Spirit. The Spirit searches all things, even the deep things of God. For who among men knows the thoughts of a man except the man's spirit within him? In the same way no one knows the thoughts of God except the Spirit of God. We have not received the spirit of the world but the Spirit who is from God, that we may understand what God has freely given us. This is what we speak, not in words taught us by human wisdom but in words taught by the Spirit, expressing spiritual truths in spiritual words. (1 Cor. 2:6–13)

Communion with God Takes Away Our Fears

Have mercy on me, O God, have mercy on me, for in you my soul takes refuge. I will take refuge in the shadow of your wings until the disaster has passed. (Ps. 57:1)

God is our refuge and strength, an ever present help in trouble. Therefore we will not fear, though the earth give way and the mountains fall into the heart of the sea, though its waters roar and foam and the mountains quake with their surging. (Ps. 46:1–3)

Communion with God Gives Us Strength

For the eyes of the LORD range throughout the earth to strengthen those whose hearts are fully committed to him. (2 Chron. 16:9a)

Cast your cares on the LORD and he will sustain you; (Ps. 55:22a)

This is what the Sovereign LORD, the Holy One of Israel, says: "In repentance and rest is your salvation, in quietness and trust is your strength," (Isa. 30:15a)

He giveth power to the faint; and to *them that have* no might he increaseth strength. Even the youths shall faint and be weary, and young men shall utterly fall: But they that wait upon the Lord shall renew *their* strength; they shall mount up with wings as eagles; they shall run, and not be weary; *and* they will walk, and not faint. (Isa. 40:29–31 KJV)

I pray that out of his glorious riches he may strengthen you with power through his Spirit in your inner being. (Eph. 3:16)

And the God of all grace, who called you to his eternal glory in Christ, after you have suffered a little while, will himself restore you and make you strong, firm and steadfast. (1 Pet. 5:10)

Jesus needed to be strengthened during His time of trial, and while He was praying in Gethsemane, "An angel from heaven appeared to him and strengthened him." (Luke 22:43)

Communion with God Provides Comfort, Consolation, and Encouragement

The word *parakleesis* appears in the Greek New Testament. In *Vine's Expository Dictionary of New Testament Words, parakleesis* is the first word listed under at least three different English words: comfort,[4] consolation,[5] and encouragement.[6] Literally *parakleesis* means "a calling to one's side." If we call on the Lord in our trouble, He will be with us.

Praise be to the God and Father of our Lord Jesus Christ, the Father of compassion and the God of all *comfort*, who comforts us in all our troubles, so that we can comfort those in any trouble with the *comfort* we ourselves have received from God. For just as the sufferings of Christ flow over into our lives, so also through Christ our *comfort* overflows. (2 Cor. 1:3–5)

There are some passages from the Old Testament that carry the same idea:

When anxiety was great within me, your consolation brought joy to my soul. (Ps. 94:19)

This is my comfort *and* consolation in my affliction: that Your word has revived me *and* given me life. (Psalm 119:50 AMP)

"Because he loves me," says the Lord, "I will rescue him; I will protect him, for he acknowledges my name. He will call upon me, and I will answer him; I will be with him in trouble, I will deliver him and honor him." (Ps. 91:14, 15)

But now, this is what the Lord says he who created you, O Jacob, he who formed you, O Israel: "Fear not, for I have redeemed you; I have summoned you by name; you are mine. When you pass through the waters, I will be with you; and when you pass through the rivers, they will not sweep over you. When you walk through the fire, you will not be burned; the flames will not set you ablaze. For I am the Lord, your God, the Holy One of Israel, your Savior . . . Do not be afraid for I am with you." (Isa. 43:1–3a, 5a)

"I, even I, am he who comforts you.
  Who are you that you fear mortal men,
  the sons of men, who are but grass. (Isa. 51:12)

If I had not known affliction, I would not have experienced the sweetness of His consolation.

OBEDIENCE

God does not really need anything that we can do for him. Consider Paul's words to the Athenians:

The God who made the world and everything in it is the Lord of heaven and earth and does not live in temples built by hands. And he is not served by human hands, as if he needed anything, because he himself gives all men life and breath and everything else. (Acts 17:24, 25)

If we keep silent, if we do not praise Him, the stones will cry out. (Luke 19:40)

God does however, expect our obedience. When we are obedient, it reflects the attitudes in our hearts (2 John 6). There are several reasons to be obedient. The first one that most Christians become aware of is fear. They realize that judgment is prepared for the ungodly. Perhaps the next reason for obedience that they appreciate is gratitude. After becoming Christians, they become thankful for their salvation, for what Jesus did for them in providing it. Several years ago I realized a third reason. We need to be obedient to the Lord because it is in our own best interest for a rich, satisfying life (Jer. 32:39). More recently I have understood a fourth reason. Obedience is necessary if we are to have a close relationship with the Father.

> If anyone turns a deaf ear to the law, even his prayers are detestable. (Prov. 28:9)

Psalm 119 contains many references to obedience. In that psalm, knowledge of God's word, obedience, gaining wisdom, and obtaining God's mercy are all tied together.

> Oh, how I love your law! I meditate on it all day long. Your commands make me wiser than my enemies, for they are ever with me. I have more insight than all my teachers, for I meditate on your statutes. I have more understanding than the elders, for I obey your precepts. I have kept my feet from every evil path so that I might obey your word. I have not departed from your laws, for you yourself have taught me. How sweet are your words to my taste, sweeter than honey to my mouth! I gain understanding from your precepts; therefore I hate every wrong path. (Ps. 119:97–104)

Obedience is a sign of our love for God and is a requirement for fellowship with Him.

> Jesus replied, "If anyone loves me, he will obey my teaching. My Father will love him, and we will come to him and make our home with him. He who does not love me will not obey my teaching." (John 14:23, 24a)

> As the Father has loved me, so have I loved you. Now remain in my love. If you obey my commands, you will remain in my love, just as I have obeyed my Father's commands and remain in his love. I have told you this so that my joy may be in you and that your joy may be complete. (John 15:9–11)

We know that we have come to know him if we obey his commands. The man who says, "I know him," but does not do what he commands is a liar, and the truth is not in him. But if anyone obeys his word, God's love is truly made complete in him. This is how we know we are in him: Whoever claims to live in him must walk as Jesus did. (1 John 2:3–6)

It is God's will that you should be sanctified: that you should avoid sexual immorality; that each of you should learn to control his own body in a way that is holy and honorable, not in passionate lust like the heathen, who do not know God; and that in this matter no one should wrong his brother or take advantage of him. The Lord will punish men for all such sins, as we have already told you and warned you. For God did not call us to be impure, but to live a holy life. Therefore, he who rejects this instruction does not reject man but God, who gives you his Holy Spirit. (1 Thess. 4:3–8)

Consider also this passage from I Peter:

So then, those who suffer according to God's will should commit themselves to their faithful Creator and continue to do good. (1 Pet. 4:19)

Consider Jesus' example:

but the world must learn that I (Jesus) love the Father and that I do exactly what my Father has commanded me. (John 14:31a)

Although he was a son, he learned obedience from what he suffered and, once made perfect, he became the source of eternal salvation for all who obey him. (Heb. 5:8, 9)

I have learned that it is hard for me to approach the throne of grace with confidence, so that I may receive mercy and find grace to help me in my time of need, if I have a guilty conscience.

FAITH AND TRUST

As we go through tribulation, it helps us if we have the faith to trust that God will work out what is best for us. If we get in the habit of trusting God when we are young, when the problems usually aren't so major, then it will make it easier to do so later, when we are older and life becomes more difficult.

If you do not stand firm in your faith, you will not stand at all.' (Isa. 7:9b)

Who among you fears the LORD and obeys the word of his servant? Let him who walks in the dark, who has no light, trust in the name of the LORD and rely on his God. (Isa. 50:10)

everything that does not come from faith is sin. (Rom. 14:23b)

Now faith is being sure of what we hope for and certain of what we do not see. (Heb. 11:1)

And without faith it is impossible to please God, because anyone who comes to him must believe that he exists and that he rewards those who earnestly seek him. (Heb. 11:6)

Consider it pure joy, my brothers, whenever you face trials of many kinds, because you know that the testing of your faith develops perseverance. Perseverance must finish its work so that you may be mature and complete, not lacking anything. If any of you lacks wisdom, he should ask God, who gives generously to all without finding fault, and it will be given to him. But when he asks, he must believe and not doubt, because he who doubts is like a wave of the sea, blown and tossed by the wind. That man should not think he will receive anything from the Lord; he is a double-minded man, unstable in all he does. (James 1:2–8)

But if you suffer for doing good and you endure it, this is commendable before God. To this you were called, because Christ suffered for you, leaving you an example, that you should follow in his steps. "He committed no sin, and no deceit was found in his mouth." When they hurled their insults at him, he did not retaliate; when he suffered, he made no threats. Instead, he entrusted himself to him who judges justly. (1 Pet. 2:20b–23)

ACCEPTANCE

Acceptance is said to be the final stage of grief and it may be the most difficult to accomplish. How do we enter God's rest?

One day, I saw a woman in the office. She was not in her usual good mood. She was fussing about her daughter-in-law, whom she did not like. Then she began fussing about the time change. We had just gone from Eastern Daylight to Eastern Standard Time. Rather quickly she said that she would just have to accept the time change. It was evident she could do nothing about it. I suggested to her that she needed to accept her daughter-in-law just as she had accepted the time change.

For some people submission to God in a situation and acceptance of that situation may occur at the same time, but it seems to me that they are different. Submission is an act of the will, whereas acceptance is a condition of the heart. People who have accepted their difficult situations are at peace.

Acceptance may come about because of a change in perspective. I can offer some personal examples from my own experiences. I was the Battalion Surgeon for the 1/69 Armor (tanks) in Vietnam for 6 1/2 months. The Scout Platoon had a mascot, a little black dog who was very friendly. The dog became ill, and over a matter of a few days, died. There was something strange about how the dog acted during those final few days. Its head was sent off to Saigon. As a result of tests performed on the dog's head, the diagnosis of rabies was confirmed. It was the responsibility of the tankers to do the mechanical work on their own tanks. Most of them had minor lacerations on their hands, and the dog had been licking the hands of those tankers. After we found out the dog had died of rabies, members of the Scout Platoon began showing up at my door, expressing concerns about how the dog had licked their hands, including the places where there were breaks in the skin.

All told, it appeared that fourteen members of the Scout Platoon needed prophylactic injections of the rabies antitoxin.

There were too many men involved to hold them all in base camp for the injections. The battalion commander decided I should fly out to the field every day, in a helicopter, to give them their injections. I was not happy about the idea, but I followed orders. Each day we flew out from Camp Radcliff in An Khe. Once we were in the air, the pilot would radio the Scout Platoon. The men would use their armored vehicles to trample down the grass over a large circular area. The vehicles would then circle the perimeter. The helicopter would land in the middle of the circle. I would jump out of the helicopter and give the men their injections. Then I would reboard the helicopter, and we would return to base camp. The whole trip took perhaps an hour or more.

One day it rained heavily. We could not get a helicopter. I had to go out in an armored personnel carrier. There was high monkey grass on both sides of the road. The road was not much wider than the vehicle on which we were riding. The trip took all day. I was scared to death the entire time. The next day, when I went out in the helicopter, it hardly bothered me at all! I was relieved to be able to use the helicopter again. I moved from submission (simply following orders) to acceptance (being at peace) because of a change in my perspective. The situation itself had not really changed.

In 1994, the physicians in Tennessee were most upset about a new form of Medicaid, state funded medical care for the poor. It was called Tenncare. It did not bother me so much that we would be expected to give care for very little money. I was used to that. What bothered me was that it seemed we would have no control over the numbers of new patients we would have to take. It seemed as if the insurance companies would have the power to make us take patients. I was afraid that the Tenncare patients would crowd out the rest of my practice. Reluctantly, because of my social conscience and the initiative taken by some primary care physicians at our hospital, I did sign up for Tenncare.

In October 1994, my wife Barbara and I went with a People to People delegation to the former U. S. S. R. It was a trip for nephrologists. We met with the physicians there and others who cared for patients with kidney disease in Saint Petersburg and Moscow in Russia, as well as in Minsk, Belarus and Vilnius and Kaunas in Lithuania. While we were there we saw buildings that were deteriorating because of lack of funds for upkeep. We met physicians who were working full time for a salary of fifty dollars a month. After having dinner with us one evening at a hotel in Saint Petersburg, a plastic surgeon, the chief of staff at his hospital, had to leave early. He could not afford a car and had to walk home in the cold. We spoke with nurses in Vilnius who had contracted hepatitis B because they were dialyzing patients without the benefit of gloves. The hospital could not afford to buy them. In Kaunas, we heard about patients who were receiving inadequate dialysis because the health care facilities could not afford to do the lab work necessary to measure dialysis adequacy. The despair exhibited by the medical staff at one pediatric hospital in Minsk, was overwhelming.

After I returned home from Eastern Europe, some of the things I had previously been fretting about did not seem so important. Tenncare did not bother me at all. My *situation* had not changed, but my *perspective* had changed.

Jesus Accepted What Could Not Be Changed

When Jesus was in Gethsemane he prayed, "My Father, if it is possible, may this cup be taken from me. Yet not as I will but as you will." That was submission but, in my mind, it was not acceptance. He was still not at peace about the situation. He was still sweating drops of blood. I do not believe that Jesus accepted his coming crucifixion until He saw the people in the arresting party approaching. Consider His words after He saw them:

"Rise, let us go! Here comes my betrayer!" (Matt. 26:46)

To Judas: "Friend, do what you came for." (Matt. 26:50a)

To Peter after he cut off the ear of the high priest's servant: "Put your sword back in its place, for all who draw the sword will die by the sword. Do you think I cannot call on my Father, and he will at once put at my disposal more than twelve legions of angels? But how then would the Scriptures be fulfilled that say it must happen in this way?" (Matt. 26:52–54).

Also to Peter: "Shall I not drink the cup the Father has given me?" (John 18:11b).

I believe the change in the tone of Jesus' words was the result of a change in His perspective. When He prayed, "May this cup be taken from me," He was focusing on the moment. When He asked the rhetorical question, "How then would the Scriptures be fulfilled that say it must happen in this way?" He was focusing on the events with an eternal perspective.

We Can Accept What We Cannot Change

How do we develop acceptance? How are we able to see things from an eternal perspective? As I see it, we are able to do so by the Spirit of God. Consider Jesus' words:

> Come to me, all you who are weary and burdened, and I will give you rest. Take my yoke upon you and learn from me, for I am gentle and humble in heart, and you will find rest for your souls. For my yoke is easy and my burden is light. (Matt. 11:28–30)

There are other passages that tell us about having peace:

> My soul finds rest in God alone; my salvation comes from him. He alone is my rock and my salvation; he is my fortress, I will never be shaken. (Ps. 62:1, 2)

> The fear of the LORD leads to life: Then one rests content, untouched by trouble. (Prov. 19:23)

> You will keep in perfect peace him whose mind is steadfast, because he trusts in you. (Isa. 26:3)

The fruit of righteousness will be peace; the effect of righteousness will be quietness and confidence forever. (Isa. 32:17)

This is what the Lord says—your Redeemer, the Holy One of Israel: "I am the Lord your God, who teaches you what is best for you, who directs you in the way you should go. If only you had paid attention to my commands, your peace would have been like a river, your righteousness like the waves of the sea." (Isa. 48:17, 18)

This is what the LORD says: "Stand at the crossroads and look; ask for the ancient paths, ask where the good way is, and walk in it, and you will find rest for your souls. (Jer. 6:16a)

I [Paul] have learned to be content whatever the circumstances. I know what it is to be in need, and I know what it is to have plenty. I have learned the secret of being content in any and every situation, whether well fed or hungry, whether living in plenty or in want. I can do everything through him who gives me strength. (Phil. 4:11b–13)

The men of faith in Hebrews 11 had an eternal perspective about their respective situations. Consider a quote from that chapter.

All these people were still living by faith when they died. They did not receive the things promised; they only saw them and welcomed them from a distance. And they admitted that they were aliens and strangers on earth. (Heb. 11:13)

As we spend time with Jesus, we need to have the faith that He will heal our damaged spirits (Ps. 147:3), but we should not get too impatient. It may take some time.

Jesus is there to help us get through the daily struggle, to help us have peace. Our proper response to tribulation is to love God and follow through with the attitudes and actions that love for God entails. If we love God, then our difficult situations will work themselves out for our ultimate good (Rom. 8:28).

15

OUR PROPER RESPONSE TO TRIBULATION: BEAR FRUIT

C onsider the words of Jesus: "You did not choose me, but I chose you and appointed you to go and bear fruit—fruit that will last" (John 15:16a). "This is to my Father's glory, that you bear much fruit, showing yourselves to be my disciples" (John 15:8). "Let your light shine before men, that they may see your good deeds and praise your Father in heaven." (Matthew 5:16b).

We see people all around us who are able to bear fruit in a special way because of the particulars of their own tribulation. Joni Eareckson Tada is a prime example. When Joni was a teenager, she had a diving accident that left her a quadriplegic. She has written several books about her experiences. Just a few of her titles include *Joni, Choices and Changes, Heaven: Your Real Home, and More Precious Than Silver*. She spends her time giving encouragement to those who are disabled. Wheels for the World is an outreach program of her Joni and Friends Ministries. It collects discarded wheelchairs, refurbishes them, and distributes them both locally and worldwide in developing countries. Each overseas recipient also receives a Bible in his own language.

Corrie ten Boom spent Christmas 1944 in a hospital barracks at Ravensbruck concentration camp. As she wrote in *Corrie's*

Christmas Memories, "Dark it was in my heart, and darkness was around me."[1] In the middle of the night Corrie heard the crying of a feebleminded child named Oelie. That night, Corrie told Oelie about Jesus. Oelie accepted Christ as her Savior. As Corrie said in the last line of the story: "Then I knew why I had to spend this Christmas in Ravensbruck."[2]

We each are able to bear special fruit in our own tribulation. If in no other way, our own affliction is an opportunity to demonstrate to the world how a Christian should act in such circumstances. "Whatever happens, conduct yourselves in a manner worthy of the gospel of Christ" (Phil. 1:27a). In 1817, *Letters Addressed to Christians in Affliction* was published in Glasgow, Scotland. A couple of the letters were written from a Mr. F to a Mrs. H on the occasion of the death of her husband. He had previously lost his oldest son. He wrote, "I thought I was now called upon to bear witness for God to all about me; to testify by my spirit and conduct, that the gospel was sufficient to support a Christian under the heaviest of worldly losses. I have professed, said I, to take the Lord for my portion: but if on the loss of created comforts I should be inconsolable, should I not give the lie to my profession?"[3]

The Bible contains many references to those who bear good fruit.

> But blessed is the man who trusts in the Lord, whose confidence is in him. He will be like a tree planted by the water that sends out its roots by the stream. It does not fear when heat comes; its leaves are always green. It has no worries in a year of drought and never fails to bear fruit. (Jer. 17:7, 8)

> Make a tree good and its fruit will be good, or make a tree bad and its fruit will be bad, for a tree is recognized by its fruit . . . For out of the overflow of the heart the mouth speaks. The good man brings good things out of the good stored up in him, and the evil man brings evil things out of the evil stored up in him. (Matt. 12:33–35)

Even in old age, our bodies may be as good as dead, but we can still bear good fruit.

The righteous will flourish like a palm tree,
they will grow like a cedar of Lebanon;
planted in the house of the Lord,
they will flourish in the courts of our God.
They will still bear fruit in old age,
they will stay fresh and green,
proclaiming, "The Lord is upright;
he is my Rock, and there is no wickedness in him." (Ps. 92:12–15)

PERSEVERANCE

At the hospital I see many people who are hurting. Recently I saw a woman I had known from high school days. Her elderly father was ill. She reminded me of a meeting we had had a couple of months previously. She had been worn out with trying to look after her father. She was worn out from all the repeated trips back to the hospital. She related to me that I had told her, "You have to persevere." She recalled how my words had initially angered her. She said under her breath, "What do you think I've been doing?" When she told me about her initial response, I became very uncomfortable. She continued her story. She told how my words had haunted her for almost a full day. Finally she realized that all she could do was persevere.

Consider what Paul had to say about perseverance in Romans chapter five.

Not only so, but we also rejoice in our sufferings, because we know that suffering produces perseverance; perseverance, character, and character, hope. And hope does not disappoint us, because God has poured out his love into our hearts by the Holy Spirit, whom he has given us. (Rom. 5:3–5)

Perseverance has to do with steadfastness, fortitude, or endurance in a difficult situation. It has to do with keeping on keeping on in spite of hardship, weariness, or discouragement. As we spend time with God and are renewed by the Spirit each day, we are able to persist in doing what we are supposed to do. The Greek word *hupomonee* means *"patience, endurance, fortitude, steadfastness, perseverance . . .* especially as they are shown in the enduring of toil and suffering . . . *Christ-like fortitude,* i.e. a fortitude that comes from communion with Christ . . . *perseverance in doing what is right."*[4]

Romans 12:12 tells us to be patient in affliction. We are to endure hardship like a good soldier of Christ Jesus. (2 Tim. 2:3). The battle is not ours, but God's (2 Chron. 20:15)

When I was in practice in Roanoke, Virginia I became acquainted with a nephrologist who was a real comedian. He could tell stories in such a way as to hold everyone's attention. Several years later, I ran into him at a meeting in Miami. We had breakfast together. He explained to the people at our table how he had become a runner, and had run in several marathons. He described one particular time when he ran the Boston Marathon. Those 26.2 miles were not easy. Heartbreak Hill is part of the course of the Boston Marathon. It is only mastered with great difficulty. His description of going up Heartbreak Hill was hilarious. He was straining. His eyes were bulging. His legs were about to come out from under him. He was short of breath. His chest felt as if it were caving in. He could hardly make it up the hill. He was in agony.

I reflected on the reason why he was willing to endure such difficulty. He did it so that he could finish the race. He was looking forward to the finish line. He had no other goal. He was not going to win. He was not going receive any prize. He just wanted to finish the race, to be able to know that he had run in a Boston Marathon and completed the course. Even though my friend may not have been going to win a prize, we have a prize certainly waiting for us if we persevere.

> Blessed is the man who perseveres under trial, because when he has stood the test, he will receive the crown of life that God has promised to those who love him. (James 1:12)

Jesus spoke of perseverance in His explanation of the parable of the sower:

But the seed on good soil stands for those with a noble and good heart, who hear the word, retain it, and by persevering produce a crop. (Luke 8:15)

Consider Jesus' example:

Therefore, since we are surrounded by such a great cloud of witnesses, let us throw off everything that hinders and the sin that so easily entangles, and let us run with perseverance the race marked out for us. Let us fix our eyes on Jesus, the author and perfecter of our faith, who for the joy set before him endured the cross, scorning its shame, and sat down at the right hand of the throne of God. Consider him who endured such opposition from sinful men, so that you will not grow weary and lose heart. (Heb. 12:1–3)

The Lord Gives Us the Ability to Persevere
In Revelation 1:9 John wrote to fellow believers that he was their companion in the suffering and patient endurance that were his and theirs in Jesus. Consider what Paul wrote to the Thessalonians:

And pray that we may be delivered from wicked and evil men, for not everyone has faith. But the Lord is faithful, and he will strengthen and protect you from the evil one. We have confidence in the Lord that you are doing and will continue to do the things we command. May the Lord direct your hearts into God's love and Christ's perseverance. (2 Thess. 3:2–5)

It Helps Us When We Remember God's Past Blessings
One thing that helps us to remain steadfast is remembering what the Lord has done for us in the past. Matthew 16 tells of a time when the disciples forgot to take bread. They were hungry and demonstrated some concern about the situation. Jesus rebuked them for their lack of insight, for not remembering.

You of little faith, why are you talking among yourselves about having no bread? Do you still not understand? Don't you remember the five loaves for the five thousand, and how many basketfuls you gathered? Or the seven loaves for the four thousand, and how many basketfuls you gathered? (Matt. 16:8b–10)

Encouragement Helps Us Persevere and Gives Us Hope

You hear, O LORD, the desire of the afflicted; you encourage them, and you listen to their cry, (Ps. 10:17)

For everything that was written in the past was written to teach us, so that through endurance and the encouragement of the Scriptures we might have hope. (Rom. 15:4)

We are comforted by believers who have been through similar trials (2 Cor. 1:6). We are encouraged by instruction from our spiritual leaders (Titus 2:1, 2).

Perseverance Authenticates Our Faith, Helps Us Mature, and Furthers Our Ministry

As we live our lives, we are supposed to test ourselves, to examine ourselves to see if we are in the faith (2 Cor. 13:5). I trust we will not fail the test. Certain things result as we persevere. Steadfastness proves our faith genuine. It results in praise, honor, and glory (1 Pet. 1:6, 7). Perseverance helps us become mature and complete (James 1:4). Our generosity results in thanksgiving to God as it supplies the needs of God's people (2 Cor. 9:10–15). Our endurance commends us to others and furthers our ministry (2 Cor. 6:3–10).

Those Who Persevere Receive the Promises

Perseverance causes us to be blessed by God (James 5:11). Steadfastness allows us to receive God's promises.

Remember those earlier days after you had received the light, when you stood your ground in a great contest in the face of suffering. Sometimes you were publicly exposed to insult and persecution; at other times you stood side by side with those who were so treated. You sympathized with those in prison and joyfully accepted the confiscation of your property, because you knew that you yourselves had better and lasting possessions. So do not throw away your confidence; it will be richly rewarded. You need to persevere so that when you have done the will of God, you will receive what he has promised. For in just a little while, "He who is coming will come and will not delay. But my righteous one will live by faith. And if he shrinks back, I will not be pleased with him." (Heb. 10:32–38)

LOVE FOR OTHERS

About five weeks after Barbara was diagnosed with cancer, her condition deteriorated. She developed severe pain in her left hip and was unable to stand. Because I had read that it might lead to codependency, I didn't want either one of my sons to feel responsible for the care of his mother. I made it plain to them that she was my responsibility, not theirs. I quit work and took care of her. I was with her all the time.

When people are together all of the time, it is hard to be nice all of the time. Occasionally cross words are exchanged. One Sunday morning we were watching church on television. The pastor said that he was going to read from Philippians four; I thought to myself, "I don't need to hear about Philippians four. I've heard that fifty times." But as the passage was being read, a little phrase caught my attention: "Let your gentleness be evident to all" (verse 5). I count that revelation as one of God's many acts of grace during our times of difficulty. I realized I needed to let my gentleness be evident to all, especially to Barbara.

The two greatest commandments are to love God and to love our neighbor as ourselves. According to Vine, *agapee* is the "characteristic word of Christianity."[5] "Love can be known only from the actions it prompts."[6] "Christian love, whether exercised toward the brethren, or toward men generally, is not an impulse from the feelings, it does not always run with the natural inclinations, nor does it spend itself only upon those for whom some affinity is discovered."[7]

Consider what love does:

> Love is patient. Love is kind. It does not envy, it does not boast, it is not proud. It is not rude, it is not self-seeking, it is not easily angered, it keeps no record of wrongs. Love does not delight in evil but rejoices with the truth. It always protects, always trusts, always hopes, always perseveres. (1 Cor. 13:4–7)

Consider these words from Paul about love:

> Let no debt remain outstanding, except the continuing debt to love one another, for he who loves his fellowman has fulfilled the law. (Rom. 13:8)

> The entire law is summed up in a single command: "Love your neighbor as yourself. (Gal. 5:14)

Consider these words of John about God's love:

> This is love: not that we loved God, but that he loved us and sent his Son as an atoning sacrifice for our sins. Dear friends, since God so loved us, we also ought to love one another. (1 John 4:10, 11)

FORGIVENESS

To be healthy spiritually, we need to be able to forgive others. In the New Testament the main word for forgive is the Greek word *aphieemi*. According to Bauer, Arndt, and Gingrich, it means leave, let go, or send away.[8] It is the word used for leave in Matthew 4:20 when Peter and Andrew left their nets to follow Jesus. It is the word used for canceling a debt. If we have an oppressive feeling of bitterness for someone, we need to forgive and let it go. It removes a tremendous burden from our shoulders.

Let me share an example of a time when Barbara and I needed to forgive and let go of oppressive feelings. We started building our current house in 1981. Those were the days of sixteen to eighteen percent interest rates. After the ordeal of building the house, all the arrangements and all the decisions, we had a sixty thousand-dollar overrun, money that was spent over and beyond the money from other sources. After we moved into the house, there were several things that needed more attention. It was a struggle to get the contractor to come back and fix them. When we did get him back, we would give him a list of eight or ten things that needed correction. He would fix one of them, and then we would not hear from him again until we called him. We were becoming upset over and over and over again. Finally I decided that the only way we could have any peace of mind was to accept the house as it was, forgive the contractor for things he should have done but didn't, and if there was other work needed for the house, to hire another contractor to come in and take care of it. Once we decided to do that, a tremendous weight lifted off our shoulders.

The New Testament appeals to us to forgive others on several different levels. We are encouraged to forgive on the basis of love. Ideally when we forgive, it should be spontaneous, not forced.

> Therefore, although in Christ I could be bold and order you to do what you ought to do, yet I appeal to you on the basis of love. I then, as Paul—an old man and now also a prisoner of Christ Jesus—I appeal to you for my son Onesimus, who became my son while I was in chains. Formerly he was useless to you, but now he has become useful both to you and to me. I am sending him—who is my very heart—back to you . . . So if you consider me a partner, welcome him as you would welcome me. If he has done you any wrong or owes you anything, charge it to me. (Philem. 1:8–12, 17, 18)

The debt that that other person owes us is insignificant compared with the debt we owe God.

> Therefore the kingdom of heaven is like a king who wanted to settle accounts with his servants. As he began the settlement, a man who owed him ten thousand talents was brought to him. Since he was not able to pay, the master ordered that he and his wife and his children and all that he had be sold to repay the

debt. The servant fell on his knees before him, "Be patient with me," he begged, "and I will pay back everything." The servant's master took pity on him, canceled the debt and let him go. But when that servant went out, he found one of his fellow servants who owed him a hundred denarii. He grabbed him and began to choke him. "Pay back what you owe me!" he demanded. His fellow servant fell to his knees and begged him, "Be patient with me, and I will pay you back." But he refused. Instead, he went off and had the man thrown into prison until he could pay the debt. When the other servants saw what had happened, they were greatly distressed and went and told their master everything that had happened. Then the master called the servant in. "You wicked servant," he said, "I cancelled all that debt of yours because you begged me to. Shouldn't you have had mercy on your fellow servant just as I had on you?" In anger his master turned him over to the jailers to be tortured, until he could pay back all he owed. This is how my heavenly Father will treat each of you unless you forgive your brother from your heart. (Matt. 18:23–35)

Jesus said that if we do not forgive others, the Father will not forgive us:

For if you forgive men when they sin against you, your heavenly Father will also forgive you. But if you do not forgive men their sins, your Father will not forgive your sins. (Matt. 6:14, 15)

If we do not forgive, it gives Satan a foothold in our lives. Consider Paul's words:

"In your anger do not sin." Do not let the sun go down while you are still angry, and do not give the devil a foothold . . . Do not let any unwholesome talk come out of your mouths, but only what is helpful for building others up according to their needs, that it may benefit those who listen . . . Get rid of all bitterness, rage and anger, brawling and slander, along with every form of malice. Be kind and compassionate to one another, forgiving each other, just as in Christ God forgave you. (Eph. 4:26–32)

We need to keep Satan from gaining a foothold in our lives. The soul and spirit of a Christian should not be like a household that is divided against itself. We need to keep the devil from establishing a place in our hearts. We are reminded in Colossians 1:13 that the Father has rescued us from the dominion of darkness. If we are angry and resentful, it is difficult to have fellowship with God. It is futile to be bitter toward our fellow man.

Consider Jesus' example. When he was on the cross, Jesus forgave those who crucified him:

> When they came to the place called the Skull, there they cruci-fied him, along with the criminals—one on his right, the other on his left. Jesus said, 'Father forgive them for they do not know what they are doing." (Luke 23:33, 34a)

If it seems impossible to forgive someone, we need to think about why we cannot forgive. We may be too full of pride to for-give. If we have trouble forgiving that other person, we need to find some way to submit to Almighty God and let it go.

Here are some suggestions to help you forgive:
1. Make a decision to forgive.
2. Make a commitment to forgive.
3. Humble yourself before God.
4. Confess lack of forgiveness as a sin.
5. Abide in Christ. "Apart from me you can do nothing." (John 15:5)
6. Ask for deliverance from a sense of hostility toward the other person.
7. Ask the Lord for success in forgiving; be persistent. (Luke 11:5–13)
8. Based on faith, believe you will be successful in forgiving. (Matt. 17:20)
9. Pray for that person. (Matt. 5:44; Luke 6:28)
10. Go to that person about the matter. (Matt. 18:15)

11. Treat him as though you have forgiven him. (Matt. 5:46, 47; Luke 6:27, 35)
12. Purpose to seek that other person's welfare. (1 Cor. 13:4–6)
13. Your feelings should change.

SERVICE TO OTHERS

Jesus called them together and said, "You know that the rulers of the Gentiles lord it over them, and their high officials exercise authority over them. Not so with you. Instead, whoever wants to become great among you must be your servant, and whoever wants to be first must be your slave–just as the Son of Man did not come to be served, but to serve, and to give his life as a ransom for many." (Matt. 20:25–28)

We Should Serve Others During Their Tribulation

In a particular situation it may be within God's providence for us to be a helper for others during their time of difficulty. If we identify with others, we are more likely to get involved when they are in trouble. We should be able to share with others the comfort that comes from God (2 Cor. 1:3–6). In addition to spiritual help, we should also be ready to meet others' physical needs.

If anyone has material possessions and sees his brother in need but has no pity on him, how can the love of God be in him? Dear children, let us not love with words or tongue but with actions and in truth. (1 John 3:17, 18)

Service to others glorifies God. Consider some of the results of that service:

This service that you perform is not only supplying the needs of God's people but is also overflowing in many expressions of thanks to God. Because of the service by which you have proved yourselves, men will praise God for the obedience that accompanies your confession of the gospel of Christ, and for your generosity in sharing with them and with everyone else. And in their prayers for you their hearts will go out to you, because of the surpassing grace God has given you. Thanks be to God for his indescribable gift! (2 Cor. 9:12–15)

We Should Continue to Be of Service as Long as We Are Able

We should continue to be of service to others during our own difficulty. Our own tribulation does not negate Jesus' command for us to love our fellowman and be of service to others. As people develop health problems, staying productive and charitable to others helps them maintain their own mental attitude. When we are in a trial and reach out to serve, it gives us something else to think about besides our own problems. It helps keep us from dwelling on negative things.

People who are ill and whose functional capacity is impaired may need some help in their efforts to stay productive. My father-in-law lived with us the last ten years of his life. One of the things he "had to do" every spring was plant a garden. The last couple of years, he was not really in good enough health to do so. My wife and I had no interest in planting a garden, but we helped him because we realized that for his own sense of well being, he needed to do it. Helping him with the garden was a way to be of service to him and for him to be of service to us.

My wife has significant residual disability from her bony metastases. She has a good mental attitude. One thing that helps her maintain a good mental attitude is being of service to others. She cooks for us. Barbara is not really able to do the cooking by herself. I help her. I cut up food. I reach for things from the high shelves. I get things from the other refrigerator on the other side of the house. I wash dishes. All of this is to help her maintain her sense of well being. It pays tremendous dividends.

Is not this the kind of fasting I have chosen: to loose the chains of injustice and untie the cords of the yoke? Is it not to share your food with the hungry and to provide the poor wanderer with shelter—and when you see the naked, to clothe him, and not to turn away from your own flesh and blood? Then your light will break forth like the dawn, and your healing will quickly appear; then your righteousness will go before you, and the glory of the

Lord will be your rear guard. Then you will call, and the Lord will answer; you will cry for help, and he will say: Here am I. If you do away with the yoke of oppression, with the pointing finger and malicious talk, and if you spend yourselves in behalf of the hungry and satisfy the needs of the oppressed, then your light will rise in the darkness, and your night will become like the noonday. The Lord will guide you always; he will satisfy your needs in a sun scorched land and will strengthen your frame. You will be like a well-watered garden, like a spring whose waters never fail. (Isa. 58:6–11)

PERSEVERANCE AND HOPE

For everything that was written in the past was written to teach us, so that through endurance and the encouragement of the Scriptures we might have hope. (Rom. 15:4)

We know that suffering produces perseverance; perseverance, character; and character, hope. (Rom. 5:3b, 4)

The Greek word for character is *dokimee*. It refers to "the quality of being approved."[9] *Dokimee* is a word related to *dokimazo*, which means to "prove by testing."[10] *Dokimazo* is the word translated "test" in the following passage:

For no one can lay any foundation other than the one already laid, which is Jesus Christ. If any man builds on this foundation using gold, silver, costly stones, wood, hay, or straw, his work will be shown for what it is, because the Day will bring it to light. It will be revealed with fire, and the fire will test the quality of each man's work. If what he has built survives, he will receive his reward. If it is burned up, he will suffer loss; he himself will be saved, but only as one escaping through the flames. (1 Cor. 3:11–15)

If we are doing what God wants us to do, we can take confidence in His promises. Romans 12:1, 2 tells us about how to learn God's will:

Therefore, I urge you, brothers, in view of God's mercy, to offer your bodies as living sacrifices, holy and pleasing to God—this is your spiritual act of worship. Do not conform any longer to the pattern of this world, but be transformed by the renewing of your mind. Then you will be able to test and approve what God's will is—his good, pleasing and perfect will.

Consider these words of David:

Find rest, O my soul, in God alone; my hope comes from him. He alone is my rock and my salvation; he is my fortress, I will not be shaken. My salvation and my honor depend on God; he is my mighty rock, my refuge. Trust in him at all times, O people; pour out your hearts to him, for God is our refuge. Selah (Ps. 62:5–8)

Jesus is our hope. We are to share this hope with others.

But in your hearts set apart Christ as Lord. Always be prepared to give an answer to everyone who asks you to give the reason for the hope that you have. But do this with gentleness and respect. (1 Pet. 3:15)

Tribulation is inevitable. We are children of Adam, and suffering is inescapable to members of the human race. However, Jesus gives us the ability to overcome. He is the one who has and will overcome Satan (Col. 2:13–15; Heb. 2:14, 15; I Cor. 15:24; Rev. 20:10). We are told not to be overcome by evil but to overcome evil with good (Rom. 12:21). Everyone who is born of God overcomes the world. Our faith has overcome the world. He who believes that Jesus is the Son of God overcomes the world (1 John 5:4, 5).

Jesus addressed seven churches in Revelation, chapters two and three. He made mention of tribulation several times. He listed hardships, afflictions, poverty, slander, persecutions, and death. But He also mentioned perseverance. He told some of them not to be afraid of what they were about to suffer. Jesus made promises to those in the seven churches about those who would overcome. There would be a great reward for those overcomers.

Ephesus: "To him who overcomes, I will give the right to eat from the tree of life, which is in the paradise of God."

Smyrna: "He who overcomes will not be hurt at all by the second death."

Pergamum: "To him who overcomes, I will give some of the hidden manna. I will also give him a white stone with a new name written on it, known only to him who receives it."

Thyatira: "To him who overcomes and does my will to the end, I will give authority over the nations—'He will rule them with an iron scepter; he will dash them to pieces like pottery'—just as I have received authority from my Father. I will also give him the morning star."

Sardis: "He who overcomes will . . . be dressed in white. I will never blot out his name from the book of life, but will acknowledge his name before my Father and his angels."

Philadelphia: "Him who overcomes I will make a pillar in the temple of my God. Never again will he leave it. I will write on him the name of my God and the name of the city of my God, the new Jerusalem, which is coming down out of heaven from my God; and I will also write on him my new name."

Laodicea: "To him who overcomes, I will give the right to sit with me on my throne, just as I overcame and sat down with my Father on his throne."

Promises are made to those who overcome. Without tribulation there would be nothing to overcome. And if there were no struggle, there would be no victory!

16

CONCLUSION

S everal months ago, I was speaking with one of my dialysis patients. He is retired after forty years of being a Methodist minister. These were his words: "John Wesley said you should be dead to this world." Then he added, "Sometimes you have to go through a lot to get there."

There is a phrase in 1 Peter 4:1 (KJV) that never did make much sense to me: "For he that hath suffered in the flesh hath ceased from sin." I knew a lot of people who had suffered and were still sinning. Note how 1 Peter 4:1, 2 is phrased in The Living Bible:

> Since Christ suffered and underwent pain, you must have the same attitude he did; you must be ready to suffer too. For remember, when your body suffers, sin loses its power, and you won't be spending the rest of your life chasing after evil desires but will be anxious to do the will of God.

To believe, in the scriptural sense, carries the idea of trust. Tribulation helps us trust our fate to Jesus Christ as it helps us realize that there is nothing else or no one else in whom to trust.

> Yet I am always with you; you hold me by my right hand. You guide me with your counsel, and afterward you will take me into

glory. Whom have I in heaven but you? And earth has nothing I desire besides you. My flesh and my heart may fail, but God is the strength of my heart and my portion forever. (Ps. 73:23–26)

In the Hebrew, the word for *portion* means "share, lot, or territory."[1] It refers to one's share of an inheritance. The sense I get from what I read about taking God as our portion is that if we have Him, we don't really need anything else.

I cry to you, O Lord; I say, "You are my refuge, my portion in the land of the living." (Ps. 142:5)

Because of the Lord's great love we are not consumed, for his compassions never fail. They are new every morning; great is your faithfulness. I say to myself, "The Lord is my portion; therefore I will wait for him." The Lord is good to those whose hope is in him, to the one who seeks him; it is good to wait quietly for the salvation of the Lord. (Lam. 3:22–26)

This book has been written to try to make some sense out of misery and grief and pain. It was written to try to reconcile the apparent contradiction of how a loving God could allow us to hurt. It was also written to help console people during difficult situations and to make some suggestions about what to do in the middle of those situations. It was written to help people to grow spiritually and to give them hope.

When Satan participated in the events leading up to Jesus' crucifixion (Luke 22:3, 4), he thought he was going to win a victory. God turned the events into Satan's ultimate defeat. When Satan afflicts us, he thinks he is going to beat us. If we allow God to do so, He will turn our afflictions into something beautiful. There are a few more thoughts I would like to share with you.

WE NEED TO LEARN TO TRUST GOD

As we deal with tribulation, we need to keep in mind that God is sovereign. God is working out His purposes, and we need to trust

Him in that. God may deliver a person from his tribulation, and He may not. Just because we pray for something does not mean that our prayer will be answered in the way we ask. Through His sacrifice, Jesus Christ has given us the right to approach the throne of grace with boldness and confidence, and we may receive mercy and find grace to help us in our time of need (Heb. 4:14–16). However, we do not have the right to demand what we want (Ps. 78:17–19).

WE NEED TO LEARN TO BE CONTENT IN ALL SITUATIONS

We need to learn to deal with both good times and bad.

When times are good, be happy; but when times are bad, consider: God has made the one as well as the other. (Eccles. 7:14a)

I form the light and create darkness, I bring prosperity and create disaster; I, the Lord, do all these things. (Isa. 45:7)

It seems to me that most Christians are willing to accept the blessings that come to them because of God's purposes, the things that they want, like, and enjoy. If we accept the blessings from God that we enjoy, then we should be able to accept everything that happens to us that fits in with God's plan, including adversity.

WE NEED TO REMEMBER THAT WE HAVE
A SURE FOUNDATION

As Christians, there are several things we need to remember in our struggles. We need to remember the Lord (Neh. 4:14) and how we have worshipped Him in the past, His past deeds (Exod. 13:3) and judgments (Ps. 105:5) and how He has taken care of us (Ps. 106:7; Ps. 143:5). Psalm 77 is a psalm of Asaph. Early in the psalm he mentioned several things. He cried to the Lord for help. He was in distress; his soul refused to be comforted. Verses 5–12 record how his thinking changed:

I thought about the former days, the years of long ago; I remembered my songs in the night. My heart mused and my spirit inquired: 'Will the Lord reject forever? Will he never show his favor again? Has his unfailing love vanished forever? Has his promise failed for all time? Has God forgotten to be merciful? Has he in anger withheld his compassion?' Then I thought, 'To this I will appeal: the years of the right hand of the Most High.' I will remember the deeds of the Lord; yes I will remember your miracles of long ago. I will meditate on all your works and consider all your mighty deeds.

We need to remember what God expects of us and what He has promised us (Num. 15:37–41; Isa. 64:5; Mal. 4:4; Josh. 21:45; 2 Pet. 1:3, 4). We need to keep in mind that God is our Rock and our Redeemer (Ps. 78:35). I talked to one man who went through a long period of depression after his wife left him. As he was trying to make it through each day, Bible verses that he had memorized over the years would come to mind. These verses sustained him. One passage that was particularly meaningful to him was Psalm 40:2:

He brought me up also out of an horrible pit, out of the miry clay, and set my feet upon a rock. (KJV)

The man said that his experience gave him the assurance that the Christian message was reliable. The same thing has happened to me. During my difficult experiences I have been made all the more confident that God is right here with me. I had received the assurance that God's promises are true.

The Lord your God goes with you; he will never leave you nor forsake you. (Deut. 31:6b)

In the middle of his tribulation, Job could make the following statement:

I know that my redeemer lives, and that in the end he will stand upon the earth. And after my skin has been destroyed, yet in my flesh I will see God. (Job 19:25, 26)

Consider these words of Jesus:

"Therefore everyone who hears these words of mine and puts them into practice is like a wise man who built his house on the rock. The rain came down, the streams rose, and the winds blew and beat against that house; yet it did not fall, because it had its foundation on the rock. But everyone who hears these words of mine and does not put them into practice is like a foolish man who built his house on sand. The rain came down, the streams rose, and the winds blew and beat against that house, and it fell with a great crash." (Matt. 7:24–27)

When Paul was in the jail cell writing his second letter to Timothy, he knew that he did not have long to live. He penned these words:

I know whom I have believed, and am convinced that he is able to guard what I have entrusted to him for that day. (2 Tim. 1:12b)

GOD HAS A TENDER HEART

God loves us.

This is how God showed his love among us: He sent his one and only Son into the world that we might live through him. This is love: not that we loved God, but that he loved us and sent his Son as an atoning sacrifice for our sins. (1 John 4:9, 10)

In the Old Testament, God was concerned about the affliction the Children of Israel were experiencing in Egypt. He expressed that concern when He spoke to Moses from the burning bush.

The Lord said, "I have indeed seen the misery of my people in Egypt. I have heard them crying out because of their slave drivers, and I am concerned about their suffering. So I have come down to rescue them from the hand of the Egyptians and to bring them up out of that land into a good and spacious land, a land flowing with milk and honey . . . And now the cry of the Israelites has reached me, and I have seen the way the Egyptians are oppress-ing them. So now go. I am sending you to Pharaoh to bring my people the Israelites out of Egypt." (Exod. 3:7–10)

When the Children of Israel were about to enter the promised land, God had some concerns about their future and expressed that concern to Moses.

Oh, that their hearts would be inclined to fear me and keep all my commands always, so that it might go well with them and their children forever! (Deut. 5:29)

During the time of the Judges, the Israelites experienced a recur-ring cycle of apostasy, servitude, repentance, and deliverance. God punished the Children of Israel, but He was not happy about it.

Then they got rid of the foreign gods among them and served the Lord. And he could bear Israel's misery no longer. (Judg. 10:16)

God later used the Babylonians to discipline the Children of Israel. He looked for reasons not to have to do so, but their wicked-ness was so detestable and they profaned His name so greatly, He turned away from them in disgust (Ezek. 23:18).

I [the Lord] looked for a man among them who would build up the wall and stand before me in the gap on behalf of the land so I would not have to destroy it, but I found none. (Ezek. 22:30)

There are several other passages in the Old Testament that describe God's care and concern for His people.

When Israel was a child, I [God] loved him, and out of Egypt I called my son. But the more I called Israel, the further they went from me. They sacrificed to the Baals and they burned incense to images. It was I who taught Ephraim to walk, taking them by the arms; but they did not realize it was I who healed them. I led them with cords of human kindness, with ties of love; I lifted the yoke from their neck and bent down to feed them. (Hos. 11:1–4).

Yet the Lord longs to be gracious to you; he rises to show you compassion. (Isa. 30:18a)

He [the Sovereign Lord] tends his flock like a shepherd: He gathers the lambs in his arms and carries them close to his heart; he gently leads those that have young. (Isa. 40:11)

In all their distress he [the Lord] too was distressed, and the angel of his presence saved them. In his love and mercy he redeemed them; he lifted them up and carried them all the days of old. (Isa. 63:9)

Since my people are crushed, I [the Lord] am crushed; I mourn, and horror grips me. Is there no balm in Gilead? Is there no physician there? Why then is there no healing for the wound of my people? Oh, that my head were a spring of water and my eyes a fountain of tears! I would weep day and night for the slain of my people. (Jer. 8:21–9:1)

First Thessalonians 3:3 tells us that we are destined for our trials. God allows us to be wounded, but He will heal us.

The moon will shine like the sun, and the sunlight will be seven times brighter, like the light of seven full days, when the Lord binds up the bruises of his people and heals the wounds he inflicted. (Isa. 30:26)

See now that I myself am He! There is no god besides me. I put to death and I bring to life, I have wounded and I will heal, and no one can deliver out of my hand. (Deut. 32:39)

Speak tenderly to Jerusalem, and proclaim to her that her hard service has been completed, that her sin has been paid for. (Isa. 40:2a)

Though in anger I [the Lord] struck you, in favor I will show you compassion. (Isa. 60:10b)

God is grieved over the pain we experience when it is necessary for Him to discipline us.

Jesus has compassion for His children:

> O Jerusalem, Jerusalem, you who kill the prophets and stone those sent to you, how often I have longed to gather your children together, as a hen gathers her chicks under her wings, but you were not willing. (Matt. 23:37)

Consider His response when Lazarus died:

> When Jesus saw her [Mary of Bethany] weeping, and the Jews who had come along with her also weeping, he was deeply moved in spirit and troubled. "Where have you laid him [Lazarus]?" he asked. "Come and see, Lord," they replied. Jesus wept. Then the Jews said, See how he loved him!" (John 11:33–36)

GOD IS COMPELLED BY HIS NATURE TO RESPOND APPROPRIATELY TO SIN

The Bible tells us that God does what He wants to do (Ps. 115:2, 3; Ps. 135:6). There are many things God does for us that are "for His own sake." Were it not so, the way He treats us might be more in line with what we deserve. We would be in a worse condition than we are.

It seems to me that at times God does things He would rather not do. God is not capricious. He is compelled by His nature to respond appropriately to sin. The righteous man does what is right even when it hurts (Ps. 15:4); so does God. Consider these words from God concerning His punishment of Israel:

> Therefore this is what the Lord Almighty says: "See, I will refine and test them, for what else can I do because of the sin of my people?" (Jer. 9:7)

God did not really want to send the Children of Israel into captivity. In Jeremiah 42:10b he said, "I am grieved over the disaster I have inflicted on you."

God did not really want to destroy Jerusalem in 70 A. D. Jesus foresaw that time.

> As he approached Jerusalem and saw the city, he wept over it and said, "If you, even you, had only known on this day what would bring you peace—but now it is hidden from your eyes. The days will come upon you when your enemies will build an embankment against you and encircle you and hem you in on every side. They will dash you to the ground, you and the children within your walls. They will not leave one stone on another, because you did not recognize the time of God's coming to you." (Luke 19:41–44)

Jesus did not really want to go to the cross.

> "Father, if you are willing, take this cup from me; yet not my will but yours be done." An angel from heaven appeared to him and strengthened him. And being in anguish, he prayed more earnestly, and his sweat was like drops of blood falling to the ground. (Luke 22:42–44)

The Lord takes no pleasure in the death of the wicked. God is not willing that any should perish.

> Say to them, "As surely as I live, declares the sovereign Lord, I take no pleasure in the death of the wicked, but rather that they turn from their ways and live. Turn! Turn from your evil ways! Why will you die, O house of Israel?" (Ezek. 33:11)

> Your Father in heaven is not willing that any of these little ones should be lost. (Matt. 18:14b)

> The Lord is not slow in keeping his promise, as some understand slowness. He is patient with you, not wanting anyone to perish, but everyone to come to repentance. (2 Pet. 3:9)

GOD PAID A HIGH PRICE FOR OUR RECONCILIATION

When it comes to our reconciliation with God, God Himself paid a price for that reconciliation that is far beyond anything we can imagine. At least we will never be able to understand it in this life. It seems to me that for God, it was not a very profitable trade-off. All He gets out of the deal is us.

OUR CONDUCT SHOULD BE ABOVE REPROACH

"Whatever happens, conduct yourself in a manner worthy of the gospel of Christ" (Phil. 1:27a). Present your body as a living sacrifice (Rom. 12:1, 2). Stand firm, a sign that you will be saved (Phil. 1:27, 28). Assume the attitude of a servant (2 Pet. 1:1). Let your gentleness be evident to all (Phil. 4:5a). By faith, turn your weakness to strength (Heb. 11:34). Conduct yourself so that later you will not be ashamed (Phil. 1:20). Wrong response to tribulation is sin. By the Spirit of God, we must master it (Gen. 4:7; Rom. 6:14). We must rely on Christ so that we will be able to overcome and win the victory (Eph. 6:10–18).

OUR CONDUCT REFLECTS ON GOD

How we act in times of trouble reflects on God to the world around us. People see what we do. We are also on display to the angels:

> There is rejoicing in the presence of the angels of God over one sinner who repents. (Luke 15:10b)

Our conduct reflects on God to all the heavenly hosts (Job 1, 2). If we act appropriately during our affliction, we glorify God.

> For it seems to me that God has put us apostles on display at the end of the procession, like men condemned to die in the arena.

We have been made a spectacle to the whole universe, to angels as well as to men.(1 Cor. 4:9)

Therefore, since we are surrounded by such a great cloud of witnesses, let us throw off everything that hinders and the sin that so easily entangles, and let us run with perseverance the race marked out for us. (Heb. 12:1)

His intent was that now, through the church, the manifold wisdom of God should be made known to the rulers and authorities in the heavenly realms, according to his eternal purpose which he accomplished in Christ Jesus our Lord. (Eph. 3:10, 11)

In his commentary on this passage in Ephesians, William MacDonald makes the following statement: "One of God's present purposes . . . is to reveal His manifold wisdom to the angelic hosts of heaven . . . God is the teacher. The universe is the classroom. Angelic dignitaries are the students . . . The church is the object lesson. From heaven the angels are compelled to admire His unsearchable judgments and marvel at His ways."[2]

As a Psychiatrist I know once said, "Observed behavior changes." Realizing we are being watched should affect what we do.

GOD ALLOWS US TO PARTICIPATE IN WHAT HE IS DOING

God's purpose is "to bring all things in heaven and on earth together under one head, even Christ" (Eph. 1:9, 10). Our appropriate response to tribulation is a witness to others and serves to advance the Gospel.

Now I want you to know brothers, that what has happened to me has really served to advance the gospel. As a result, it has become clear throughout the whole palace guard and to everyone else that I am in chains for Christ. Because of my chains, most of the brothers in the Lord have been encouraged to speak the word of God more courageously and fearlessly. (Phil. 1:12–14)

263

But thanks be to God, who always leads us in triumphal procession in Christ and through us spreads everywhere the fragrance of the knowledge of him. (2 Cor. 2:14)

GOD DESIRES OUR ULTIMATE GOOD

There are things that God allows to happen to us that seem unpleasant at the time, but for those who know and love the Lord, these things are for our ultimate good. Just as Jesus' suffering made him complete, our suffering makes us complete. Suffering helps us grow to spiritual maturity. In our tribulation we need to ask God for help (Matt. 7:9–11; James 4:2b). We need to pray persistently (Luke 11:5–10). In our tribulation we need to find out what is the will of God and do it wholeheartedly.

For his anger lasts only a moment, but his favor lasts a lifetime; weeping may remain for a night, but rejoicing comes in the morning. (Ps. 30:5)

There can be only one "captain of the ship" of each of our lives. Believers learn to trust God in this life as we find that nothing else in life is permanent and that nothing is secure except our relationship with our heavenly Father. God allows suffering. In doing so He gives us a world where nothing but Jesus truly satisfies the inner longings of our souls and spirits.

WE CAN HAVE JOY IN SPITE OF AND
BECAUSE OF OUR AFFLICTION

My first experience of inexpressible joy in the middle of affliction was during the lawsuit. My reputation was at risk, but I didn't much care, because of the new level of fellowship I was experiencing with the Lord. When we were going in for the deposition with the plaintiff attorney, I was able to tell my attorney that the experience of the previous three years had been difficult, but I would not have missed it for anything.

I have had the same joy since Barbara has been ill. I do not have joy because of her cancer, but I do have joy over what my experience as an informal caregiver has brought me. Rather than just being an observer of the truth of having joy in affliction, I now have experienced it, and I can testify to the truth in some of those Scripture passages I passed on to my patients over the years.

> Consider it pure joy, my brothers, whenever you face trials of many kinds, because you know that the testing of your faith develops perseverance. Perseverance must finish its work so that you many be mature and complete, not lacking anything. If any of you lacks wisdom, he should ask God, who gives generously to all without finding fault, and it will be given to him. (James 1:2–5)

> In this you greatly rejoice, though now for a little while you may have had to suffer grief in all kinds of trials. These have come so that your faith—of greater worth than gold, which perishes even though refined by fire—may be proved genuine and may result in praise, glory, and honor when Jesus Christ is revealed. Though you have not seen him, you love him, and even though you do not see him now, you believe in him and are filled with an inexpressible and glorious joy, for you are receiving the goal of your faith, the salvation of your souls. (1 Pet. 1:6–9)

WE CAN FACE THE FUTURE WITH CONFIDENCE

We are not to worry (Matt. 6:25–34). We have not been given a spirit of fear (2 Tim. 1:7). If we persist in doing what is right, we show God we love Him. God has a plan, and He alone knows what is best. Our mortal bodies stand in contrast to what is incorruptible in our lives right now: the Word of God (1 Pet. 1:23), our new birth (1 Pet. 1:3–5; 1:23), our spirit (Rom. 8:10, 16), our love for Christ (Eph. 6:24), and our inheritance (1 Pet. 1:4). Our faith gives us courage.

> Even to your old age and gray hairs I am he, I am he who will sustain you. I have made you and I will carry you; I will sustain you and I will rescue you. (Isa. 46:4)

Lift up your eyes to the heavens, look at the earth beneath; the heavens will vanish like smoke, the earth will wear out like a garment and its inhabitants die like flies. But my salvation will last forever, my righteousness will never fail. (Isa. 51:6)

. . . the truth, which lives in us . . . will be with us forever. (2 John 2)

Therefore we do not lose heart. Though outwardly we are wasting away, yet inwardly we are being renewed day by day. For our light and momentary troubles are achieving for us an eternal glory that far outweighs them all. So we fix our eyes not on what is seen, but on what is unseen. For what is seen is temporary, but what is unseen is eternal. (2 Cor. 4:16–18)

Doxology:

To him who is able to keep you from falling and to present you before his glorious presence without fault and with great joy— to the only God our Savior be glory, majesty, power, authority, through Jesus Christ our Lord, before all ages, now and forevermore! Amen. (Jude 24, 25)

EPILOGUE

As I was preparing the revised edition of this book, it occurred to me that some of the readers might be curious as to what happened to my wife Barbara. While pondering the issue, I spoke with my medical assistant who told me that "tons of people" who have read the book call the office to find out about her. This epilogue is a brief account of Barbara's final year.

Finding Strength in Weakness was first published in 2001, just prior to the Christian Bookseller's Association Convention in July. Barbara's breast cancer was well enough under control that we were able to go to Atlanta for that convention. She was also well enough for us to work together in an exhibit booth several weeks later at the American Association of Christian Counselors Convention at the Opryland Convention Center in Nashville. At the A.A.C.C. Convention, Barbara was very active in sharing with others our message of hope. She spent a lot of time talking with hurting people. She always advised people to read *Finding Strength in Weakness* from the beginning. In the fall, we attended the Focus on the Family conference for physicians at Focus headquarters in Colorado Springs.

Barbara did reasonably well through the fall of 2001, but eventually she started having trouble with significant pain in her left hip.

We suspected that her radiation therapy had something to do with the arthritis. As I've heard some of my patients say, it was "bone on bone." Barbara was optimistic about the future. She wanted a more normal existence and opted for a total hip replacement. The original scheduling of the procedure was for January 2002, but the procedure was postponed because of a low-grade fever. The procedure was also postponed once or twice more because of other problems. She eventually had her hip replacement in April. She was in the hospital for four days and in the rehabilitation unit for five more. After two weeks at home, she was back in the hospital with a subdural hematoma. She required left frontal and parietal burr holes for evacuation of the hematoma. After a hospital stay of five days and then ten more in the rehabilitation unit we returned home once again. During the spring, the main thing besides her illness and my working that occupied our waking hours, was the preparation for our son Ryan's wedding to Leslie on May 18. Those were real times of joy for her. As she said, "I didn't realize it would be so much fun to help them out." At the groom's dinner, the night before the wedding, we formally released Ryan to his new bride. On the day of the wedding, we didn't realize that Barbara had only five weeks left to live. I believe that the excitement of planning the wedding prolonged her life.

On June second, Barbara was admitted for her first of three hospitalizations for obscure illness. During these episodes, she would appear at the point of death. She would be brought into the hospital, treated with intravenous fluids, corticosteroids, and antibiotics, stabilize, and then be discharged after 4–6 days, only to have to return to the hospital after a couple of days, very ill again. We did not know what we were treating. For that third trip to the hospital, I had to call for ambulance transport. She was too ill for me to take her to the hospital myself. Always before, her widespread metastasis had been limited to the bones. During that last hospitalization, we found evidence of cancer in the liver. Further testing also demonstrated metastasis to the meninges, membranes that envelop the brain. Her oncologist said that treatment for the meningeal involvement would kill her.

That last morning in the hospital, I helped her up to the bed-side commode. Later, in trying to get her back into bed, I almost dropped her on the floor. I called for help, and three of us could hardly get her back in bed without dropping her. I realized that I could not handle her any longer. We made arrangements for her to be transferred to St. Mary's Residential Hospice in Halls. She was transported by ambulance. I drove out by myself. She told me that she wanted a chocolate malt, not a milkshake. There were only a couple of places in town where we could get a malt. I stopped at Sonic Drive-In on the way out. I arrived at the residential hospice at about 11:30 AM, shortly after the ambulance did.

After Barbara was settled in her room, I left to go home, shower, shave, and put on clean clothes. I had not cleaned up or changed clothes in three days. Barbara had not wanted me to leave her. On my way out, I saw several familiar faces among the hospice person-nel. I spent too much time chatting with them. Eventually, as I was getting into my car, one of Barbara's friends came out and told me that Barbara had become very restless as soon as I walked out of the room. I decided that I had better hurry up and do what I needed to do. I drove home and showered as quickly as I could. While I was shaving, the telephone rang. Barbara had taken a turn for the worse. I was notified that if I wanted to see Barbara, I had better get back there right away. During the frantic drive back to the hospice facility, I prayed that Barbara would not die before I arrived.

When I returned to Barbara's room, she did not look as bad as I expected, but I made up my mind that I was not going to leave her side again. Soon thereafter, Barbara calmed down. She rallied. She perked up and became conversant. I fed the chocolate malt to Barbara with a spoon. She sat up and we had the nicest con-versation with Ryan and Leslie for about an hour. She did so well that I began to have serious doubts about what we were doing in a residential hospice. After that conversation, she lay back down and proceeded to die.

Barbara was about the same for most of the night. At 4:00 AM, I was awakened by a nurse coming into the room. Barbara had fever and was sweating. Axillary temperature was 101.4 degrees. It was more of a struggle for her to breathe. Barbara was given morphine and Ativan. The nurse told me that Barbara had started the active process of dying, that it was the beginning of the end. I sat at the bedside and held Barbara's hand. The nurse advised me to tell Barbara that she was free to leave, and so I did. I lied!

At 7:15 AM, Barbara's axillary temperature was 102.5 degrees. Her feet were cold. I told her I loved her. I looked at the Thicken Up, the thickening material to put in her liquids to keep her from aspirating. I realized we would have no use for it. At 7:40 AM, I told her once again that I loved her. She opened her eyes. I feel certain she knew I was there. My emotions were very unsettled. My judgment was impaired. I realized I needed to try less to control the situation and look more to the advice of the people at the facility. The nurse started the morphine pump. Barbara continued about the same for several hours.

At 2:40 PM the hospice staff gave Barbara a bath. Soon thereafter, our son Jason and Michelle, his significant other, came for a visit. Barbara brightened up for an instant when she realized Jason was there and again for Michelle. Later on in the afternoon, Barbara became restless and was given Ativan. Her blood pressure was unobtainable.

Early the morning of June 22, Barbara was given more morphine. Her chest was more congested. At 6:30 AM, I called Jason and Ryan and told them that their mom probably had only a few hours left. She developed more difficulty breathing. At 10:45 AM our Rector and his wife came in. He read prayers for the dying. At 11:30 AM, Barbara was having agonal (ineffective) respirations. Her husband, both sons, and their significant others were at her bedside. At 11:49 AM Barbara died.

Barbara's funeral was at Church Of The Good Shepherd in Fountain City. We had been members of that church for years, but I had never before been to a funeral in an Episcopal church. The funeral was more of a celebration of Barbara's home-going than it was a time of grieving our loss. Our rector eulogized Barbara, telling about her faith and about her sense of contentment as she approached the end of her life. He told about speaking with her after she realized she was about to die. She said calmly, "That's the way the cookie crumbles." The pain of losing Barbara was the worst pain I had ever felt. It was especially acute during the funeral. In spite of the pain I was experiencing, I felt God's hand holding me up. I felt a sense of peace, of having done what I was supposed to do.

Of course, for several days after Barbara died, my emotions were very meteoric. In the initial publication of this book, I had written about how spousal caregivers, after the deaths of their mates, may look for excuses to feel guilty. I had warned against excessive introspection and allowing the Enemy of Souls to gain a stronghold in our lives through feelings of guilt over something we could not control. Even though I warned people not to do that, I did it myself anyway. A few days after Barbara was gone, I began brooding inordinately over giving Barbara the morphine and Ativan and how they may have contributed to her death. Finally, I telephoned one of the hospice physicians for reassurance. During the conversation he reminded me that the doses of medication used by the hospice staff were relatively small and that this treatment really did allow someone to die with much less suffering. I also remembered how Barbara had told me not to allow her to suffer during her final hours. I was finally able to work through those negative feelings.

During the last several months of Barbara's life, there had been times when she apologized to me for what her illness had done to me. I couldn't see it, but it seemed that almost everyone else did. Some time after Barbara was gone, people started telling me how much better I looked. There had also been times when she wanted to talk about what I would do after she was gone. She let me know that she expected me to remarry. She didn't want me to marry someone who had never been married, because she thought that person would not have much patience with our sons. She also said that she didn't want me to marry someone who had been divorced.

A few months after Barbara died, someone recommended to me the book *Final Gifts* by Maggie Callahan and Patricia Kelly. The book was a comfort to me. On page 23, they write, "Though it can be grief and stress-laden, death can occur in a context of completion and closure." After reading this book, I had the assurance that, when the right time had come, Barbara had been able to get on with dying because she had no unfinished business.

A Christmas Letter 2001

For the Christmas season, 2001, Barbara wrote a thirteen page Christmas letter. As a tribute to her, I would like to list a few quotes from that letter:

"In spite of everything that has happened, we have been and continue to be very blessed."

"Many years ago, I read that a good grandmother provides three things that every child needs: time, undivided attention, and unconditional love. We decided that parents should do that too as often as possible. We wanted them (Jason and Ryan) to understand the concept of being valued by God and figured the best way to do that was to be sure that they knew we valued them."

"This letter comes straight from my heart . . . I want my life to be a testimony of the things I believe down deep in my heart and soul."

ENDNOTES

Preface

1. Walter Bauer, William F. Arndt, F. Wilbur Gingrich, *A Greek—English Lexicon of the New Testament* (Chicago: The University of Chicago Press, 1957), 531, 532.
2. Richard Ingrams, *Muggeridge—The Biography* (New York: HarperCollins Publishers, 1995).
3. Malcolm Muggeridge, *Something Beautiful for God—Mother Teresa of Calcutta* (New York: Walker and Company, 1971).
4. Harold J. Sala, *Joyfully Single in a Couple's World* (Camp Hill, Pennsylvania, 1998), 24.

Part One: Understanding Tribulation

Chapter 1 The Reality of Tribulation

1. Walter Bauer, William F. Arndt, F. Wilbur Gingrich, *A Greek—English Lexicon of the New Testament* (Chicago: The University of Chicago Press, 1957), 362, 363.
2. Paul Tillich, *The Courage To Be* (New Haven: Yale University Press, 1952).
3. Gail Sheehy, *Passages* (New York: E. P. Dutton & Co., 1976).
4. Ibid.

Chapter 2 How Tribulation May Affect Us

1. K. A. Matthews, J. F. Owens, L. H. Kuller, K. Sutton-Tyrrell, L. Jansen-Mc-Williams, Are Hostility and Anxiety Associated with Carotid Atherosclerosis in Healthy Postmenopausal Women?, *Psychosom Med*, 1998; 60:633–638.
2. Susan A. Everson, George A. Kaplan, Debbie E. Goldberg, Timo A. Lakka, Juhani Sivenius, Jukka T. Salonen, Anger Expression and Incident Stroke, *Stroke*, 1999; 30:523–538.
3. Ichiro Kawachi, David Sparrow, Avron Spiro III, Pantel Vokonas, Scott T. Weiss, A Prospective Study of Anger and Coronary Heart Disease, *Circulation*, 1996; 94:2090–2095.
4. Murray A. Mittleman, Malcolm Maclure, Jane B. Sherwood, Richard P. Mulry, Geoffrey H. Tofler, Sue C. Jacobs, Richard Friedman, Herbert Benson, James E. Muller, for the Determinants of Myocardial Infarction Onset Study Investigators, Triggering of Actue Myocardial Infarction Onset by Episodes of Anger, *Circulation*, 1995; 92:1720–1725.
5. Richard Schulz, Scott R. Beach, Caregiving as a Risk Factor for Mortality, *JAMA*, 1999; 282:2215–2219.
6. Janice K. Kiecolt-Glaser, Ronald Glaser, Chronic Stress and Mortality Among Older Adults, *JAMA*, 1999; 282:2259, 2260.
7. J. William Worden, *Grief Counseling and Grief Therapy* (New York: Springer Publishing Company, 1991), 4.

Chapter 3 Negative Reactions to Tribulation

1. James D. Mallory, Jr., *The Kink & I* (Wheaton: Victor Books, 1965).
2. Tim LaHaye, *Spirit-Controlled Temperament* (Wheaton: Tyndale House Publishers, 1955), 183–187.

Chapter 4 Adverse Behavior During Tribulation

1. William MacDonald, *The Believer's Bible Commentary—Old Testament* (Nashville: Thomas Nelson Publishers, 1992), 183.
2. R. Laird Harris, Gleason L. Archer, Jr., Bruce K. Waltke, *Theological Wordbook of the Old Testament* (Chicago: Moody Press, 1980), 581.
3. Vernon E. Johnson, *I'll Quit Tomorrow—A Practical Guide to Alcoholism Treatment* (New York: Harper-Collins Publishers, 1980), 19.
4. Ibid., 35.
5. Ibid., 44.
6. Robert Hemfelt, Frank Minirth, Paul Meier, *Love Is a Choice* (Nashville: Thomas Nelson Publishers, 1989), 11.
7. Robert Hemfelt, Paul Warren, *Kids Who Carry Our Pain* (Nashville: Thomas Nelson Publishers, 1990).

Chapter 5 Causes of Tribulation

1. Walter Bauer, William F. Arndt, F. Wilbur Gingrich, *A Greek—English Lexicon of the New Testament* (Chicago: The University of Chicago Press, 1957), 495.
2. Ibid., 493, 494.
3. F. LaGard Smith, *The Narrated Bible In Chronological Order* (Eugene, Oregon: Harvest House Publishers, 1984).

Chapter 6 How God Uses Tribulation in Our Lives

1. A. N. Wilson, *C. S. Lewis: A Biography* (New York: W. W. Norton & Co., 1990).
2. Marilyn Baker (as told to Janet Hall), *Another Way of Seeing* (Reading: Word (UK), Ltd, 1988).
3. James Strong, *A Concise Dictionary of the Words in the Greek Testament* (New York: Abingdon—Cokesbury Press, 1890), 56.
4. Walter Bauer, William F. Arndt, F. Wilbur Gingrich, *A Greek—English Lexicon of the New Testament* (Chicago: The University of Chicago Press, 1957), 646.
5. Ibid., 18.
6. W. E. Vine, *A Comprehensive Dictionary of the Original Greek Words with their Precise Meanings for English Readers* (McLean, Virginia: MacDonald Publishing Company), 318.
7. Walter Bauer, William F. Arndt, F. Wilbur Gingrich, *A Greek—English Lexicon of the New Testament* (Chicago: The University of Chicago Press, 1957), 809.
8. Ibid., 608.
9. Francis Brown, *The New Brown—Driver—Briggs—Gesenius Hebrew and English Lexicon* (Peabody, Massachusetts: Henddrickson Publishers, 1979), 415, 416.
10. Walter Bauer, William F. Arndt, F Wilbur Gingrich, *A Greek—English Lexicon of the New Testament* (Chicago: The University of Chicago Press, 1957), 248, 249.

Part Two: Understanding God's Nature, Purposes, Works

Chapter 7 Characteristics of God

1. Francis Brown, *The New Brown—Driver—Briggs—Gesenius Hebrew and English Lexicon* (Peabody, Massachusetts: Hendrickson Publishers, 1979), 872.

2. W. E. Vine, *A Comprehensive Dictionary of the Original Greek Words with Their Precise Meanings for English Readers* (MacLean, Virginia: MacDonald Publishing Company), 623, 979.

3. D. Martyn Lloyd-Jones, *The Plight of Man and the Power of God* (Grand Rapids: Baker Bookhouse, 1982), 67.

4. W. E. Vine, *A Comprehensive Dictionary of the Original Greek Words with Their Precise Meanings for English Readers* (MacLean, Virginia: MacDonald Publishing Company), 1181.

5. Walter Bauer, William F. Arndt, F. Wilbur Gingrich, *A Greek—English Lexicon of the New Testament* (Chicago: The University of Chicago Press, 1957), 45.

6. *Merriam—Webster's Collegiate Dictionary* (Springfield: Merriam Webster, Incorporated, 1993), 69.

7. W. E. Vine, *A Comprehensive Dictionary of the Original Greek Words with Their Precise Meanings for English Readers* (MacLean, Virginia: MacDonald Publishing Company), 702.

8. Ibid., 412.

9. Walter Bauer, William F. Arndt, F. Wilbur Gingrich, *A Greek—English Lexicon of the New Testament* (Chicago: The University of Chicago Press, 1957), 728.

10. *Merriam—Webster's Collegiate Dictionary* (Springfield: Merriam Webster, Incorporated, 1993), 727.

11. Ibid., 234.

12. Ibid., 1194.

13. Ibid., 376.

14. W. E. Vine, *A Comprehensive Dictionary of the Original Greek Words with Their Precise Meanings for English Readers* (MacLean, Virginia: MacDonald Publishing Company), 742.

Chapter 8 God's Purposes

1. C. H. Spurgeon, *The Treasury of David, Volume I* (Nashville: Thomas Nelson Publishers), 365.

2. Francis Brown, *The New Brown—Driver—Briggs—Gesenius Hebrew and English Lexicon* (Peabody, Massachusetts: Hendrickson Publishers, 1979), 320.

3. R. Laird Harris, Gleason L. Archer, Jr., Bruce K. Waltke, *Theological Wordbook of the Old Testament* (Chicago: Moody Press, 1980), 289.

Chapter 9 Why the Wicked Prosper

1. *Encyclopedia Britannica* (Chicago: William Benton, Publisher, 1966), Volume 2, 951.
2. Ibid., 967.
3. F. LaGard Smith, *The Narrated Bible In Chronological Order* (Eugene, Oregon: Harvest House Publishers, 1984), 1209–1221.
4. William Whitson, *The Works of Josephus* (New York: Oakley, Mason and Co., 1870), Volume 2, 253–256.
5. *Encyclopedia Britannica* (Chicago: William Benton, Publisher, 1966), Volume 1, 576.
6. Henry H. Halley, *Halley's Bible Handbook* (Grand Rapids: Zondervan Publishing House, 1965), 402, 403.
7. Lancelot C. L. Brenton, *The Septuagint with Apocrypha: Greek and English* (Peabody, Massachusetts, 1992), Preface.
8. Ibid., i.
9. Ibid., iii.
10. Ibid., Preface.
11. Ibid., iv.
12. Henry H. Halley, *Halley's Bible Handbook* (Grand Rapids: Zondervan Publishing House, 1965), 152.
13. *Encyclopedia Britannica* (Chicago: William Benton, Publisher, 1966), Volume 1, 576.
14. Ibid.
15. Ronald Brownrigg, *Who's Who in the New Testament* (New York: Bonanza Books, 1971), 135.
16. *Encyclopedia Britannica* (Chicago: William Benton, Publisher, 1966) Volume 11, 441.
17. Ibid., 440.
18. Ibid., 441.

Chapter 10 God's Providence

1. R. Laird Harris, Gleason L. Archer, Jr., Bruce K. Waltke, *Theological Wordbook of the Old Testament* (Chicago: Moody Press, 1980), 823.
2. Henry Clarence Thiessen, *Introductory Lectures in Systematic Theology* (Grand Rapids: William B. Eerdmans Publishing Company, 1949) 177.
3. *Merriam—Webster's Collegiate Dictionary* (Springfield: Merriam Webster, Incorporated, 1993), 940.
4. W. E. Vine, *A Comprehensive Dictionary of the Original Greek Words with their Precise Meanings for English Readers* (McLean, Virginia: MacDonald Publishing Company), 909.

5. J. Graham Miller, *Calvin's Wisdom* (Carlisle, Pennsylvania: The Banner Of Truth Trust, 1992), 275–278.
6. J. Vernon McGee, First and Second Chronicles (Nashville: Thomas nelson Publishers 1991), 259, 260.
7. C. H. Spurgeon, *The Treasury of David, Volume II* (Nashville: Thomas Nelson Publishers), 71.
8. Edward W. Goodrick, John R. Kohlenberger III, *The NIV Exhaustive Concordance* (Grand Rapids: Zondervan Publishing House, 1990), 937.
9. Francis Brown, *The New Brown—Driver—Briggs—Gesenius Hebrew and English Lexicon* (Peabody, Massachusetts: Hendrickson Publishers, 1979), 340.
10. Isaac Watts, *Twelve Sermons, on Various Subjects, Divine and Moral: Designed for the Use of Pious Families, as Well as for the Hours of Devout Retirement; with a Hymn, Suited to Each Subject* (Montpelier: Wright & Sibley, 1811), 286.
11. Ibid., 287.
12. Ibid.
13. Ibid., 288.

Chapter 11 God's Grace

1. James Strong, *A Concise Dictionary of the Words in the Greek New Testament* (New York: Abingdon—Cokesbury Press, 1890), 77.
2. W. E. Vine, *A Comprehensive Dictionary of the Original Greek Words with Their Precise Meanings for English Readers* (MacLean, Virginia: MacDonald Publishing Company), 510.
3. *Merriam—Webster's Collegiate Dictionary* (Springfield: Merriam Webster, Incorporated, 1993), 505.
4. Francis Brown, *The New Brown—Driver—Briggs—Gesenius Hebrew and English Lexicon* (Peabody, Massachusetts: Hendrickson Publishers, 1979), 337.
5. Walter Bauer, William F. Arndt, F. Wilbur Gingrich, *A Greek—English Lexicon of the New Testament* (Chicago: The University of Chicago Press, 1957) 886.
6. James Strong, *A Concise Dictionary of the Words in the Greek New Testament* (New York: Abingdon—Cokesbury Press, 1890), 77.
7. W. E. Vine, *A Comprehensive Dictionary of the Original Greek Words with Their Precise Meanings for English Readers* (MacLean, Virginia: MacDonald Publishing Company), 487.
8. James Dobson, *Hide or Seek* (Grand Rapids: Fleming H. Revell, 1974).
9. William D. Hendricks, *Exit interviews* (Chicago: Moody Press, 1993).

Chapter 12 The Man Of Sorrows

1. James Strong, *A Concise Dictionary of the Words in the Hebrew Bible* (New York: Abingdon—Cokesbury Press, 1890), 54.
2. Francis Brown, *The New Brown—Driver—Briggs—Gesenius Hebrew and English Lexicon* (Peabody, Massachusetts: Hendrickson Publishers, 1979), 468.
3. Walter Bauer, William F. Arndt, F. Wilbur Gingrich, *A Greek—English Lexicon of the New Testament* (Chicago: The University of Chicago Press, 1957), 702.
4. Frank Charles Thompson, *The New Chain—Reference Bible; The New Comprehensive Bible Helps* (Indianapolis: B. B. Kirkbride Bible Co., Inc., 1934), 260–263.
5. William MacDonald, *Believer's Bible Commentary; New Testament* (Nashville: Thomas Nelson Publishers, 1990), 159.
6. F. LaGard Smith, *The Narrated Bible In Chronological Order* (Eugene, Oregon: Harvest House Publishers, 1984), 1410.

Part Three: Understanding Our Appropriate Response To Tribulation

Chapter 13 A Personal Assessment

1. James A. Mackay, *The Complete Works of Robert Burns* (Ayr, Scotland: Alloway Publishing Ltd., 1986), 222.
2. J. William Worden, *Grief Counseling & Grief Therapy* (New York: Springer Publishing Company, 1991), 21.
3. Ibid., 70.
4. Ibid., 1.
5. Ibid., 40.
6. Ibid., 32.
7. Ibid.
8. Ibid., 10–18.

Chapter 14 Our Proper Response to Tribulation—Love God

1. Keith Beasley-Topliffe, *A Longing for Holiness: Selected Writings of John Wesley* (Nashville: Upper Room Books, 1997), 65.
2. Samuel Rutherford, *Letters of Samuel Rutherford* (Edinburgh: The Banner of Truth Trust, 1973), 189.

3. Ibid., 78.
4. W. E. Vine, *A Comprehensive Dictionary of the Original Greek Words with their Precise Meanings for English Readers* (McLean, Virginia: MacDonald Publishing Company), 209.
5. Ibid., 233.
6. Ibid., 366.

Chapter 15 Our Proper Response to Tribulation—Bear Fruit

1. Corrie ten Boom, *Corrie's Christmas Memories* (Old Tappan, New Jersey: Fleming H. Revell Company, 1976), 55.
2. Ibid., 57.
3. *Letters Addressed to Christians in Affliction* (Glasgow: M. Ogle, 1817), 14.
4. Walter Bauer, William F. Arndt, F. Wilbur Gingrich, *A Greek—English Lexicon of the New Testament* (Chicago: The University of Chicago Press, 1957), 854.
5. W. E. Vine, *A Comprehensive Dictionary of the Original Greek Words with Their Precise Meanings for English Readers* (MacLean, Virginia: MacDonald Publishing Company), 702.
6. Ibid., 703.
7. Ibid.
8. Walter Bauer, William F. Arndt, F. Wilbur Gingrich, *A Greek—English Lexicon of the New Testament* (Chicago: The University of Chicago Press, 1957), 125.
9. Ibid., 201.
10. Ibid.

Chapter 16 Conclusion

1. R. Laird Harris, Gleason L. Archer, Jr., Bruce K. Waltke, *Theological Wordbook of the Old Testament* (Chicago: Moody Press, 1980), 293.
2. William MacDonald, *Believer's Bible Commentary; New Testament* (Nashville: Thomas Nelson Publishers, 1990), 744.

To order additional copies of

Send $14.95 plus $4.95 shipping and handling
and/or $1.00 for each additional copy of the book to:

WILLIAM D. BLACK, M. D.
939 EMERALD AVE, SUITE # 610
KNOXVILLE, TN 37917
(865) 637-8635
E-MAIL – ckwdblack@comcast.net

CPSIA information can be obtained
at www.ICGtesting.com
Printed in the USA
JSHW020656121019
1897JS00003B/3